SPORTS AS SOUL-CRAFT

Paul Marcus

SPORTS AS SOUL-CRAFT

HOW PLAYING AND WATCHING SPORTS ENHANCES LIFE

www.marquette.edu/mupress/

LIBRARY OF CONGRESS CATALOGING-IN-PUBLICATION DATA

Marcus, Paul, 1953-
Sports as soul-craft : how playing and watching sports enhances life / by Paul Marcus. — First Edition.
pages cm
Includes bibliographical references and index.
ISBN 978-1-62600-046-9 (paperback : alk. paper) — ISBN 1-62600-046-8 (paperback : alk. paper)
1. Sports—Psychological aspects. 2. Conduct of life. I. Title.
GV706.55.M35 2015
796.01'9—dc23

2014044714

∞The paper used in this publication meets the minimum requirements of the American National Standard for Information Sciences—Permanence of Paper for Printed Library Materials, ANSI Z39.48-1992.

MARQUETTE UNIVERSITY PRESS
MILWAUKEE

The Association of Jesuit University Presses

TABLE OF CONTENTS

ACKNOWLEDGMENTS

I would like to thank my wife, Irene Wineman-Marcus, a child and adult psychoanalyst, and my good friend, William B. Helmreich, Professor of Sociology, for reading the entirety of my book and offering me many constructive criticisms. Likewise, I have sent each chapter to a sports specialist scholar and would like to express my gratitude for their willingness to read and critique my work in a collegial manner: Ed Winters (soccer), Peter J. Schwartz (baseball), Stuart Rachels (chess), Mark W. Foreman (tennis), David McNaron (golf), and Peter M. Hopsicker (cycling). I alone, of course, take full responsibility for everything written in my book. I would also like to thank Stefanie Bendik for doing such a lovely job copyediting my book.

DEDICATION

To my dear friend Harry,
who has taught me how to love playing.

"It's good sportsmanship to not pick up lost golf balls while they are still rolling."

Mark Twain

CHAPTER I

INTRODUCTION

The French Nobel Prize-winning author, Albert Camus, who played goalkeeper for the University of Algiers junior soccer team, reflected on the powerful meaning of his athletic experience: From "sports…I learned all I know about ethics" (1960, p. 242).[1] What Camus was getting at is that from the moral perspective, soccer, like all sports that are played honorably, should have the same objective as great art. "The aim of art, the aim of a life can only be to increase the sum of freedom and responsibility to be found in every man and in the world" (ibid., p. 240). Indeed, the main premise of this book is that what makes sports so compelling, beyond the entertainment of watching the amazing physical and mental prowess of athletes as they compete, is the fact that each sport taken as a totality of circumstances is a "parable of life" that superbly depicts the existential challenges and dilemmas that ordinary people face as they attempt to fashion the "good life." Most importantly, perhaps, by viewing sports as "parables of life" we can access the landscape of diverse emotions and a rich vocabulary in which sports' connection to personal and social narratives can be examined (Goldblatt, 2006, pp. 732, 790). Sports, conceived as a magical amalgamation of visual art, theater, civic religion and science, have become an important resource for many to shape a personal and collective identity. By "good life" I mean, following Freud, a life of deep and wide love, creative and productive work, one that is guided by reason and ethics and is aesthetically pleasing (that is, attentive and appreciative of sensuous experiences). Similar to the way that Jesus uses a simple story in the Gospels to illustrate a profound moral or spiritual lesson, each sport has its own aura, that is, its own controlling "storylines" that tell a unique "moral fable" that is pertinent to the art

1 I take up Camus's views of soccer in Chapter 2.

of living the "good life." There are, of course, certain similarities among sports—for example, sports psychologists describe the need for athletes to train their minds in mental toughness, positive thinking and visualization (Agassi, 2010, p. 74) to dovetail their physical ability—but what makes sports so commanding in all cultures is the fact that they convey "deep" insights about the human condition that go beyond an athlete's physique, conditioning level and the maximization of his competitive advantage. That is, when looked at from a metaphorical angle of vision, one that is lodged in a psychoanalytic sensibility but also draws from the reflections of sports-writing philosophers and literati, sports are pregnant with insights that speak to what "really" matters in life, questions of character and values, as well as how best to negotiate common, everyday human experiences associated with "space, improvisation, challenge, loss and belief" (Turnbull, 2008, p. xiii), among other problematics that constitute the art of living the "good life."

In each of these illustrative chapters on soccer, baseball, chess (which some consider to be a sport and not merely a game), tennis, golf and cycling, I provide a "thick description," the details, conceptual structures and inner meanings of what it is like to engage in these activities skillfully, with the fullness of one's being, and always with an eye to discerning insights into the art of living the "good life." Moreover, as with any thick description, I have tried to not only delineate the literal behavior that constitutes the sport in question, but also its broader psychological and social context, such that someone who has never engaged in, for example, a soccer game or tennis match would understand and appreciate their complexities and evocative sway. To further enhance this empathic, "experience-near" approach with a freshness of authentic detail, and to stimulate the visual imagination, I have deliberately quoted from many athletes and fans. My claim is that whether one plays or spectates, Plato's psychological insight applies: "You can discover more about a person in an hour of play than in a year of conversation" (Brooke, 2006, p. 56).[2]

---

2 I am aware that while there are many overlapping aspects to performing a sport and spectating there are also differences; however, in this book I regard the "family resemblances" and common ground between the two stances to allow for reasonable generalizations (Arnold, 1985, pp. 1–7).

Defining Psychoanalysis

In the remainder of this introductory chapter, I will briefly contextualize the gist of my focus and methodology by providing a few comments on what I mean by psychoanalysis and artful self-fashioning of the "good life."

I conceive of psychoanalysis as a form of life, a way of being, a resource for individuals who can appropriate the life- and identity-defining narrative of psychoanalysis when they seek to understand, endure and conquer the problems that beset the human condition: despair, loss, tragedy, anxiety and conflict. In effect, individuals in psychoanalysis try to synthesize or come to grips with the emotionally painful experiences of life through a psychoanalytic outlook. In other words, psychoanalysis can be viewed as what Michel Foucault called a "technology of the self": "an exercise of the self, by which one attempts to develop and transform oneself, and to attain a certain mode of being" (1989, p. 433). As philosopher Pierre Hadot notes about ancient Greek philosophy in another context, psychoanalysis can be understood as a "spiritual exercise" (1997, p. 83), a tool for living life skillfully and wisely. The aim of a spiritual exercise is to foster a deep modification of an individual's way of "seeing and being" (ibid., p. 103), a decisive change in how he lives his practical, everyday life. The main objective of a spiritual exercise is "a total transformation of one's vision, life-style, and behavior" in the service of increased personal freedom and peace (ibid., p. 14). According to this view, as philosopher Emmanuel Levinas described "Jewish Humanism," psychoanalysis is "a difficult wisdom concerned with truths that correlate to virtues"—in other words, it is a powerful tool for the art of living a "good life" (1989, p. 275), as one construes and fashions it.

Thus, while being mindful of the corrupt side of organized sport—its hyper commercialization, industrialization and sanitized form of play (e.g., playing without inspiration, joy or panache), and, of course, the pervasive doping—my overall aim of this study is to use the best of sports, both playing and watching them, as a point of entry into a vast repository of practical wisdom on how to more aptly fashion the "good life," one that can help promote greater autonomy, integration and humanity in those who skillfully engage this culturally universal activity. As Foucault said, amidst the depersonalizing, dehumanizing and normalizing "mass" society we have to promote new forms of experience, pleasure and meaning that counter these toxic social forces: "we have to create ourselves as a work of art" (1987, p. 237). Meandering for a while in various sport cultures and appropriating the best of sports as metaphor and practical illustration is a fertile breeding ground for later artful and ethical self-fashioning.

CHAPTER 2

SOCCER: THE BEAUTIFUL GAME

"Magic and Dreams are finished in football."

Carlos Alberto Parreira (Mason, 1995, p. 154)[1]

"It can cause young men to faint, holy men to swear and strong men to become impotent for a day," said Samuel Ekpe Akpabot, the great Nigerian composer, about soccer in his country (Goldblatt, 2006, p. 649). Indeed, soccer is the sport that is regarded as the global game, as "[n]o other game is played by as many people and no other sport has the numbers of spectators that this sport attracts" (Moore, 2000, p. 117). For example, Juventus Football Club, based in Turin, the most successful Italian team, has about 12 million fans in Italy and 173 million worldwide (Borghini & Baldini, 2010, p. 306). While most spectators are by far men, it has been estimated that about 10% to 20% of worldwide soccer spectators are female, and the numbers are rapidly increasing (Hoyningen-Huene, 2010, p. 9). Moreover, soccer's appeal transverses most other socio-economic fault lines. For example, while soccer has long appealed especially to European working class young men, in fact, it is one of the main global "hubs of urban popular culture" (Goldblatt, 2006, p. 656),[2] and has captured the imaginations of

1 Parreira was a former Brazilian manager whose team won the 1994 World Cup, among other competitions. The excerpted quote was taken from a 1994 New York *Times* interview that read: "We will play in the way today's football demands. Magic and dreams are finished in football. We have to combine technique and efficiency."

2 Part of soccer's appeal to the urban working class has to do with the fact that there are no socioeconomic requirements (e.g., you don't need expensive equipment to play) that discourage playing as in other sports.

a number of prominent intellectuals. Consider, for instance, Jean-Paul Sartre who was an avid devotee to soccer, and even wrote a complicated passage about relationships between soccer players in his *Critique of Dialectical Reason*. Reflecting on the theme of "otherness," Sartre noted, "In football everything is complicated by the presence of the opposite team." In other works he discussed the nature of refereeing, suggesting that in understanding the ideal referee we can get a glimpse into the dynamics of authentic decision-making, responsibility and contingency in highly ambiguous circumstances that have applicability beyond the pitch (Crowe, 2010, p. 347). As already quoted in my introductory chapter, Camus's assertion, "After many years during which I saw many things, what I know most surely about morality and the duty of man I owe to sport [i.e., soccer] and learned it in the RUA" (Racing Universitaire Algerios) (www.camus-society.com, retrieved 4/5/14),[3] and the personal and political reflections on soccer by Martin Amis, Salman Rushdie, Umberto Eco and Gunter Grass (Goldblatt, 2006, p. 687), all speak to the powerful meanings that soccer can have on positively shaping individual and collective identity. Finally, the great rhapsodist of soccer, the Uruguayan journalist and novelist, Eduardo Galeano, wrote a highly regarded ode to soccer's beauty and immortality, *Soccer in Sun and Shadow*. He wrote, "But those of us who were lucky enough to see [Pelé] play received alms of extraordinary beauty: moments so worthy of immortality that they make us believe immortality exists" (2009, p. 152).

In this chapter I first describe what it is about soccer, conceived as a sport that "re-enacts the drama of life" (Hoyningen-Huene, 2010, p. 12), in both its best and worse ways, that has earned it the nickname the "beautiful game." I then suggest a plausible analogy that by understanding the individual and collective "nuts and bolts," the physical, psychological and spiritual elements that constitute beautiful soccer, one can derive important insights from why playing and watching the sport has a hold on the psyche of so many as well as learn how to live one's everyday life in a more beautiful manner. As Nietzsche famously said in *The Birth of Tragedy*, "it is only as an aesthetic phenomenon that existence and the world are eternally justified" (Kilpatrick, 2010, p. 39). That is, the capacity to live in a more aesthetically pleasing and impressive manner is what, in part, constitutes the art of living the "good life." While I agree that playing and watching soccer is a practical

3 This is a different translation of the same passage cited in my introduction.

way to get some of "the skills and character" that are necessary to effectively function in contemporary life (Lambert, 2010, p. 217), and certainly learning to play a "team" sport is wisely emphasized in most school systems, it can be much more than this: for soccer can be both a venue and rich resource for creative self-fashioning and self-regeneration, fellowship-building, and even "spiritual communion" (Turnbull et al., 2008, p. 222). As journalist Reed Johnson of the *Los Angeles Times* noted, beautiful soccer "is the athletic equivalent of stream-of-consciousness writing, and its all-time greatest artists...practically scribbled *Finnegans Wake* in the sod with their cleats" (ibid., p. 63).

I. THE EROTIC CHARGE OF KICKING A BALL

"We played until it was dark," said philosopher Jacques Derrida reflecting on his childhood, "I dreamt of becoming a professional footballer" (www. notespublication.com, retrieved 3/12/14). Somewhat similarly, British rock singer and songwriter Rod Stewart noted, "I'm a rock star because I couldn't be a soccer star" (www.pinterest.com, retrieved 1/30/14). Indeed, soccer's global appeal suggests that it is touching something deep inside a person that feels irresistible, and as psychoanalysis has taught us, this almost always has its origins in childhood. As English novelist Nick Hornby wrote in his award-winning, coming-of-age soccer memoir, *Fever Pitch*, the circumstances that led to his life-long obsession with his beloved Arsenal were best described as a "Freudian drama" (1992, p. 9). He was age 11 when he first watched Arsenal play. Hornby was a rather glum and miserable child as his parent's marriage had just ended, he and his mother were homeless for a time and had to live with neighbors, and he was in need of some nurturing and stable psychological ground, especially in terms of his troubled relationship with his father. Arsenal, and everything around the club, became his psychological anchor and the modulating bridge between him and his father, a passion in which he and his father could get together to talk and bond. In short, becoming a devoted soccer fan, specifically of Arsenal, became Hornby's way of re-claiming his inner center of gravity during a tough time in his formative life: it was his "childhood comforter, [his] security blanket," a "way of coping with it all" (ibid., p. 92).

While a person's passion for a sport is always a highly idiosyncratic, multi-determined psychological trajectory, it is usually lodged in earlier family dynamics, and as we will see in our study of baseball, for example, in the case of boys, it is often connected to their relationship with their father. Hornby and his friend Pete first became season-ticket holders, with money they did not easily have, because they had an incredibly intense real and fantasized relationship with their beloved Arsenal and the manager George Graham, who was equated in Hornby's conscious mind with his own less effective and less impressive father: "George is my dad, less complicated but much more frightening than the real one....In dreams, as in life, he is hard, driven, determined, indecipherable: usually he is expressing disappointment in me for some perceived lapse, quite often of a sexual nature, and I feel guilty as all hell" (ibid., p. 161). For Hornby, his central fantasy, what he calls the "impossible dream," of a 1991 championship season guided by the all-knowing wisdom of manager Graham, was symbolically connected to resurrecting his ambivalent and feeble relationship with his father: "Perhaps little boys want fathers to be this way [like the victorious Graham], to act but never explain the actions, to triumph on our behalf and then to be able to say, 'You doubted me but I was right, and now you must trust me.' It is one of football's charms that it can fulfill this kind of impossible dream" (ibid., p. 162).[4]

It is worth mentioning that in soccer, the theme of father/son bonding has been poignantly expressed by many players. Cristiano Ronaldo, the great Portuguese forward who plays for Real Madrid, said, "When I win awards, I think of my father" (www.ronaldo7.net, retrieved 1/28/14). Pelé recalls, "I always had a philosophy which I got from my father. He used to say, 'Listen, God gave to you the gift to play football. This is your gift from God. If you take care of your health, if you are in good shape all the time, with your gift from God no one will stop you, but you must be prepared" (www.thegoaldiggers.weebly.com, retrieved 1/28/14). Former Australian goalkeeper Mark Bosnich noted after losing 6–0 to Brazil, "I said to my dad: 'How can I tell people I played well when I let in six goals?' He said that if I'd

4 Talking about an "impossible dream," soccer has its fair share of zany fans. Galeano tells the story of how a Boca Juniors fan on his deathbed declared his last wish—he wanted to be draped in a flag of an enemy club River Plate so that when he died, "he could celebrate with his final breath the death of 'one of them'" (2009, p. 125). In another tragicomic moment, a referee begins the match with the fans mourning the death of his mother. He is shortly thereafter cursed and jeered by them when a decision opposes their club (http://betweenthelines.in/2014/01/book-review-soccer-sun-shadow-eduardo-galeano-translated-mark-fried/, retrieved 1/30/14).

played badly it would have been 12–0" (www.goalkeepersaredifferent.com, retrieved 4/3/14). Also worth mentioning is that Hope Solo, American soccer goalkeeper who won two Olympic gold medals, noted, "My father was never around. But I glorified my father, and I was always daddy's little girl. He was my first soccer coach" (www.npr.org, retrieved 1/28/14).

While for Hornby, finding soccer was a way of "re-finding" an improved version of his father after his family's dislocation, there are many other childhood psychological antecedents to soccer's adult appeal. Pelé, for instance, said that his father, who was a semi-professional soccer player, had undergone a serious knee injury that terminated his career, leaving Pelé feeling obligated to earn extra money for the family, who lived in a poor and sometimes violence-prone neighborhood. He describes being only age ten and selling newspapers, becoming a shoemaker's apprentice, and even collecting cigarette butts to resell as handmade cigarettes at soccer matches. Pelé's mother and grandmother were so worried for his physical safety that they infrequently came to watch him play. "In all her life," said Pelé, his mother came to see him "play at the stadium maybe three times...She always prefer[red] to stay at home and pray" (Turnbull et al., 2008, p. 124).

Despite these early hardships and numerous challenges in his career, Pelé's "final word" on the game was aptly captured in the title of his autobiography, *My Life and the Beautiful Game* (Pelé, with Fish, 1977) (in fact, it was probably Pelé who nicknamed soccer the affectionately called "beautiful" game). As I shall later discuss in greater detail, while soccer has its violent side, "In football you sometimes have beauty and cruelty together, and I think that's why we all love the game as much as we do" (Ferris, 2001, n.p.), said the great Danish goalkeeper Peter Schmeichel, at its best it is beautifully sublimated aggression.

Following Hornby, what I want to suggest is that soccer, and everything associated with it, especially in childhood, but also in adulthood, is not so much an escape from life's outrageousness, or even a form of thrilling entertainment, but more profoundly, it is a "different version of the world," an "alternative universe" that one can reside in, one that is analogous to performing in or watching "glorious theatre." And like great theatre, soccer playing and disciplined spectatorship is "as serious and stressful as work, with the same worries and hopes and disappointments and occasional elations" (1992, pp. 156, 127).[5] In this section I offer a few reflections on the childhood basis of soccer's appeal to both player and fan, this being a context for better understanding the "language game," the "form of life," the way of being, to quote Ludwig Wittgenstein (Grimwood & Miller, 2010, p. 384), that makes soccer the "beautiful" game it can be.

As Freud wrote, there is "sexual pleasure in movement," that is, there is an "infantile connection between romping and sexual excitation." Most importantly, continues Freud, the use of "games" in "young people...replaces sexual enjoyment by pleasure in movement—and forces sexual activity back to one of its auto-erotic components" (like masturbation) (Freud, 1949, p. 203). For adults who play and watch soccer, these early infantile pleasures are partially satisfied, but what is it about the soccer-specific "movements" that make the game uniquely erotically pleasurable?

As Goldblatt notes in his wonderful history of soccer, kicking a ball has always had an appeal:

> It is an irresistible act; to spy the object, to imagine its future trajectory, to shape and balance one's body and then to take a mighty swing. Better still there comes the delicious moment of impact and the always extraordinary sensation of energy and motion passion from one's leg to the inanimate object. It soars into the air. It scuds across the ground. It finds its target or perhaps it bounces, tumbling, spinning on an unimagined course.
>
> This is not football. This is play. (2006, p. 4)

While Goldblatt does not rigorously psychologically define what he means by play, I assume it at least refers to an activity, the opposite of adult work, which "is done for its own sake, without any serious aims and ends" (Rycroft, 1995, p. 134). He further notes, "No game embraces both the chaos and uncertainty and the spontaneity and reactivity of play like football" (Goldblatt, 2006, p. 907), these aspects of the game metaphorically depicting some of the most troubling features of contemporary society—its sense of radical disarray and the need for skillful improvisation and adaptation to survive, let alone flourish.

5 Galeano also describes soccer using a theatre metaphor: he calls it "the great theater of soccer," in which "suddenly, whoosh, up jumps the player and the miracle of the resurrection occurs" (2009, p. 15).

Early soccer balls were made from animal bladders or stomachs, suggesting the game's sociobiological roots are lodged in our primeval past, though because the balls would quickly disintegrate from being kicked too much they evolved into the resilient ones they are today. Exactly what a ball symbolizes in the context of the historical pre-cursors of modern soccer in ancient Japan and China is open to many interpretations, but it is plausible to suggest that on some unconscious level, the ball is a sex organ equivalent, or at least it contains evocative sexual imagery that both player and spectator intuit and enjoy.[6] For example, in dreams a "ball" can symbolize testicles, a phallus or a breast. Swiss writer Philippe Dubath describes soccer as a way to understand a unique form of male self-assertion and self-knowledge. He mentions the ultra-finessed, humiliating-to-the-opponent move, *le petit pont,* "the little bridge," which involves passing the ball through a defender's legs (Turnbull et al., 2008, p. 245)[7] (perhaps unconsciously symbolizing "castrating" the opponent). The legendary Brazilian right-winger and striker Garrincha, possibly the greatest dribbler in soccer history, had as his signature move "the capacity to find every way to pass his opponent with the ball. Sometimes he enjoyed it so much he would, on beating his man, turn back and do it all over again" (Goldblatt, 2006, p. 375) (perhaps a form of exquisite "sadistic" pleasure at humiliating his opponent). In soccer, this fancy footwork and other such kinesthetically and esthetically impressive moves are highly regarded for their own sake, for in their dazzling talent we sense the players' masculine self-affirmation rooted, at least in part, in his and our exhibitionistic pleasure in being looked at, his dramatic self-display and showing

---

6 That the soccer ball is pregnant with symbolic meanings is suggested by the fact that Brazilian Portuguese has about forty synonyms for the soccer ball (ibid., p. 797).

7 The term in English for "the little bridge" is "nutmeg" (used both as a noun and verb). It has been suggested that this derives from "nuts," referring to the testicles of the player to whom the ball has been passed (Edward Winters, personal communication, 5/6/14). Turnbull mentions other soccer-specific male vocabulary that is designed to humiliate its opponents, such as *le grand pont* (the "big bridge," passing the ball around an opponent to oneself); *l'aile de pigeo* ("the pigeon's wing," sideways-flicking the ball with the leg raised behind, in a wing-like motion); *la bicyclette* (the "bicycle," executing an overhead kick); *la lucarne* ("the skylight," shooting the ball into one of the goal's upper corners); and *le rateau* ("the rake," placing one's foot on the ball and dragging it out of an opponent's reach.

off (Rycroft, 1995, p. 52), especially as the examples above suggest, of his magician-like, manly aggressive prowess. For Freud, exhibitionism was one of the "component" or "partial"[8] instincts in childhood that accompany normal infantile sexuality, expressing the child's wish to exhibit the body, most notably his genitals, and most evidently during the phallic phase, ages three to six. Later in life, this genital wish can become a more generalized desire to attract attention and adoration to the self, to display one's physical attributes or entire body, in a more derivatively displaced form, to attain attention through one's achievements (Moore & Fine, 1990, p. 69), like being a soccer star.

An outrageously brilliant variation on this masculine self-assertion/exhibitionism theme occurred in the 1938 World Cup semifinal between Italy and Brazil. Giuseppe Meazza, the great Italian center forward, was chosen to take a penalty kick. The Brazilian goalkeeper Walter, who was notorious for mesmerizing his adversaries by staring them down and for saving penalty shots, haughtily asserted that he was sure he would hypnotize Meazza and save his shot. Meazza was not intimidated by the arrogant Walter. As Galeano notes, "Meazza was the dandy of the picture. A short, handsome Latin lover and an elegant artilleryman of penalties, he lifted his chin to the goalkeeper like a matador before the final charge. His feet, as soft and knowing as hands, never missed" (2009, p. 80). However, as he stepped up to take the penalty kick, with perfect tragicomic timing, his shorts fell down, probably because the elastic band around his waist had previously been pulled and torn by a Brazilian defender. Meazza, without missing a beat, pulled up his shorts with one hand and shot past the utterly puzzled and disarmed Walter, who was still laughing at the absurd happening. The utterly memorable goal allowed Italy to progress into its second consecutive World Cup final.

The other childhood-based aspect of soccer that is noteworthy is that except for the goalkeeper, the players are not allowed to touch the ball with their hands. If they do so, they are penalized, even expelled from the field of play ("red carded"). Thus, in soccer the player and the

---

8 A "component" or "partial" instinct is a term from classical Freudian theory. According to Freud, the adult sexual instinct "gradually develops out of successive contributions from a number of component instincts which represent particular erotogenic zones," those areas of the body especially sensitive to sexual stimulation, like the mouth, anus and phallus (Rycroft, 1995, p. 83).

spectator are allowed to have a highly displaced, sublimated version of infantile sexual pleasure, one that can be masturbatory and/or exhibitionistic in character, though it need not be: The player can touch the erotically-tinged ball only with his feet, and even then, it is a brief pleasure before he is aggressively challenged by a defender who wants to "steal" the ball from him and render him impotent, or one might say in psychoanalytic parlance, castrated. As Freud said, masturbation was the "primary addiction," the basis for various types of substance abuse, expressing a wide range of conscious and unconscious feelings and fantasies that can be developmentally progressive and adaptive or the opposite (Moore & Fine, 1990, p. 117), depending on the totality of circumstances of a person's inner and outer life. As we have seen, in Hornby's case, it was his relationship with Arsenal and manager Graham that was itself "masturbatory" in character; that is, it was inordinately self-absorbed and self-indulgent: "It was no use pretending any longer that football was a passing fancy, or that we were going to be selective with our games," rather it was a sign that [we] "had to come to terms with the hopelessness of our addiction" (Hornby, 1992, p. 160). This being said, Hornby's obsession with Arsenal, Graham and soccer in general also had a number of positive psychological functions such as strengthening his relationship with his father and consolidating his masculine identity.

I am well aware that the above formulations may appear rather preposterous to the non-Freudian reader, but as we have seen, there is some "soft" evidence that soccer's modern appeal is related to its displaced, sublimated expression of childhood-emanating erotic wishes along the lines described above. Most often, however, players and fans are not so much re-enacting these more deeply repressed, unconscious infantile "component" or "partial" satisfactions, at least not in "pure form," but rather they are incorporated, elaborated and ultimately transformed into more adult-like erotic longings. In particular, finessing the ball is equated with making love to an alluring, passionate woman. In a sense this mirrors child development, for while in children the ball (and more generally, the game) may have its infantile exhibitionistic/sadistic and masturbatory meanings, in adults they have psychologically progressed to mature object relations such that these auto-erotic psychosexual wishes are mere "leftovers"—that is, they are assimilated into an adult outlook on the game which intensifies its appeal. As Galeano notes,

> in Brazil no one doubts the ball is a woman. Brazilians call her pudgy, *gorduchinha,* or baby, *menina,* and they give her names like Maricota, Leono, or Margarita. Pelé kissed her in Maracana when he scored his thousandth goal and Di Stefano built her a monument in front of his house, a bronze ball with a plaque that says, *Thanks, old girl.* (2009, p. 22)

Indeed, the famed Brazilian midfielder, nicknamed Didi, known for his "deep" passing and his "dry leaf" kicks (in which the ball gracefully veered seemingly downwards at the apt moment, resulting in a goal), expresses what many soccer players and spectators consciously and/or unconsciously feel about the ball, that it is not an inanimate object, but rather, it is "alive," it is a feeling entity, and must be respectfully related to like one does to a cherished woman. If not, the ball, like a "scorned" woman, can become aggressively retaliatory. In an interview Didi elaborates his erotically-charged relationship with the ball:

> I always felt a lot of affection for her. Because if you don't treat her with affection, she won't obey. When she'd come, I'd take charge and she'd obey. Sometimes she'd go one way and I'd say, "Come here, child," and I'd bring her along. I'd take care of her blisters and warts and she'd always sit there, obedient as can be. I'd treat her with as much affection as I give my own wife. I had tremendous affection for her. Because she's fire. If you treat her badly, she'll break your leg. That's why I say, "Boys, come on, have some respect. This is a girl that has to be treated with a lot of love..." Depending on the spot where you touch her, she'll choose your fate. (ibid., p. 121)

Galeano further describes the players' erotically-charged relationship to the ball in a section called "The Idol": "The ball seeks him out, knows him, needs him. She rests and rocks on the top of the foot. He caresses her and makes her speak and in the tête-à-tête millions of mutes converse" (ibid., p. 5).[9] The legendary Italian forward, Roberto Baggio, expressed similar sentiments, "Please, give me the ball back, each time I get it from you I must weep its tears" (www.philosophyfootball.com, retrieved 3/21/14).

The great Argentine attacking midfielder, Maradona, known for his protruding tongue when he was on the attack and when he scored his

---

9 Pelé expressed a similar sentiment: "Football is like a religion to me. I worship the ball. I treat it like a god. Too many players think of a football as something to kick. They should be taught to caress it, and treat it like a precious gem" (www.pitchero.com, retrieved 4/22/14).

amazing goals (perhaps an "upward" phallic displacement), "by night slept with his arms around a ball and by day performed miracles with it" (Hornby, 1992, p. 161). In this instance, one can surmise that for Maradona, he and the ball had a perfectly reciprocal, affectionate relationship. At night he lovingly cradled the ball and by day the ball gave back love by letting Maradona produce fabulous plays with her. Roy Keane, the former captain of Ireland and Manchester United noted, "I don't believe skill was, or ever will be, the result of coaches. It is a result of a love affair between the child and the ball" (www.topendsports.com, retrieved 1/27/14).

Dubath also describes how the legendary French attacking midfielder, Zidane, played so artistically that the "ball rolls as if it had the pleasure of giving itself to wherever it's going." Dubath continues,

> [The players] are millionaires, but they pass the ball to each other just like the naked children of Africa's bare fields. They all, we all, belong to Zidane, some part of us, because, even if our own ball doesn't always purr happily, it often rolls on charged with good intentions. We love to receive [sweet affection] like that, we do, all ready for us, all adapted to our speed, to our slowness, to our thoughts. (2008, p. 247)

Similar erotically-charged sentiments were explicitly verbalized by the famed English striker and one of the greatest English managers of all time, Brian Clough, who begrudgingly commented on Arsenal's victory over his Nottingham Forest's unbeaten record: they "caress a football the way I dreamed of caressing Marilyn Monroe" (www.news.bbc.co.uk, retrieved 3/18/14).

Finally, we come to the symbolic meanings of scoring a goal. Galeano and Hornby are quite clear on what it signifies to them: "The goal," says Galeano, "is soccer's orgasm. And like orgasm, goals have become an ever less frequent occurrence in modern life" (2009, p. 9). Hornby notes, after watching Arsenal amazingly score four times in sixteen minutes after lagging behind the majority of the game, that he felt for "a quarter of an hour...a kind of sexual otherworldliness" (1992, p. 222). Hornby amusingly opines on the problematic nature of the goal/orgasm metaphor:

> The trouble with the orgasm as metaphor here is that the orgasm, though obviously pleasurable, is familiar, repeatable (within a couple of hours if you've been eating your greens), and predictable,

> particularly for a man—if you're having sex then you know what's coming, as it were....Even though there is no question that sex is a nicer activity than watching football (no nil-nil draws, no offside trap, no cup upsets, and you're warm), in the normal run of things, the feelings it engenders are simply not as intense as those brought about by a once-in-a-lifetime last-minute Championship winner. (ibid.)

Hornby is probably rhetorically magnifying his point for humorous effect, but the main thrust of what he is saying has at least a grain of truth, namely, that compared to most of everyday life there are soccer moments that are so extraordinarily pleasurable that they feel as if reality had been unexpectedly flipped inside out (Shenk, 2006, p. 2): "sometimes soccer," says Galeano, "is a pleasure that hurts" (2009, p. 270). As Hornby concludes, it is soccer's capacity to suddenly transport a player and spectator to a different dimension of the spirit, to a consciousness-busting realm, that makes it so magically transformational. "We [fans] do not lack imagination, nor have we had sad and barren lives; it is just that real life is paler, duller, and contains less potential for unexpected delirium" (1992, p. 223). If one has gone to a soccer game, especially between rival teams in a jam-packed stadium, one knows that delirium is just the right word, a state of violent excitement or emotion: "*Goaaaaaaaal*," the frenzied Spanish-speaking announcer melodically sings. Moreover, some of this extreme excitement can be experienced in more improvised settings. As one Colombian sociologist notes, the weeknight and weekend change of Colombian city streets into makeshift stadiums becomes ad hoc places "where men of all ages vent their aggressive impulses and psychic eroticism" (Turnbull et al., 2008, p. 119).[10]

"The creation of something new," said Carl Jung, "is not accomplished by the intellect but by the play instinct acting from inner necessity. The creative mind plays with the object it loves" (Nachmanovitch, 1990, p. 42). Indeed, what is clear from the numerous above quotations is that the typical soccer player and fan loves the game, as if it was a beloved girlfriend, wife, mother or significant other. In fact, Hornby begins his book with the words, "I fell in love with football as I was later to fall in love with women: suddenly, inexplicitly, uncritically, giving no thought to the pain or disruption it would bring with it" (1992, p. 7). As a

---

10 Turnbull notes that until 1986, in Colombia female physical education students were not permitted to play soccer.

result of this passionate and joyful intimate inner relation with the sport, the player is able to do amazing things with the ball and with his teammates. Likewise, the fan is able to do amazing things in his mind with the observed movements, patterns and rhythms. He experiences the exquisite order, harmony and proportion before him as uplifting and instructive, especially of his favorite club. In both instances the player and fan experience the aesthetic-intellectual aspects of the game as erotically-charged, as containing invigorating hidden presences, and therefore with rapturous pleasure. Thus, one of the important take home points from this discussion of the childhood sexual origins and imagery associated with soccer is the need to become more attuned to the role of Eros in everyday life, to the invisible sensuous or even "divine-like" presences, that as we shall see underlie ordinary reality and give it palpable pleasure and meaning. I am suggesting the advantages of embracing the rudiments of the best of the Freudian outlook, that is, the drive theory, and most importantly, the version of the world connected with it—man as pleasure-seeking in an erotically-tinged universe (Weinstein, 1990, p. 26). To achieve that sense of renewal, that freedom from the imprisoned self with its deadening perceptions, a vital part of the art of living the "good life," we must be receptive to the erotically-tinged nature of both the animate and inanimate objects around us. While in a sense, soccer, like all sports, is pure escapism and utterly pointless—a group of grown adults chasing a ball[11]—it has hidden erotically-tinged presences (and ultimately, important life-affirming lessons) that are discernible to the cultivated and attuned eye and thus provide much joy.[12] Football is perhaps the last great sacred ritual in modern society[13] and it is to this subject that I turn.

II. SOCCER AS A SECULAR RELIGION

English writer and composer Anthony Burgess quipped, "Five days shalt thou labour, as the Bible says. The seventh day is the Lord thy

11 As Pope John Paul II quipped, "Amongst all unimportant subjects, football is by far the most important" (www.philosophyfootball.com, retrieved 4/1/14).

12 On a lighter note, it has been reported that the coach of Brazil's "national team announced that his players could sleep with wives and girlfriends before World Cup matches this summer, so long as there are no possibly injurious 'acrobatics'" (*The Week*, 4/25/14, p. 4).

13 I am paraphrasing Italian film director and poet, Pier Paolo Pasoloni.

God's. The sixth day is for football" (Gill, 2005, p. 135). Indeed, soccer has been described as a "secular religion" (Kilpatrick, 2010, p. 37), a "civic religion" (Goldblatt, 2006, pp. 514, 428) and a "lay religion" (Turnbull et al., 2008, p. 239). As Kilpatrick claims, "Soccer, more than any other sport, is the global phenomenon that has most fully replaced religion in modern life" (2010, p. 37). A secular religion is dictionary defined as those ideas, theories or philosophies that involve no spiritual component yet possess qualities similar to those of a religion. Like any religion sociologically conceptualized, a secular religion "provides a shared, collective way of dealing with the unknown and unknowable aspects of human life, with the mysteries of life, death, and existence, and the difficult dilemmas that arise in the process of making moral decisions." Religion also provides a foundation for "social cohesion and solidarity" (Johnson, 1995, p. 232).

While it is beyond the scope of this chapter to unpack the controversial subject of what constitutes a "secular religion," let alone to detail the claim that soccer can be described as such, what is most important in this chapter is that individual players and spectators seem to describe their relationship to the game in a manner that calls to mind so-called "religious" or "quasi-religious" experiences. For example, as Turnbull and colleagues note, strong "belief" is a "vital intangible" in soccer in which players, managers and fans intensely believe that victory is possible, even feeling that it is their club's "destiny" (2008, p. 221). As Hornby noted, "The main thing was that you were a believer" (1992, p. 14). That is, ecclesiastical language is often used to express this communal conviction, this secular faith in their club's capacity to win. Thus, it is not entirely coincidental that Liverpool fans begin every game by singing their club anthem, "You'll Never Walk Alone," while in Old Trafford Stadium, the home of Manchester United Football Club, there is a banner that reads "MUFC: For every Manc a religion."

What makes soccer a "heavenly game" that is "spectacular to watch" (Nuttall, 2008, p. 280)? To the typical player and fan, soccer is part of their everyday lives from early on and therefore by the time the child fan becomes an adult he has been acculturated into soccer, especially in his favorite club, which includes a quasi-religious sensibility and relation to his club and, more generally, to the game. Soccer, in other words, has acquired for the fan, and somewhat differently for the player, an "inflated solidarity and obsession with the club," the "core of an entire lifestyle" (Goldblatt, 2006, p. 554). Arthur Hopcraft, the

English scriptwriter, notes, "The point about football in Britain is that it is not just a sport people take to like cricket or tennis. It is built into the urban psyche, as much a common experience to our children as are uncles and school. It is not a phenomenon: it is an everyday matter" (www. digitalcommons.mcmaster.ca, retrieved 3/19/14). Former German-American soccer defender Thomas Dooley noted, "In Europe [compared to America], it's different, you eat soccer, you breathe soccer, you drink soccer. Everything is about soccer" (www. izquotes.com, retrieved 1/30/14). In certain ways soccer has become a good substitute for creating a robust social identity and sense of group cohesion, especially among the millions of young fans who are estranged from traditional political and religious forms of affiliation.

Thus, similar to how people used to be socialized into religion and enjoyed its individual and communal aspects, today many people turn to soccer (and other sports) to experience the joys associated with a heartfelt religious outlook. For example, as with religion, soccer has its seemingly "other-worldly" moments, most often of offensive genius. Consider what has been voted the "Goal of the Century," in which during the 1986 quarter finals of the World Cup, Maradona seized the ball inside his own half of the pitch and made a 60-meter (~197 feet), ten-second dash, in which he dodged five English opponents and dribbled around the goalkeeper to score a goal. Maradona was henceforth nicknamed *Barrilete Cósmico*, "Cosmic Kite." The name was given to him by a prominent Uruguayan radio announcer, Victor Hugo Morales, and was first heard by the Argentine public just after Maradona scored: "Cosmic Kite. What planet have you come from?" Morales yelled. Many years later Morales noted that he "believed Maradona's dribbling was so unpredictable that for opponents it must have been like chasing a kite in the wind" (www.footballtoptens.wordpress.com, retrieved 3/23/14).

Maradona is also known for his "Hand of God" goal that he got in the same game before the above-mentioned goal, in which he deceptively used his hand to get a goal while the referees ruled it was not an infringement. In an interview, Maradona, known to be a "rascal" in his style of play, famously accounted for his goal as "a little with the head of Maradona and a little with the hand of God." Deception of various types has a long and quasi-accepted history in soccer; for example, a dive to draw a penalty, faking fouls and stalling to maintain a one-goal lead (Dura-Vila, 2010, pp. 142, 147). I will discuss the moral lapses, ambiguities and virtues associated with the game in the next section.

With similar religious undertones, Portuguese goalkeeper Costa Pereira points to the seemingly "other-worldly" nature of the incomparable Pelé: "I arrived hoping to stop a great man, but I went away convinced I had been undone by someone who was not born on the same planet as the rest of us" (www.fifa.com/world-match-centre/.../7/, retrieved 1/27/14). Italy defender Tarcisio Burgnich, who marked Pelé in the Mexico 1970 final, noted that intimidation is an operative dynamic in soccer: "I told myself before the game, 'he's made of skin and bones just like everyone else.' But I was wrong" (ibid.). Indeed, as already quoted, Pelé's father told him he had been given "a gift from God," and thus he played with a sense of "divine" inspiration that gave him, and all of us who were graced by his supreme artistry, a glimpse of immortality: "Pelé doesn't die. Pelé will never die. Pelé is going to go on forever" (www.theguardian.com, retrieved 1/28/14). In the headline in the *Sunday Times* after Brazil's Word Cup victory it read, "How do you spell Pelé? G-O-D" (www.fifa.com, retrieved 1/28/14).[14]

In equally celestial language, one BBC Sports commentator, Alan Parry, said of the incomparable Ronaldo, "He's a gift from heaven, he is truly a gift from heaven. Whatever he touches turns to gold" (www.ronaldo7.net, retrieved 1/27/14). Another English centre-half, Sidney Owen, described playing a top-notch Hungarian team that beat them 7 to 1 (the worst international defeat in English soccer) in decidedly "other-worldly" terms: "It was like playing people from Outer Space" (Imre, 2010, p. 290), while one newspaper editorialist described the play of Xavi, Iniesta and Messi as such: "Only in paradise can you see soccer like this" (Nguyen, 2010, p. 274). Uros Zupan, a great Slovenian poet, noted that "Red Star's subsequent victory over Marseille in the finals took us straight to paradise." Reflecting on the 2000 European Championships, he hoped that "a new era was beginning for soccer—a lighter more beautiful era, whose path would be better marked and laid out and that would lead to the creation of what we might call an

14 Of interest is that while Pelé was nicknamed *O Rei*, "the King," in Brazil, he was viewed as remote, as if from another world, a perfect one, Garrincha was called *O alegria de povo*, "the joy of the people," of this imperfect world, that is, he was "disabled, drunk, fragile and ultimately" a "broken" person. As Goldblatt further notes, "The King was and is revered but Garrincha was loved" (2006, p. 377).

empty space, of beauty achieved, of inner light" (Zupan, 2008, p. 178). Acclaimed German writer Christian Delius, the son of a rural pastor, recalls the first time he heard a soccer announcer describe a match. The announcer profusely used such words as "miracle," "thank God... this is what we all hoped and prayed for." Delius listened with stunned fascination at "the word '*believe*'" being used with "more intensity than a preacher or religion class teacher." And the words, "Turke, you're a devil of a fellow, you're a Soccer God," were so blasphemous to this pastor's son that he was embarrassed to be enjoying them (Delius, 2008, p. 252). "Paradise," "inner light," "miracle," "thank God," "believe" and many other such religiously infused terms that are used to describe aspects of soccer and soccer culture all point to the psychological connection between soccer and religious sentiments in the mind and hearts of players and fans.

Other ecclesiastical language and categories have also been used by scholars to describe aspects of soccer that suggest its connection to religious experiences. For example, shouting fans in a soccer stadium or sports bar have been characterized as expressing a form of "prayer that might miraculously get answered." Similar to authentic prayer, fans feel that they are embedded in the action (Winters, 2010, p. 149), and that what they pray for matters to a hard-to-pin-down, usually unconsciously conceived and invested Transcendent Reality or Higher Authority. Soccer historian Nicholas Fishwick noted that after World War II, English soccer had become "the Labour Party at prayer" (Goldblatt, 2006, p. 333). As Hornby notes, "Football is a context where watching *becomes* doing" (1992, p. 178), and when one's team wins (or loses), it is experienced as a personal victory (or failure), as the level of identification with the team has become organically connected to things that are judged to be of "ultimate concern," similar to how the religious believer feels about his local church, community and tradition.

It has been suggested that "today the cathedral has been replaced by the stadium," especially globally speaking, the soccer stadium, where as we have seen, players are "worshipped" in the context of a communally produced "shared narrative," similar to how religion is said to sociologically function for vast groups of people (Kilpatrick, 2010, p. 37).[15]

15 Edward Winters (personal communication, 5/6/14) noted that pictures of soccer stars or teams replace religious pictures on the walls of soccer fans and on the walls of the bars where they drink. Scarves, pendants and other

As Vargiu notes, "'to contemplate' comes from '*templum*,' a Latin word meaning 'temple.' Haven't people compared the great stadiums with temples more than once? Isn't the *Maracana* [a famous open-air stadium in Rio de Janeiro, Brazil] known as the 'temple of world soccer?'... May we not say the same for Wembley, Azteca, San Siro, Santiago Bernabeu...?" (2010, p. 175). In his discussion of the fan, Galeano also describes the stadium as a "temple," as a "sacred place," where "divinities are "on display" and the fan can "see his angels in the flesh doing battle with the demons of the day" (Galeano, 2009, p. 7). Worth mentioning is the nineteenth World Cup that took place in South Africa soon after its transition from apartheid to democracy. It was in "the most beautiful of stadiums," one that drew from the symbolic life-affirming power of Eros. The stadium was in the shape of a flower, a common symbol of love and resurrection, and it "opened its immense petals above a bay" named after Nelson Mandela (ibid., p. 263). As Mandela noted in a speech, "Sport has the power to change the world. It has the power to inspire. It has the power to unite people in a way that little else can. Sport can awaken hope where there was despair" (www.fansided.com, retrieved 3/26/14).

For sure, not everyone can relate to soccer with the quasi-religious sensibility and devotion as do the many players and fans described above. However, their capacity to do so not only is enviable in the way that anyone who can throw themselves completely into something beautiful is enviable, but even more profoundly, such devotion to the game's beauty and immortality suggests something often overlooked about the art of living the "good life." As Galeano notes, likely tongue-in-cheek, "How is soccer like God? Each inspires devotion among believers and distrust among intellectuals" (ibid., p. 36). That is, the royal road to "heaven's glory," as Galeano calls soccer playing and spectatorship (ibid., p. 3), requires the cultivation of a certain way of looking at the game, and for that matter, an angle of vision that has applicability beyond soccer. Soccer, like anything not obviously beautiful, such as a brilliant sunset or an impressionist painting, requires considerable literacy and disciplined observation to fully grasp and enjoy it. In general, knowledge enhances pleasure. As English novelist J.B. Priestly

pieces of memorabilia adorn mantelpieces and pub shelves in the same way that religious memorabilia once occupied the same places. Indeed, in Catholic countries like Spain and Italy and those of Latin America, soccer memorabilia sit comfortably side by side with religious memorabilia.

noted, "To say that these men paid their shillings to watch twenty-two hirelings kick a ball is merely to say that a violin is wood and catgut, and that Hamlet is so much paper and ink" (Hutchinson, 2000, p. 3). Thus, what is needed is a "gracious" mode of engagement to life, one that acknowledges the "sacred zone" around each person, activity and thing, whether it is a soccer game or something else one encounters. To cultivate such a reverential way of being, O'Donohue notes, requires a deferential attitude before the mystery of life, especially to the depth presences of the ordinary, one that is always mindful of "the secret law of balance" that "insists on the proper proportion of the human presence in the light of the eternal." Such a way of being does not mean embracing a heaviness or severity to one's comportment or assuming a dull and boring piety. Rather, as we have seen in the context of soccer, playfulness, humor, and even the anarchic are constituent parts of a reverential way of being. Thus, when one's mode of engagement to the other, even to the otherness of a mere soccer game, is "respectful, sensitive and worthy," transcendent-pointing gifts of beauty, creativity, challenge and healing suddenly reveal themselves. Such surprising grace-infused moments, as they are called in religious language, a kind of sublimated spirituality, make the moment feel nothing short of luminous (O'Donohue, 2004b, pp. 24, 31, 23). To be able to create and find these luminous moments in soccer and in life is the art of living the "good life."

III. SOCCER AS A METAPHOR FOR WAR

There is more than a grain of truth to George Orwell's famous quip, "International football is the continuation of war by other means" (www. hdfootballwallpaper.com, retrieved 1/28/14). In fact, Orwell observed, "Football has nothing to do with fair play. It is bound up with hatred, jealousy, boastfulness, disregard of all rules and sadistic pleasure in witnessing violence: in other words, it is war minus the shooting" (www.4dfoot.com, retrieved 4/1/14). One only has to remember Uruguayan soccer star "Perucho" Petrone, whose kick was so forceful it knocked out goalkeepers and tore through nets (Galeano, 2009, p. 67). Galeano also describes soccer as "choreographed war" and as a "metaphor for war" (ibid., pp. 18, 49). These observations are supported by the fact that in international soccer matches (and at all American baseball games) the national anthems are played before a match begins, which amplifies the fan's sense of solidarity and patriotism. Soccer, similar to chess, symbolizes a wide range of important social and political situations, including elements of war (Shenk, 2006, p. 72).

In this section I briefly elaborate the analogy between soccer and war and suggest that soccer played at its best it requires some of the warrior skills that are associated with the military, including their praiseworthy valuative attachments. Unlike war, soccer is a beautifully sublimated form of aggressive discharge that does not seriously hurt anyone; in fact, like all sublimations it represents a progressive psychic accomplishment and self-enhancement, a vital defensive requirement of living the "good life." Consider the famous advice given to his team by Nereo Rocco, the great Italian midfielder and coach. Rocco, the exponent of *catenaccio* ("door bolt/chain"), a well-organized and effectual backline defense that aimed to neutralize opponents' attacks and thwart their chances of scoring goals, told his team, "Kick everything that moves; if it is the ball, even better" (Goldblatt, 2006, pp. 432, 433). Soccer, like all competitive sports, involves the sublimation of aggressive impulses which can also be thinly veiled violent wishes.

While soccer usually reduces the expression of blatant aggression to a tolerable degree, it is not without its fair share of it. Like the military, the game and culture has its "dark" side. This is not surprising, in part because compared to all other sports, soccer requires the longest period of uninterrupted action—two halves of 45 minutes each, and the clock never stops. Players, managers and fans, like soldiers on the battlefield, get tired, more easily riled up and stressed, and therefore they are more prone to "act out" their raw aggression (Kent, 2010, p. 54). Three examples, the first two from players and the last one from a referee, are illustrative of this defensive breakdown against aggressive impulses.

One infamous expression of blatant aggressive disregard for a fellow player, clearly provoked but ultimately self-destructive, was done by one of the greatest players in the history of the game, French attacking midfielder, Zinedine Zidane, nicknamed "Zizou." Zizou had announced that he would retire after the 2006 World Cup in Germany against Italy. One of the Italian players, Marco Materazzi, known for his provocative and excessively aggressive behavior on the pitch (he was nicknamed "The Matrix" due to his erratic personality and has been ranked as the ninth dirtiest player in the history of the game, having received 60 "yellow cards" and 25 "red cards" in his career), repeatedly insulted Zizou's sister and mother in saying something like, "I would prefer your whore of a sister"; you're "the son of a terrorist whore." Said Zizou after the game, "You hear those things once and you try to walk away....That's what I wanted to do because I am retiring. You hear it a second time and then a third time..." In extra-time, and with the score even at 1 to 1, Zizou finally reacted to the verbal provocation and shirt-pulling from Materazzi, and he deliberately forcefully shoved his head into Materazzi's chest, head-butted him, and sent him crashing to the ground. Zidzou's head-butt, viewed thousands of times on YouTube (and counting), got him ejected from the game by Argentinean referee Horacio Marcelo Elizondo. Zizou's exit has become the best example of the worst career exit of all time. Incidentally, without Zizou, Italy won the match 5-3 on penalties to become world champions for a fourth time (www.worldsoccer.about.com, retrieved 3/28/14).

A second example of player's violence on the pitch was notoriously perpetrated by French forward/midfielder Eric Cantona in 1995 while playing for Manchester United. Cantona was at an away match against Crystal Palace and was ejected by the referee for kicking Palace defender Richard Shaw after Shaw had neutralized him during a clearance, which included tugging at his shirt. As Cantona was escorted to the locker room, he initiated a "kung-fu"-like kick at Crystal Palace fan Matthew Simmons, who had dashed down over ten rows of stairs to verbally abuse Cantona, reportedly saying something like, "Fuck off back to France, you French motherfucker." Cantona followed the karate kick with a barrage of punches at Simmons. He was arrested, convicted for assault, and given a two-week prison sentence that was eventually overturned, resulting in 120 hours of community service (Simmons was later fined £500 by the court for threatening language and behavior).[16]

16 During a press conference Cantona strangely explained his outrageous behavior by saying, in a trance-like manner, the now famously puzzling words: "When the seagulls follow the trawler, it's because they think sardines will be thrown into the sea. Thank you very much." Cantona stood up from his chair and slowly departed the press conference, leaving the audience utterly confused. About the kung-fu incident Sir Alex Ferguson, the celebrated manager of Manchester United, noted that "over the years since then I have never been able to elicit an explanation of the episode from Eric, but my own feeling is that anger at himself over the ordering-off and resentment of the referee's earlier inaction combined to take him over

It is not altogether surprising that with any "high-octane" competitive sport there are bound to be moments of ugliness, even violence on the part of players and fans, the latter of whom are totally identified with their club, where the generally superb self-control and self-mastery of the player breaks down. As Sir Alex Ferguson noted, "Well, football is a hard game; there's no denying it. It's a game that can bring out the worst in you, at times" (www.shortlist.com, retrieved 3/29/14). This being said, judging from these and other examples, there may be at least some validity to the popular definition of soccer: "a gentlemen's game played by thugs, whereas rugby is a thug's game played by gentlemen" (Turnbull et al., 2008, p. xi).

In soccer the referee has been aptly described in terms of his "loneliness" (and as we shall see in the next section, so has the goalkeeper, who watches the game alone, from a distance). As in other sports, some referees are sticklers, others dodge making tough decisions, some are frustrated players and others are "poseurs" or "tough guys" (Crowe, 2010, p. 347). In one recent instance, a referee in Santa Ines, Brazil got horribly swept into the aggression of soccer. Referee Octavio da Silva "told player Josenir dos Santos Abreu...that he was out of the game. The two began to scuffle, and da Silva pulled a knife and stabbed the player to death." Even worse, "Fans armed with rocks poured onto the field, stoned da Silva to death, and tore his body into quarters. Local media reported that the spectators then decapitated da Silva and stuck his head on the pike in the field" (*The Week*, 7/19/13, p. 6). This grotesque occurrence calls to mind the fact that soccer, as we know the game, "purportedly began somewhere in Medieval England with the severed head of an opposing army's leader being kicked around" (Ilundain-Argurruza & Torres, 2010, p. 196). Indeed, as with war, the sociobiological origins of soccer, of our "Soccer Tribe," are rooted deep within our primordial, instinctual past.

---

the brink" (www.theguardian.com, retrieved 3/28/14). However, in another statement Ferguson may have inadvertently revealed what motivated Cantona: "If ever there was one player, anywhere in the world, that was made for Manchester United, it was Cantona. He swaggered in, stuck his chest out, raised his head and surveyed everything as though he was asking: 'I'm Cantona. How big are you? Are you big enough for me?'" (www.theguardian.com, retrieved 3/28/14). With this kind of puffed up ego it is no wonder that when things did not go his way on the pitch, both with the referee and fans, narcissistic rage was Cantona's response.

While these above examples express the ugly and violent side of soccer and its culture, the fact is that at its best soccer is, as I have called it, a beautifully sublimated version of a war game. While this subject deserves a discussion the length of a book,[17] I want to mention their main similarity. As in war, soccer is saturated with the use of strategy and tactics. In the military context, strategy refers to the art and science of planning and conducting a war or a military campaign. In soccer, strategy is concerned with collective actions designed to achieve an overall aim, namely victory over one's opponent. Tactics—organizing and maneuvering forces in battle to achieve a limited or immediate aim—are also an important aspect of playing great soccer. Thus, soccer requires strategy, that is, long-term, whole-game thinking and tactics, as well as the short-range, move-by move maneuvering in a skillful way (Shenk, 2006, p. 78).

This being said, as in war, in soccer (and for that matter, in ordinary life), there is a "fog" that permeates these social contexts. That is, they are experienced with a high degree of complexity, contingency, change and contradiction. In fact, Freud noted, "neurosis is the inability to tolerate ambiguity" (Wilkinson, 2006, p. 146). This chaotic, messy sense to war, soccer and ordinary life is in part connected to the wide range of options and choices that are present at any point in time. "Battle," said General George S. Patton, "is an orgy of disorder" (Tsouras, 2005, p. 47). The great philosopher of war, Carl von Clausewitz, defined the "friction" of war as the disruptive aspect of the battlefield experience, present within the perceived and felt discrepancy between plans and what actually occurs. Friction thus describes the "uncertainties, errors, accidents, technical difficulties, the unforeseen, and...their effects on decisions, morale, and actions," the situational variables to which one must continually adapt (Paret, 1986, p. 202). General Dwight D. Eisenhower's observation pertaining to war is also applicable to soccer and everyday life: "In preparing for battle I have always found that plans are useless, but planning is indispensable" (Charlton, 2002, p. 5). Even more famous are the pithy words of Field Marshal Helmuth von Moltke, "No battle plan survives contact with the enemy" (Holmes, 1999, p. 77). As in war, soccer and ordinary life, all strategies are not only provisional but highly limited in their effectiveness. In fact, as the pre-eminent military historian Martin van Creveld noted, "An

17 For a study of the artful use of military strategy in everyday life, see Marcus, 2014.

intellectual system sufficiently powerful to encompass all of...["the dilemmas of strategy"], and thus provide a complete guide to the employment of force, does not exist" (1991, p. 116).

All great strategic military masters in history have affirmed that war is characterized by fog, friction, unpredictability and chance. And as I have argued, so is soccer, but in an enjoyable way. What makes soccer a beautiful game is its mixture of "ability" and "chance," a combustible combination that often ends in terrible injustices on the pitch. The Dutch manager and former soccer player, Ruud Gullit, explained the "rough justice" after a defeat: "We must have had 99 percent of the game. It was the other three percent that cost us the match" (www.backpagefootball.com, retrieved 1/30/14).

Indeed, perhaps more than most sports, soccer has an unavoidable susceptibility to chance or luck, in part because the final scores of a soccer match are relatively small compared to other sports (e.g., basketball). That is, the greater the numbers of the final score, the greater the likelihood that the score results are mostly due to ability since on a statistical level chance is averaged out. While this chance factor can be rather troubling to some, it adds to the depth, thrill and overall pleasure of the game (Eylon & Horowitz, 2010, p. 12; Hoyningen-Huene, 2010, p. 21). The secret to experiencing soccer "as a beautiful game" is precisely "its variability in the mixture of these two elements" (Hoyningen-Huene, 2010, pp. 2, 15), ability and chance. Like successfully prosecuting a war, playing great soccer requires negotiation of this dynamic interplay of ability and chance, which means being steeped in the practical wisdom of military strategy (though in the soccer world it is not consciously thought of this way), which is a particular way of "seeing" the world. As Isaiah Berlin notes about military masters,

> These great men are wiser, not more knowledgeable; it is not their deductive or inductive reasoning that makes them masters; their vision is "profounder." They see something the others fail to see; they see the way the world goes, what goes with what, and what never will be brought together; they see what can be and what cannot; how men live and to what ends, what they do and suffer, and how and why they act, and should act, thus and not otherwise.

Thus, this practical wisdom involves many of the psychological qualities that are stressed in both great military strategy and great soccer, like intuition, adaptation to change, improvisation, versatility and the like. However, even more so, says Berlin, what is needed is a "special sensitiveness to the contours of the circumstances in which we happen to be placed; it is a capacity for living which cannot be either altered, or even fully described or calculated; an ability to be guided by rules of thumb...this sense of cosmic orientation is the sense of reality, the 'knowledge' of how to live" (2009, pp. 70, 69).

Berlin's astute characterization of the great military strategist's outlook dovetails with how the great soccer players go about their war game, and even more importantly, it suggests what is necessary to artfully live the "good life." The great Northern Ireland international soccer player, the late Danny Blanchflower, famously commented on what the game meant to him in terms of personal expression and striving for excellence:

> The great fallacy is that the game is first and last about winning. It is nothing of the kind. The game is about glory, it is about doing things in style and with a flourish, about going out and beating the other lot, not waiting for them to die of boredom. (www.dailymail.co.uk, retrieved 2/10/14)

The key words here are "style," or elegance and sophistication, and "flourish," a bold or extravagant gesture or action, made especially to attract the attention of others. Indeed, great soccer players personify this glorified playing, an exquisite form of sublimation that looks as if it comes naturally and automatically. Ronaldo, known for his offensive brilliance, noted, "I don't think about one trick or the other, they just happen" (www.ronaldo7.net, retrieved 1/28/14). Lionel Messi, the spectacular Argentinian forward, also noted, "I never think about the play or visualize anything. I do what comes to me at that moment. Instinct. It has always been that way" (www.lushquotes.com, retrieved 1/28/14). For these and other soccer greats, the aggression associated with the game has been utterly transformed into gorgeous natural playing, which points to what makes soccer the beautiful game, one that real life should emulate. Messi aptly makes this point, "In football as in watch making [and in living the "good life"] talent and elegance mean nothing without rigor and precision" (www.geniusrevive.com, retrieved 1/28/14).

Thus, there are many reasons why soccer is said to be beautiful, reasons that indicate the superb sublimatory capacities of players; for example, "the range of bodily expressions found in the sport," "the interface of body and ball is also a site of skill and grace", and "the distinct forms and techniques such as shooting, trapping, dribbling, tackling and passing" (Lambert, 2010, p. 221). Another soccer aficionado noted, "From the daring relentlessness of Lionel Messi, the ball controlling wizardry of Ronaldhino, the impenetrableness of Babi Cannavaro's defense, the completeness of Steven Gerrard, the technical mastery of Kaka, and of course, the offensive brilliance of Cristiano Ronaldo [and the rich differences between the European and South American ways of playing], the game's beauty can be spontaneously revealed" (Elcome, 2010, p. 163).[18] Perhaps most importantly, as the great Russian composer, Dmitri Shostakovich, noted, in its flow, spacing and positioning, "Football is the ballet of the masses" (www.theglobalgame.com, retrieved 1/27/14). Soccer is thus not only a way of being, one that expresses a culture, but it is itself a cultural expression, a ritualized and passionate art form. What Germaine Greer, the Australian academic and journalist, said about her country applies to many other countries: "Soccer is an art more central to our culture than anything the Arts Council deigns to recognize" (Pepple, 2010, p. 201).

The upshot of this soccer-as-war game connection revolves around the notion of sublimation of aggression being a vital psychological capacity to play beautiful soccer and live the beautiful life. For Freud, beauty was understood as a sublimation of sexual and aggressive wishes. Sublimation can be simply defined as a "mature" developmentally-based "defense mechanism whereby a repressed or unconscious drive that is denied gratification is diverted into a more acceptable channel or form of expression, as when aggression is diverted into playing or watching violent sports, or when libido is diverted into artistic or creative activity" (Colman, 2009, p. 739). Whether for soccer player, actor or any "artsy" person, sublimation has a culturally "higher" aim, one that is regarded as pro-social in character. Freud's formulation of sublimation is worth remembering:

---

18 It is noteworthy that Messi and Ronaldo have been locked in battle for about the last five years over who is the better player. Between them they have won the world player of the year award every year for the last four of five years, and they play for arch rivals Real Madrid and Barcelona. There is a barely-veiled and long-running personal animosity between them, and they're each trying to prove over and over again that they are the better player, driving them both on to gain quite astonishing records and statistics.

> Sublimation of instinct is an especially conspicuous feature of cultural development; it is what makes it possible for higher psychical activities, scientific, artistic or ideological, to play such an important part in civilized life....it is impossible to overlook the extent to which civilization is built up upon a renunciation of instinct, how much it presupposes precisely the non-satisfaction (by suppression, repression or some other means?) of powerful instincts. (1927–1931, p. 97)

What Freud is getting at is the need for all of us to rationally acknowledge and ultimately come to terms with our deepest aggressive impulses, for if they are denied, ignored or repressed they do not magically vanish. In fact, the more we treat these impulses as persona non grata, the more revenge they take against us. Adults who are bent on repression and other maladaptive defenses against their aggressive impulses, especially in the domain of the imagination and creativity, truncate their inner experience and often bring about havoc in their outer lives. Playing and appreciatively watching beautiful soccer and artfully living the "good life" thus requires an excellent capacity to neutralize the destructive aspects of aggressive instinctual energy, impulses and wishes, and transform them into something that the ego can use in the service of life affirmation and moral deepening. The Brazilian anthropologist Roberto DaMatta pointed to this conclusion when he reflected on the deep cultural importance of soccer in his country: "After all, it is better to be champion in samba, carnival and football than in war and the sale of rockets" (Goldblatt, 2006, p. 357).

IV. SOCCER AS MORAL EDUCATION

Like all sports, soccer and its culture have morally questionable if not objectionable aspects. There is, for example, the shameful hooliganism of fans hollering contemptuous chants at opponents when the game is supposed to promote human solidarity and sportsmanship. Also troubling is the extreme commercialization of the game and the crass values it perpetuates among players ("Advertisement in Motion") (Galeano, 2009, p. 108) and fans (e.g., among children, the extreme celebrity-seeking via the game). And then there is the unbridled narcissism among players; for example, the great Brazilian striker, Romario, also known for his womanizing, noted, "When I was born, God pointed at me and said 'That's the man'" (www.pinterest.com, retrieved 3/30/14). Johan Cruyff, the Dutch legend and advocate of "Total Football" (which emphasizes player ball control and tactical inventiveness) said of himself, "In a way I'm probably immortal." The word "probably" betrays his false modesty (www.isleofholland.com, retrieved 1/29/14). As with most narcissistically-compromised sports celebrities, his need for affirmation has a pathetic if not pained aspect to it. Physically battered by years of playing, when asked about retirement, Maradona confessed: "I need [the fans] to need me" (Galeano, 2009, p. 233).[19] Galeano and others have noted that soccer has become a game that is coldly efficient, "staid and standardized," full of "mechanical repetition" in how it is played, emphasizing "lightning speed and brute strength" at the expense of joy, fantasy, creative spontaneity and risk and daring. Moreover, this "efficiency of mediocrity" is motivated by the "bottom line" industry demands of the coaches, owners and gamblers who want victory at any price, including at the expense of the aesthetics of the game (ibid., pp. 2, 199, 157; Winters, 2010, p. 162). As Galeano elegiacally wrote, "I go about the world, hand outstretched, and into the stadiums I plead: 'A pretty move, for the love of God'" (2009, p. 1). Soccer, "a primordial symbol of collective identity" (ibid., p. 243), has also been exploited by dictators like Franco and Mussolini and by South American politicians to perpetuate their authoritarian rule, as well as stir up destructive ethnocentrism and nationalism. At the institutional level soccer had

---

19 On the other hand, players have expressed more measured narcissism, even a concern for the future of the game: Messi noted, for example, "Like I've said many times before, I'm always more likely to remember goals for their importance [to the team] rather than if they're beautiful or not [i.e., self-aggrandizing]. Goals scored in finals, for example"; "When the year starts the objective is to win it all with the team, personal records are secondary" (www.vanguardngr.com, retrieved 1/28/14). Ronaldo has a similar sentiment: "What I do as an individual player is only important if it helps the team to win. That is the most important thing" (www.ronaldo7.net, retrieved 1/29/14). Like any team sport, soccer highly values individual accomplishment, but never above team victory. Finally, Pelé felt a profound responsibility to the next generation: "Every kid around the world who plays soccer wants to be Pelé. I have a great responsibility to show them not just how to be like a soccer player, but how to be like a man" (www.sportsillustrated.cnn.com, retrieved 1/28/14). Even more emotionally demonstrative, after Pelé scored his historic thousandth goal, the former shoeshine boy, peanut vendor, and fourth grade drop-out (though he did eventually get a university degree), called by the Brazilian Congress the "nonexportable national treasure," wept, "remember the children, remember the poor children" (Lever, 1983, pp. 142, 141).

pre-empted Nazi expulsion of Jews from Germany's sporting organizations before it was ordered in June 1933 by the Minister of Education (Lever, 1983; Goldblatt, 2006, p. 309). Pakistan produces roughly three-quarters of the world's soccer balls, and they are stitched by very poorly paid workers, including many children, who on a productive day make about four balls at 20 cents each. The shameful irony is that without these exploited workers, the "grotesquely wealthy circus of global football grinds to a halt" (Goldblatt, 2006, p. 856).

Soccer, however, puts into sharp focus many aspects of the moral life that consciously and unconsciously resonate with fans and that are praiseworthy, uplifting and instructive to the art of living the "good life."[20] In this illustrative section, rather than focus on the superstar, goal-making strikers, I want to mainly concentrate on the goalkeeper, the player who stands in the team's goal-mouth to try to stop the other team from scoring. For in many ways, the goalkeeper's role best depicts more common vital aspects of the human condition and the challenges of living the "good life." As former Cambridge goalkeeper and famous author Vladimir Nabokov noted, "The goalkeeper is the lone eagle, the man of mystery, the last defender. Less the keeper of a goal than the keeper of a dream" (www.free-project.eu, retrieved 4/1/14). Indeed, while all of the players on the pitch chase the ball, the goalkeeper is the only one who ultimately stands against it.[21] Who has not felt like this in real life?

---

20 So-called "soccer values" include "creativity, the emphasis on skill over brute force, on technique over physical strength or the use of intelligence and vision instead of unthinking discipline" (Dura-Vila, 2010, p. 143). Soccer also perpetuates many of the familiar values associated with any sport excellence, like self-discipline and dedication, and on the pitch, the ability to adapt to change and possess inventive improvisation, as well as embrace the idea that above all else, it is the "mind" that matters (along with luck) to attain victory. In an interview, Pelé made the point that success in soccer is no accident—it is lodged in wholesome moral values: "It is hard work, perseverance, learning, studying, sacrifice and most of all, love of what you are doing or learning to do." This being said, Pelé responded to those who accounted for his playing excellence in terms of his "uncommon peripheral vision and well-placed center of gravity" by affirming that "his talents were the gift of God" (Lever, 1983, p. 141; www.360soccer.com, retrieved 1/28/14).

21 I am paraphrasing Emrah Serbes, a popular Turkish author who wrote a short story about soccer.

Camus, who played goalkeeper for his university, noted that through soccer he had "learned all I know about ethics" (1960, p. 242).[22] He explained what life lessons he learned playing goalkeeper: "That the ball never comes where you expect it, that helped me a lot in life, especially in large cities where people don't tend to be what they claim." In addition, he "learned to win without feeling like God and to lose without feeling like rubbish, skills not easily acquired" (Galeano, 2009, p. 66).[23] Goalkeepers are an unusual group, often unfairly taking the blame for a lost game. As the great English goalkeeper Gordon Banks noted, "At that level, every goal is like a knife in the ribs" (www.ifhof.com, retrieved 2/1/14).[24] The Russian goalkeeper Lev Yashin, nicknamed "The Black Spider," who is considered perhaps the greatest goalkeeper of the twentieth century, explained the secret to his defensive genius: "The trick was to have a smoke to calm your nerves, then toss back a strong drink to tone your muscles" (Galeano, 2009, p. 134).

22 Camus, born in Algiers, was raised in poverty and never knew his father who died in the beginning of the First World War, when Camus was only one year old. He was raised by his mother who was strict in her parenting, while his grandmother used to beat him frequently, which perhaps explains his early liking for playing goalkeeper in the street games. That is, there was less scuffing of the shoes, and if there was one thing that landed him a beating by his grandmother, it was scuffed shoes. But there is something utterly apt about Camus playing goalkeeper, as he was both participant and observer, a lonely position on the pitch (www.telegraph.co.uk, retrieved 4/4/14).

23 Camus's often-quoted words may refer to the "simple morality he wrote about in his early essays," such as "an ethic of sticking up for your friends, of valuing courage and fair-play." Camus thought that politicians and religious thinkers attempt to confuse people with complicated and long-winded moral systems to make things seem more complex than they really are, possibly to satisfy their own self-serving agendas. People may be wiser to consider "the simple morality of the football field than to politicians and philosophers" in terms of how to live their lives. In line with this view, Camus was once asked by his friend, Charles Poncet, which he liked better to watch, football or the theatre. Camus is said to have answered, "Football, without hesitation"(www.camus-society.com, retrieved 4/5/14).

24 Lev Yashin also felt tortured by goals that were ceded. He said, "What kind of a goalkeeper is the one who is not tormented by the goal he has allowed? He must be tormented! And if he is calm, that means the end. No matter what he had in the past, he has no future" (www.goalkeepersaredifferent.com, retrieved 4/4/14).

Former English goalkeeper John Burridge noted, "I still go to bed with my goalkeeping gloves on." Indeed, Burridge's rather exotic behavior is probably rooted in what all goalkeepers feel—a childhood-based love of the ball. As former German goalkeeper Jens Lehmann said, "Unconsciously, I fell in love with the small round sphere, with its amusing and capricious rebounds which sometimes play with me" (www.totalfootballforums.com, retrieved 4/2/14).[25]

Calling to mind the erotically-tinged nature of soccer, Icelandic singer and songwriter Björk quipped, "Football is a fertility festival. Eleven sperm trying to get into the egg. I feel sorry for the goalkeeper" (www.goalkeepersaredifferent.com, retrieved 4/1/14). Indeed, what is striking about the goalkeeper is his solitude. He is an outsider looking in (Winters, 2010, p. 160), as most of the game he is alone, watching and waiting in the goal-mouth for danger to strike. He is vulnerable and on the defensive, the "last defender," facing ten fiercely determined, advantaged, goal-hungry men who want to overwhelm him; and he is accountable, as he feels utterly responsible for what happens in terms of goals being scored. As American goalkeeper Brad Friedel noted, "For a goalkeeper, there is no hiding place" (www.goalkeepersaredifferent.com, retrieved 4/1/14). That is, there is no rhetorical "smoke and mirrors" that can conceal the fact of a scored goal, indicating that at that instant, the goal maker was superior to the goalkeeper (Goldblatt, 2006, p. 480). Thus, the goalkeeper has been described as the loneliest figure on the pitch. Consider, for example, the penalty shot or shootout when the goalkeeper faces his opponent and has "no choice and little chance" of making the save (Winters, 2010, p. 158). Moreover, if there is a missed shot it is usually because the kicker erred or the goalkeeper was simply lucky that he predicted where the ball was going (ironically, the luck factor is one of the main reasons goalkeepers lose concentration during a game). One only has to remember what is perhaps the most famous botched penalty kick between the legendary Italian forward, Roberto Baggio, and the goalkeeper, Cláudio Taffarel, in the 1994 World Cup final against Brazil, in front of over 90,000 spectators. Baggio, a great penalty kicker (he took 17 practice kicks before the game and scored every time), unbelievably and heartrendingly missed the goal (the ball sailed over the bar) and

25 While goalkeepers are a lonely group, they are probably viewed more as eccentrics, in fact there is an adage that goes, "You have to be a bit mad to be a goalkeeper."

Italy lost the championship. Baggio said, "It affected me for years. It is the worst moment of my career. I still dream about it. If I could erase a moment, it would be that one" (www.thedivineponytail.com, retrieved 4/1/14). Baggio's missed shot emphasizes the role of chance, luck and fluke in soccer, and for that matter, in life, and to nobody is this randomness, this seemingly arbitrary determinism, more evident than to the goalkeeper whose sense of control and effectiveness is felt to be radically precarious.[26]

While most goalkeepers are remembered for their mistakes, sometimes the opposite is true, which again emphasizes the role of chance and contingency in this highly unpredictable sport. One of the greatest saves judged as "The Save of the Century" was made by Gordon Banks in the first phase of the 1970 World Cup between England and Brazil: "A Jairzinho [a quick and powerful winger] cross from the right was met perfectly by Pelé who headed it down towards Gordon's bottom right corner. As the ball hit the ground in front of the goal line, he managed to flick it with his outstretched right hand as it came up. The ball rose over the bar for a corner" (www.planetworldcup.com, retrieved 4/1/14). As Banks noted many years later, "That save from Pelé's header was the best I ever made. I didn't have any idea how famous it would become, to start with, I didn't even realise I'd made it at all" (www.observer.theguardian.com, retrieved 4/1/14). In light of soccer's "stubborn capacity for surprise" (and life's capacity as well), and it being the "art of the unforeseeable," as Galeano aptly describes it (2009, p. 243), how does a great goalkeeper effectively manage to keep his inner center of gravity and perform well?

Eduardo Chillida, the famous Spanish sculptor, hit the nail on the head when he commented, "The conditions you need to be a good goal keeper are exactly the same conditions you need to be a good sculptor [and artful self-fashioner]. You must have a very good connection, in both professions, with time and space" (www.goalkeepersaredifferent.com, retrieved 4/2/14). What Chillida was getting at is the need for situational awareness, the perception of environmental elements with respect to time and/or space, the comprehension of their meaning, and the projection of their status after some variable has changed, such

---

26 Olaya et al.'s observation seems relevant here: in soccer, "[w]e learn how short and long a minute can be. We learn to suffer. We learn to rejoice. All of this happens because football is an emotional compromise" (Olaya, Lammoglia, & Zarama, 2010, p. 285).

as time or a predetermined event. Deconstructionist Jacques Derrida hinted at a similar observation when he wrote in his typically opaque style about soccer, "Beyond the touchline," the boundary line of each side of the soccer pitch, "there is nothing." That is, since there is no absolute Truth or Reality, what ultimately matters is "the terrain or foot" (www.independent.co.uk, retrieved 4/1/14), the totality of concrete circumstances that one is in at a particular point in space and time. Goalkeeper Brad Friedel put it just right: "What I do for a living may appear to be simple. Yet think about it, I have to apply an intuitive understanding of geometry and the laws of physics. I'll make continuous and instantaneous risk assessments about the action I should take in relation to the flight of a spheroid object. That's what my job is really all about" (www.how2playsoccer.com, retrieved 4/3/14).

Consider, for example, the nature of the spectacularly balletic "fingertip save," where the goalkeeper seems to be flying through space. What matters most is the timing of the desperate "leap, and of twisting and stretching within that leap, so as to maximize the chances of deflecting the ball." As Winters concludes, "the fingertip save is at the limits of what it is possible for a man to achieve in stretching himself to his proprioceptive limits" (2010, p. 152).[27] It is managing the high cross that is the ultimate test by which the best goalkeepers are judged. In short, being a good goalkeeper requires the same intuition and skillfulness as real life, namely the knack of being at the right place at the right time and in the right positional readiness when it most matters.[28]

While Chillida's goalkeeper/sculptor connection is a good one, it needs a bit of detailing, especially in terms of highlighting how the goalkeeper's outlook and skills aptly apply to the art of living the "good life." Eamonn Dunphy, the popular Irish sports pundit, noted about the nature of the goalkeeper, "Somewhere the grace of a ballet dancer joins with the strength of an SAS squaddie, the dignity of an ancient kind, the nerve of a bomb disposal officer" (www.sportplan.net, retrieved 4/2/14). One of the underappreciated links among the sculptor/ballet dancer/soccer player and the artful self-fashioner of identity

27 To some there is an erotically-tinged aspect to the goalkeeper's movements. For example, American goalkeeper Tim Howard noted, "Some goalkeepers are really sexy with their feet. I have a little sexiness with my feet, but I don't like to bring it out" (www.goalkeepersaredifferent.com, retrieved 4/2/14).

28 I am paraphrasing from Welsh, 1999.

is the need for a single-mindedness of purpose in terms of what one judges to ultimately matter. In the case of the goalkeeper, since the inception of the modern game, the superordinate aim is always the same: never to grant a goal. While in everyday life the objective may not be so concretely delineated and obvious, there are many instances where it is precisely this kind of single-mindedness, the ability to keep one's mind resolutely on one task, such as in overcoming adversity, which is needed to prevail. In the case of the goalkeeper, this fierceness of purpose, especially when combined with his power, agility and quickness,[29] can instill fear in his opponents, intimidating strikers from fully engaging the goalkeeper at key moments. As retired Danish goalkeeper Peter Schmeichel noted, "I always try to pressure the player for as long as he begins to think. As soon as the attacking player must think, I have got him!" (www.barnet123.wix.com, retrieved 4/3/14). Most importantly, such single-mindedness requires a high degree of fearlessness. Former German goalkeeper Toni Schumacher quipped, "I am often scared by my lack of fear" (www.unm.edu, retrieved 4/2/14). Indeed, despite the goalkeeper being the "last defender," he most often exudes a steadfast calmness to his team, especially when the going gets tough. His job includes being able to organize the players before him and motivate them to defensive excellence. As former German goalkeeper Sepp Maier aptly put it, this requires the capacity to "radiate peace" (http://www.goalkeepersarediffferent.com, retrieved 4/2/14) (but not so much inner peace that he loses concentration or falls asleep, as goalkeepers fear). Indeed, it is not coincidental that the goalkeeper is regarded as the "jewel in the crown," the player who most depicts the spirit of soccer at its best, for he personifies the personal autonomy and integration that is needed to win, especially with grace and style. Schumacher called it the capacity to "play like an innocent child" (www.hansleitert.com, retrieved 4/4/14). All great goalkeepers display great perseverance and courage, are highly driven and incredibly hardworking, always willing and able to meet challenges, and display what is often called character.[30] But even more, a great goalkeeper, like any artful self-fashioner of the "good life," has a way of relating to the game and to himself that seems critical in order to prevail. A fitting end to this section, Friedel aptly makes this point:

---

29 I am paraphrasing Hope Solo, the American goalkeeper.

30 I am paraphrasing Yousseff Dahha, the Canadian goalkeeper trainer.

> You are part of a team yet somehow separate; there are no grey areas, with success or failure being measured in real time; and you have a physical job which you can only do well by paying attention to your mental well-being. A great goalkeeper has to have the keys to a great mindset. To be able to work well in the box, I believe you have to be able to think outside the box. (www.how2playsoccer.com, retrieved 4/3/14)

CONCLUSION: SOCCER AS THE BEAUTIFUL GAME

As the great Liverpool manager Bill Shankly famously remarked, "Some people believe football is a matter of life and death. I'm very disappointed with that attitude. I can assure you it is much, much more important than that" (www.shankly.com, retrieved 2/1/14). For most readers, Shankly is probably overstating his case, at least a trifle. However, what is true and pertinent is that whether one is talking about the art of playing or watching beautiful soccer, or living the beautiful life, what is clear is that it requires experiencing with the fullness of one's whole being the "symbolism in action" (Shenk, 2006, p. 54) that infuses each activity with an aesthetically pleasing, if not magical, quality. While I have suggested many affect-integrating, meaning-giving, action-guiding symbolic leitmotifs throughout this chapter, I want to close by emphasizing what is perhaps the main aspect of playing beautiful soccer and living beautifully, namely, embracing a sense of what Russian literary theorist Mikhail Bakhtin called the "carnivalesque." These are the magnificently delightful moments when conventional rules and traditional order are pushed to the side, the world is upturned and the familiar routines of everyday life are abrogated. The term carnivalesque emanates from the carnival revelry in which the populace in Catholic societies put on masks and had huge street parties immediately before Lent, such as the celebration of Mardi Gras. The carnivalesque evokes "excitement, revelry, danger, and a certain topsy-turviness to the way the world works" (www.shmoop.com, retrieved 4/4/14). When we think about the difference between two great soccer traditions, the English and Latin American styles of play (www.expertfootball.com, retrieved 4/4/14), the carnivalesque becomes more obvious, including as a mode of being to emulate in life. British soccer's players, for example, are typically "physical, quick and direct" in how they play. This straightforward, no-nonsense English style includes many traditional values that have been in existence in

England since the emergence of modern soccer. Attacks are organized rapidly with few touches on the ball. Passes are direct, usually propelled over the defense. This fast-paced way of thinking and playing often leads to intense fighting over 50-50 balls. Crosses are kicked in from any obtainable position (ibid.). This terrifyingly efficient style has been critically described as "stereotypical industrialized" soccer "of simple-minded efficiency," driven by "sweat-drenched work horses" that involves "the application of sheer force," a pragmatic approach that has been an incredibly successful way of playing soccer (Goldblatt, 2006, p. 266). In contrast, Latin American soccer players are typically self-assured, outstanding dribblers and very creative, crafty and flamboyant in how they maneuver the ball. The Latin game is unique because of its possession-oriented character, including when attacking. The ball is moved spontaneously with many individual-based plays being its trademark. While Latin teams from Spain, Portugal and Argentina are typical of this Latin style, it is Brazil that most personifies the improvisational, versatile and free-flowing form of play (www.expertfootball.com, retrieved 4/4/14). As Goldblatt notes, historically, English and Latin soccer were distinguished by England's "crude utilitarianism" while the Latin Americans conceived and played their game "as art, as spectacle, as dance and as drama" (Goldblatt, 2006, pp. 266, 359).

My take home point polemically affirmed is this: While an attitude toward life that is instrumental, in certain contexts even machine-like in its efficiency, is a crucial one in terms of living the "good life," an outlook that values equally, if not more, that the aesthetic should animate one's overall comportment. In short, the Brazilians have it more right than the English: Whether on the pitch or in real life, "playing for love" is better than "playing to win," and "the cult of the dribble," of individual brilliance, creativity and spontaneity, should be valued more than "the cult of efficiency" (ibid., p. 266). In so doing, one may be lucky enough to experience some of the spells and enchantment that beautiful soccer and beautiful living have to offer. As one of the greatest soccer players who ever played the game, Ronaldo, put it, "I am living a dream I never want to wake up from" (www.manchester.com, retrieved 1/27/14).[31]

---

31 Soccer great David Beckham succinctly made a similar point in an interview: "Soccer is a magical game" (*People Magazine*, 2008).

CHAPTER 3

BASEBALL: THE IMMORTAL GAME

> "In our sundown perambulations of late through the outer parts of Brooklyn, we have observed several parties of youngsters playing 'base,' a certain game of ball…The game of ball is glorious…I see great things in baseball. It is our game, the American game."
>
> Walt Whitman (Sexton, with Oliphant & Schwartz, 2013, p. 215)

"Baseball," wrote syndicated columnist and baseball rhapsodist George F. Will, "is heaven's gift to struggling mortals" (Will, 1998, p. 64). Indeed, baseball, to some extent like other sports, is "a way of looking at life," one that teaches a subtle form of exquisite pleasure (Giamatti, 1998a, p. 82). Exactly what constitutes baseball's pleasure-giving qualities to its players and spectators, qualities that point to the possibility of glimpsing immortality, is what this chapter is mainly about. Robert Jay Lifton has described this process as striving for "symbolic immortality," an "experiential transcendence," that intense feeling when "time and death disappear." Such experiences of being enamored with existence centrally involve "losing oneself," and can occur in a number of enthralling contexts: in religious and secular forms of mysticism, "in song, dance, battle, sexual love, childbirth, athletic effort, mechanical flight, or in contemplating works of artistic or intellectual creation" (Lifton, 1976, pp. 33–34). Baseball, similar to religion, has a "systematic coherence, spiritual luminosity, and transcendent character" (Giamatti, 1998a, p. 43), which has a strong interpretive grip on millions of people, not only in the United States, but also in many other parts of the world. One Gallup poll from 2006 indicated that nearly half of Americans are baseball fans (Jones, "Nearly Half of Americans are Baseball Fans," retrieved 10/28/13), while it is one of the most popular sports in Japan and parts of Central and South America.

In addition to baseball appealing to the "common man" (and woman), its diehard fans include some notable intellectuals like the late President of Yale University and baseball commissioner, A. Bartlett Giamatti, the late Harvard paleontologist and historian of science, Stephen Jay Gould, and most recently, the President of New York University, John Sexton, who teaches a popular course on baseball as a spiritual journey. The seriousness of many intellectuals' baseball devotion is in sync with the well-known observation that baseball is the "thinking person's sport," it is "graceful, subtle, elegant, inexhaustibly interesting and fun" (Will, 1998, p. 50).While some may find baseball to be boring compared to football and basketball, the American broadcaster Red Barber quipped, "Baseball is dull only to dull minds."[1] To the aficionado, however, it is the "green fields of the mind." The great English novelist/essayist John Fowles explains, "Though I like the various forms of football in the world, I don't think they begin to compare with these two great Anglo-Saxon ball games for sophisticated elegance and symbolism. Baseball and cricket are beautiful and highly stylized medieval war substitutes, chess made flesh, a mixture of proud chivalry and base—in both senses—greed. With football we are back to the monotonous clashing armor of the brontosaurus" (izquotes.com, retrieved 9/15/13). In other words, baseball is mainly about "nuances and anticipations," while football is about "vectors and

---

1 As the former American League baseball pitcher Jim Bouton quipped, "Baseball players are smarter than football players. How often do you see a baseball team penalized for too many men on the field?" (Burman, 2012, p. 116). This being said, as national TV ratings have repeatedly shown, football and basketball have become more popular than baseball in American society. Why this is the case has to do with broader cultural trends that have fashioned America. For example, football is "louder, faster and more violent," and this facilitates more excitement, compared to baseball which is "quiet" and "slow" with flashes of excitement. In our current cultural moment such considerations appear to be more psychologically in tune with sports fans (see Mahler, "Is the Game Over?", retrieved 10/1/13). However, some baseball scholars have claimed that basketball is not a more popular sport than baseball by most measures such as viewership, attendance and revenue/team value (Peter Schwartz, personal communication, 12/20/13).

forces" (Will, 1990, p. 250).[2] Psychoanalytically speaking, we can say that baseball is about the psychological struggle between sons and fathers, while football is about sibling rivalry, brothers whacking each other in the backyard or sandlot. Most importantly for this chapter, as the wonderful baseball films like *Field of Dreams* (my favorite), *The Natural, Bull Durham,* and *It Happens Every Spring,* suggest, baseball is "one of the best settings for metaphorical tales of the human spirit and character" (Sexton, 2013, p. 160). It can aptly be conceived as a "parable of life," as a "moral fable" (Robson, 1998, pp. 3, 14), one that has much to teach us about how to live the "good life." Most importantly, this requires developing a greater baseball literacy and attunement to the way the craft is performed at its highest level of excellence, for this is the most fertile point of entry for embracing baseball's magic, its beautiful immortality.

I. HOME PLATE: THE INTERNAL PLACE WHERE YOU MUST RECKON WITH YOURSELF

Baseball has a powerful emotional bond and tie to home plate, both literally and symbolically, as it is the center of the baseball universe. It is perhaps for this reason that it is not simply called "fourth base." Home plate is the place where the batter begins his existential odyssey, that is, his high octane, "man-to-man" battle against the pitcher and secondarily, the fielders, and hopefully hits the rocketing ball and scores a run, signified when he victoriously crosses home plate. In baseball, the only safe passage around the four bases is the "home run," otherwise the challenge of safely and victoriously returning to home plate requires nearly superhuman powers. As Ted Williams, the left fielder of the Boston Red Sox (nicknamed "the greatest hitter who ever lived"), famously said, hitting a baseball is the most difficult task in any sport, it "is the only field of endeavor where a man can succeed three times out of ten and be considered a good performer" (Palmer, Gillette, & Shea, 2006, p. 7). The best hitters manage to score a bit more than 100 runs a season in roughly 650 times at bat (Kraus, 2004, p. 10).[3] Home plate is often a place of shattered dreams of greatness,

---

2 Will is quoting from Sandy Alderson, the Harvard lawyer who was the general manager of the Mets.

3 The great powerhouse Ted Williams noted about the art of hitting, "Wait-wait-wait and then quick-quick-quick." As Will notes, "quickness is

if not immortality. To quote Ted Williams again, "All I want out of life is that when I walk down the street folks will say, 'There goes the greatest hitter who ever lived'" (Will, 1990, p. 329). Interestingly, Williams psyched himself up before batting by saying to himself, "My name is Ted fucking Williams and I'm the greatest hitter in baseball" (Dickson, 2008, p. 599). Baseball, like all sports, involves the wish for immortality in its players, and in a different way, in its fans (Giamatti, 1998b, p. 15).

What is baseball's obsession with home plate all about, and what does it suggest about the art of living the "good life," including pointing to something deeper and more profound, that can plausibly be the staging ground to sensing the ineffable or transcendent (Sexton, 2013, pp. 3, 21)?

It was A. Bartlett Giamatti, a Renaissance scholar and the "metaphysician of American sport" (Will, 1990, p. 100), who has perhaps best captured the allegorical meaning of home plate in baseball. As a narrative, baseball is "an epic of exile and return, a vast, communal poem about separation, loss, and the hope for reunion." That is, says Giamatti, baseball is a "story of going home after having left home, the story of how difficult it is to find the origins one so deeply needs to find. It is the literary mode called Romance" (1998b, pp. 95, 90). Giamatti beautifully explains,

> Baseball is about homecoming. It is a journey by theft and strength, guile and speed, out around first to the fair island of second, where foes lurk in the reefs and green sea suddenly grows deeper, then to turn sharply, skimming the shallows, making for a shore that will show a friendly face, a color, a familiar language and, at third, to proceed, no longer by paths indirect but straight, to home.
>
> Baseball is about going home, and how hard to get there and how driven is our need. It tells us how good home is. Its wisdom says you can go home again but that you cannot stay. The journey must always start once more, the bat an oar over the shoulder, until there is an end to all journeying. (1998a, pp. 30–31)

---

the quality most rewarded in baseball," whether when one is batting or on the field (1990, p. 281). Wade Boggs is less clear about the art of hitting, though his words are probably more typical for the geniuses of the game: "Everyone asks me 'why' about everything. I have no idea. I see it. I swing, I hit it" (Dickson, 2008, p. 65).

Citing Homer's *Odyssey* and the many literary romances that have grown from it, Giamatti makes the thoughtful observation that while the goal of Odysseus, and the batter, is to return home and put things right, it "is rarely glimpsed, almost never attained." One of the main reasons for this is that once one leaves home, one is "thrown" into inhospitable real life, that is, one has to negotiate the many challenges and hardships, the pain and sorrow, emanating from what often feels like an uncooperative, hostile world (Giamatti, 1998b, pp. 92, 93). While residue of this "hunger for home" (Giamatti, 1998a, p. 42) may survive the ordeal of separating and venturing into the world, the home from whence one began is mainly an imagining that rarely corresponds with the reality of returning home, especially when one remains home over time. Indeed, Thomas Wolfe was on to something psychologically important when he wrote his famous novel, *You Can't Go Home Again*. In baseball, however, you can literally go home again, which is part of baseball's promise of redemption. Everyone longs "to arrive at the same place, which is where they start," home plate. While home is a literal possibility in baseball, ironically, just about everything has psychologically changed for the batter and spectator during and after this journey "of leaving and seeking home" (ibid., pp. 94, 103). It is this point that is often underappreciated by Giamatti and others who embrace baseball as an Odysseus-like, spiritual journey.

In real life, home, the place one lives permanently, is usually experienced as a refuge from the harshness of the outside world, as a place of security and happiness, of comfort and relaxation, and competence and familiarity—in short, it is unconsciously equated with a real or imagined warmth, protectiveness and love of one's mother.[4] For most people, this is only one side of being at home, especially in terms of an adult remembrance of one's childhood home. Home is also a place of familial discord, conflict, rivalry, and frustrated desires. If, as I do, you believe Freud was right, for the boy growing up in a traditional family (of baseball fanatics), home is a place of subtle, and sometimes not so subtle, fears, especially of the imposing, "larger than life" father.

4 The great outfielder Willie Mays noted, "I remember the last season I played. I went home after a ballgame one day, lay down on my bed, and tears came to my eyes. How can you explain that? It's like crying for your mother after she's gone. You cry because you love her. I cried, I guess, because I loved baseball and I knew I had to leave her" (Dickson, 2008, p. 356).

Freud conceptualized this problematic aspect of the father/son relationship with one's real or imagined, powerful and "castrating" Oedipal father, as a struggle against helplessness. Home thus can be conceived as having a duality of structure; it can be the basis of experiencing one's childhood home, to use an apt religious expression, as a "blessing"—the comforting fantasized maternal presence eluded to above—or a "curse"—the threatening side of the paternal presence. Most often, however, one's home world is regarded as situated in the "gray zone," full of emotional half-tints, that is, mixed and conflicted feelings often associated with both parents. For instance, interest in baseball is often a point of memorable father/son bonding. As Sexton noted, "Just as I had once forged a powerful bond with my father through a ball club, so too, I decided, must my son be given the opportunity to experience such wonders with me" (2013, p. 48). I have had many patients who have reported that their fondest memories of their father was playing a simple game of baseball "catch" with each other.

In baseball, this duality of structure to the felt experience of home is dramatically depicted: home plate is where one can hit a home run and feel like a conquering hero,[5] yet it is also a place where one can strike out and feel publicly humiliated and furious. Home, especially one's childhood home, is thus an ambiguous and ambivalent place of personal identity, of growth and development and the opposite. This duality of structure, in particular the two emotion clusters most associated with home plate and batting, maternally-tinged security versus paternally-tinged insecurity, a nest of self-belonging versus a crucible of fear, calls to mind Freud's notion of the uncanny, which he defined as "that class of the frightening which leads back to what is known of old and long familiar." Moreover, he said, "an uncanny experience occurs either when infantile complexes [e.g., castration and womb fantasies] which have been repressed are once more revived by some impression, or when primitive beliefs which have been surmounted seem once more to be confirmed" (1919, pp. 220, 249).[6] Freud mentions the eerie and unsettling examples of *déjà vu*, perceiving one's double, and feeling that someone who has died has come back to life.

5 A home run is also a symbolic "gift" to the adoring fans.

6 I am indebted to Joe Kraus's essay, "There's No Place Like Home!" for drawing my attention to the applicability of Freud's "uncanny" to baseball (Bronson, 2004, p. 12).

As already insinuated, in the context of baseball, the experience of the uncanny is in sharp focus during the batter's duel with the pitcher at home plate. Similar to much of ordinary life which feels like a battle, "baseball life is an endless series of skirmishes about who will control the periphery of the plate, batters or pitchers" (Will, 1990, p. 95). The great Yankees slugger Mickey Mantle once told shortstop Tony Kubek that at least once a year, and maybe more often, "I wake up screaming in the middle of the night, sweating a cold sweat, with the ball coming right at my head" (ibid., p. 176). As is well known, though often underplayed and/or denied, downright fear of the pitcher is an intrinsic aspect of batting. In fact, in Little League, children just starting to learn the game often have incredible anxiety about being hit by the ball, especially in the head. One six-year-old I treated would obsessively touch his penis before he had to bat. His visceral response to fear is no surprise, as a pitcher throws a hard ball at about 90 mph (60 mph in Little League), and yet all the batter has to defend himself with, as it were, is a thin wooden or aluminum bat and some plastic equipment. If the ball hits him it usually hurts terribly. Moreover, the speeding ball can do serious bodily harm, and it can, in a worst case scenario, actually be lethal. Not only this, the pitcher is well-aware that he is at a huge advantage in terms of the power dynamics over the batter: he is on the "mound," the small hill on which the pitcher stands, thus appearing bigger and more formidable than he actually is; he is collaborating with the catcher (and other fielders) to outsmart the batter, and the catcher is nerve-rackingly squatting directly behind the batter who is "boxed in," having to stay inside the "batter's box" while batting. To make matters even more threatening, behind the catcher is the Law, the umpire, who is an imposing figure of absolute judgment. As Will evocatively puts it, "Umpires are carved from granite and stuffed with microchips. They are supposed to be dispassionate dispensers of Pure Justice, icy islands of emotionless calculation" (ibid., p. 58). "Call 'em fast and walk away tough," home plate umpire Richie Garcia famously said (ibid., p. 64). Most importantly, the pitcher is willing and able to use fear to intimidate the batter into submission, that is, to get him out of his routine, so self-doubting that a conceptual disarray is induced. As the great pitcher Don Drysdale noted, "The pitcher has to find out if the hitter is timid, and if he is timid, he has to remind the hitter he's timid" (Dickson, 2008, p. 150). Will further notes,

> Even the most gentlemanly pitchers can be provoked to use fear. Kubek says that Sandy Koufax "who could throw a baseball maybe better than anybody in history," once threatened Lou Brock [left fielder, St. Louis Cardinals] just because Brock stole a base in a crucial situation. As Brock was dusting himself off at second, Koufax turned to him and, according to Kubek, said, "Next time you do that I'm going to hit you right in the head." Brock stole another base against Koufax. He then became the only man Koufax ever hit in the head. Brock stole no more bases off Koufax. (ibid., p. 177) [In fact, Koufax said, "Pitching is the art of instilling fear" (Price, 2006, p. 128).]

"If you've got them by the balls, their hearts and minds will follow," said President Theodore Roosevelt.[7] Indeed, intimidation is an all-important constituent of being a great pitcher, and both the pitcher and batter viscerally know this (Dickson, 2008, p. 608). Said one of the most daunting fastball pitchers, Early Wynn, "A pitcher will never be a big winner until he hates hitters...[he] has to look at the hitter as his mortal enemy" (ibid., p. 606). Ted Williams said, "There's only one way to become a hitter. Go up to the plate and get mad. Get mad at yourself and mad at the pitcher" (Seidel, 1991, p. xix). Like David facing Goliath, the batter hopes that his trusty "sling shot/bat" will protect and prevail. What makes the duel between the batter and pitcher so thrilling, if not nerve-wracking to both the batter and the spectator, is that it re-enacts the Oedipally-tinged struggle between the more powerful and "castrating" father and the weaker and near helpless son, who is fighting for his freedom to be his own person and for his self-respect, if not for his life, symbolized by returning safely and victoriously home to the "mother of all bases," home plate. Indeed, the symbols of this struggle saturate the erotically-tinged psychological context of the batter facing—"man to man"[8]—the pitcher, all within a decidedly masculine "gang up": the catcher is "behind" the batter calling to mind a sense of vulnerability to the powerful phallic father, while the ultimate symbol of paternal judgment and punishment is evoked in the

7 Some have claimed that this proverb was used first by President Lyndon B. Johnson who was known for his crude directness.

8 As Jim Bouton approvingly notes, "My wife says there is that sexy moment in baseball when the pitcher and the batter size each other up. She says football is just herds of buffalo running together into head-on collisions for no good reason" (Dickson, 2008, p. 69).

stern rulings of the heartless umpire. From the onset of the duel, the pitcher has the clear advantage of power; in the batter's unconscious mind he appears bigger, stronger and faster than the batter. He throws a "hard ball," an unconscious sex organ equivalent, at the batter who holds a small, thin bat, another unconscious reference to the phallus, and who most of the time will strike out, that is, be "struck down" by the pitcher's precise ferocity. Remember, as a Yale professor of physics noted, a pitcher's fastball is thrown with an initial velocity of 97 mph and it crosses home plate in 0.4 seconds. Batters therefore have 0.17 seconds to make the decision to swing. To make matters even more daunting, if they swing 0.0005 seconds early, they forego the maximum bat velocity. Incredible skill and timing is required of the batter like in no other sport (Will, 1998, pp. 243–244, 58). It is for this reason that the spectator has a degree of identification with the batter's underdog status, if not his helplessness, and this is why when he gets a hit, a way of "hitting back" at the Oedipal father, there is a sense of relief, if not overwhelming joy. Perhaps this moment has been best captured in the famous "called shot" of the incomparable Yankees slugger, Babe Ruth. Ruth's "called shot" was the home run he hit in the fifth inning of the third game of the 1932 World Series played at Chicago's Wrigley Field. While at-bat against pitcher Charlie Root, the Chicago Cubs' "bench jockeys" and fans were mercilessly heckling Ruth, including fans who were yelling insults and throwing lemons. Allegedly, someone even spat on Ruth's wife, Claire. Rather than paying no attention to the taunting and trash talk, the angry Ruth was ridiculing the dugout and fans through his words and gestures. With two strikes against him in a tied game, he then made a pointing gesture at either the center field bleachers, at the Cubs' dug-out, or at Charlie Root (this is hotly disputed)[9], seemingly proclaiming that he would hit a home run to that part of Wrigley Field. On the following pitch, Ruth hit a home run to center field. The fifty thousand fans watching

9 Babe has made a number of comments, sometimes contradictory, about this home run. The following quote seems to be closest to the "truth": "Aw, everybody knows that game, the day I hit the homer off Charlie Root there in Wrigley Field, the day, October 1, the third game of that 1932 World Series. But right now I want to settle all arguments. I didn't exactly point to any spot, like the flagpole. Anyway, I didn't mean to, I just sorta waved at the whole fence, but that was foolish enough. All I wanted to do was give the thing a ride…outa the park…anywhere" (Dickson, 2008, p. 473).

the game went wild. Thus, in this intensely anti-Yankees, anti-Ruth context, Ruth asserted his will to power, reclaiming his and his wife's dignity, just as his mythological status, his immortality, was guaranteed in the annals of baseball history. Indeed, what is uncanny about this is that when the Babe completed his victory run and crossed home plate, it was unconsciously understood by fans that that the Yankees "son" had slain the Cubs' "father," thus calling to mind the Oedipal struggle. The roaring spectators, even the diehard Cubs fans and dugout were cheering, thoroughly identified with the Babe's guilt-free, self-affirmation of his wish to defeat the fearful, dominating, hate-filled father/pitcher and return home as conquering hero to the loved and loving "mother," symbolically named home plate. Such inspired self-affirmation is radically transformative for both the batter and spectator. It has a transcendent spiritual intensity that makes you feel completed and perfected and want to rejoice. As the Yale professor of History and Classics and baseball lover Donald Kagan put it, "A dramatically heroic and potentially tragic confrontation stands at the heart of this most poetic game" (ibid., p. 148). The exalted melancholy of the batter's fate is that the exhilaration associated with this so-called "Oedipal victory" lasts only briefly, reminding us of the truth that nothing remains the same. More importantly, the batter and spectator are reminded that forever possessing the mother is not the way things are supposed to be. At best, we are permitted to "re-find" our mother symbolically, whether it is in the real-life choice of a partner who unconsciously calls to mind the best of one's real or fantasized mother, or hitting a home run in baseball. Indeed, the whole Oedipal drama repeats itself when the batter returns to home plate for his next at-bat.[10] Baseball loves these beautiful repetitive rhythms and patterns, especially those that signify "something more," something beyond and greater than oneself, that hints at a transcendent realm of values, meanings and feelings. It is to this subject that I now turn.

---

10 I am aware that my Oedipally-based formulation is focused on the psychology of the typical boy, leaving the question of the appeal of baseball to the typical girl unanswered. While this subject deserves its own study, my sense is that women who find baseball appealing are probably also identified with the "home/mother" symbolism and the phallic strivings that permeate hitting and pitching. The "castrating" father/pitcher may also hit her nerve, though this is probably a displacement from the girl's rivalry with the dominating mother for her father's love.

II. THE AESTHETICS OF BASEBALL

"Baseball, of course, is beautiful," wrote philosopher Eric Bronson. That is, on the elemental level it has a lilting aesthetic appeal: "The stadium and uniforms are visual treats, the sounds of the ball hitting the bat or popping into the catcher's mitt takes us back to a more innocent time, as does the smell of peanuts on a hot summer day" (Bronson, 2004, p. 319).[11] The American broadcaster Red Smith made a similar point when he famously quipped, "Ninety feet between home plate and first base may be the closest man has ever come to perfection" (Dickson, 2008, p. 504). Cohen has further elaborated what constitutes the beauty of baseball,

> The structure of baseball is its art. It's a structure that admits of infinitely complicated possibilities and combinations, within the rigid framework of rules in common, of distances to fences, of worked-out angles, of human proportions. Man is the measure of all things. The Major League ballplayer is the measure of the distances on his field of trade. Given these, he must do or die, win or lose. It's the majesty that dignity imparts. (1974, p. 3)

What these baseball mavens are implicitly saying is that to appreciate the beauty of baseball you need to learn the art of disciplined observation lodged in a repository of accumulated knowledge. The spacing of the players, the pace of the game, and the fact that there are flashes of discrete action rather than flowing action like basketball (Will, 1998, p. 241, 311) make baseball a sport that is most conducive and best appreciated via disciplined observation. It requires "thoughtfulness," that is, "attention to detail" (ibid., p. 147). "Baseball people," said poetry professor Giamatti, "have the keenest eyes for details I have ever

---

11 Actor/comedian Billy Crystal has further noted, "I've been all over the world, and the sight of Yankee Stadium for the first time on May 30, 1956, is still the most vivid in my memory. I love Dodger Stadium, but it doesn't smell like there's going to be a game that day. You walk into Yankee Stadium, and you just know, the hot dogs have been there for awhile, and even though the ball park looks different, you know there's going to be a game" (Dickson, 2008, p. 125). Second-baseman Roberto Alomar also expressed an olfactory affection for baseball; he spoke of the love of the "smell of the ballpark—hot hogs, grass...This is what God chose me to do. He sent me here to play baseball" (Will, 1998, p. 284). The sounds of baseball also evoke a similar affection, like the "crack" of the wooden bat hitting the ball and the spectator's thunderous roaring in pure pleasure.

known" (ibid., p. 211). Often this learning process takes place amidst the father/son bonding relationship when they go to watch a game. In W. P. Kinsella's *The Iowa Baseball Confederacy*, a father urges his son, Gideon, to carefully observe the exacting choreography of a play:

> Gideon, there's a lot more to watching a baseball game than keeping your eye on the ball...[t]he real movement doesn't start until the ball is in play. *After* the ball is hit, *after* it has cleared the infield, especially if it is going for extra bases, you've got to train yourself to look back at the infield. While the outfield is running down the ball, watch who is covering which base, watch to see who is backing up third and home. You'll be amazed at the amount of movements. Ah, Gideon, when everyone is in motion it's like watching those delicate, long-legged insects skim over the calm water...

The father further presses his son to see the more subtle details of the play, the "purposeful watching" that allows one to see the "game within the game" (Will, 1990, pp. 49, 288), as it has been called:

> You've got to watch the pitcher, Gideon...and you'll appreciate why baseball is a combination of chess and ballet. Watch him back up the bases, watch him get across to first on a grounder to the right side, see how the first baseman leads him, tossing to an empty sack, trusting him to be there....It takes a lot of years watching baseball to learn *not* to follow the ball every second. The true beauty of the game is the ebb and flow of the fielders, the kaleidoscopic arrangements and rearrangements of the players in response to a foul ball, an extra-base hit, or an attempted stolen base. (Sexton, 2013, pp. 19–20)

What is it about playing or watching a baseball game that feels like one is doing or watching great art, like going to a great theater performance, and having the uplifting experience of participating in the "immortal force" of beauty, as Plato described it? (Bronson, 2004, p. 319). To give a plausible answer to this important question, I need to say something about the psychological experience of beauty in terms of the analogy between doing and/or watching a great baseball player and actor performing his craft at the highest level of excellence. As Willie Mays noted, "Baseball players are no different from other performers. We're all actors, when you come down right to it, so I always thought I had to put a little acting into the game—you know, make it more interesting to the fans" (Dickson, 2008, p. 356). Giamatti pointed out, "Athletes and actors...share much." Through years of perfecting their craft they achieve "complete intensity and complete relaxation—complete coherence or integrity between what the performer wants to do and what the performer has to do." The performer has achieved a kind of absolute freedom that operates automatically and naturally (Giamatti, 1998b, p. 40).[12]

THE CALL OF BEAUTY

Beauty, most simply defined, is the combination of qualities that make something pleasing and impressive to listen to or touch, or especially to look at. While this definition is a serviceable one, it does not connote what the engagement with beauty, and its internalization in terms of one's feeling, thinking, and acting, actually means for one's general comportment, one's way of being in terms of living the "good life." As the incomparable actor, theater director and developer of "method acting," Constantin Stanislavski, advised to singers who were training as actors, "learn to see, hear, love life—carry this over into art, use it to fill out the image you create for yourself of a character you are to play" (1968, p. 31). This recommendation also applies to the baseball player.

According to Catholic philosopher and poet John O'Donohue, beauty is a kind of "invisible" and "eternal embrace," a tender but pressing call to awaken to the world of the Spirit, that vital force that characterizes a living being as he embraces life without reserve (2004b, p. 13). As Stanislavski said, "Our ideal should always be to strive for what is *eternal* in art, that which will never die, which will always remain young and close to human hearts" (1989a, p. 192). For O'Donohue, like Stanislavski, beauty is not so much a thing "out there" that we experience through our senses, though it is that too, rather, like any mystery, it erodes the sense of a distinction between "what is in me and what is before me" (Treanor, "Gabriel Marcel," retrieved 10/29/13). However, more importantly, as the actress and teacher Stella Adler described acting, the capacity to perceive, feel and create beauty is a different, more refined way of imaginatively "seeing and describing" the world and one's experience of it (Marcus & Marcus, 2011, p. 44). As O'Donohue noted, "Beauty inhabits the cutting edge of creativity—mediating between the known and unknown, light and darkness, masculine and feminine, visible and invisible, chaos and meaning, sound

12 For a psychoanalytically-informed study of acting theory and technique and its application for living the "good life," see Marcus and Marcus, 2011.

and silence, self and others" (2004b, p. 40). In this context, beauty can be adequately defined for the actor and baseball player as "human subjectivity expressed in ideal form"; in other words, "it is an aspect of experience of idealization in which an object(s), sound(s), or concept(s) is (or are) believed to possess qualities of formal perfection." In most instances, the experience of beauty is enjoyable and can evoke a gamut of emotional states, "from a gentle sense of disinterested pleasure to awe and excited fascination" (e.g., like watching a tidal wave on television). Moreover, while the observer usually believes that the beautiful object or baseball game is inherently beautiful, it is the appropriate and skillful subjective involvement in the object of beauty that is crucial to experience its beauty (Hagman, 2005, p. 87).

The capacity to experience and, most importantly, create beauty is thus a huge subjective accomplishment that implies a "high level" mode of psychological functioning. Indeed, psychoanalysis and other psychological perspectives have elaborated in thousands of books and professional articles the psychology of creativity. For our purposes, I want to simply suggest some of the internal conditions of possibility for a person to experience and create the beautiful, whether in the performing arts, in baseball, or in the art of living the "good life."

George Hagman, a psychoanalyst, has aptly summarized much of the psychoanalytic literature on the sense of beauty. He notes that the main contribution of psychoanalysis has been carefully explicating "the nature, sources, and functions of the subjective experience of beauty" (ibid., p. 94). His integrated findings are worth thinking about as they relate to acting, baseball and living the "good life," though not surprisingly, as with Stanislavski, much of what has been written by psychoanalysts on creativity has to do with unconscious processes. Stanislavski asked, "How can we come closer to this nature of creation? This has been the principle concern of my whole life." His answer: "Through the conscious to the unconscious, that is the motto of our art and technique" (1989b, p. 9). Mainly drawing from Hagman, this brief review of some of the most interesting psychoanalytic formulations about the sense of beauty are provided to give the reader a "feel" for the internal accomplishments that experiencing and creating beauty seem to entail. Whether actor, baseball player or ordinary person, Hagman's insights provide much "food for thought" in terms of understanding why baseball excellence feels so utterly beautiful to both the player and spectator.

Sublimation

For Freud, beauty was understood as a sublimation of sexual and aggressive wishes. Sublimation can be simply defined as a "developmental process by which instinctual energies [i.e., sex and aggression] are discharged in non-instinctual forms of behavior" (Rycroft, 1995, p. 176). Put differently, for any creative, artistic person, whether a baseball player or actor, sublimation is "a resolution of intraspychic conflict [conflict between two parts of the psyche] by changing the sexual and aggressive aim of an urge and finding a substitute gratification" (Person, Cooper, & Gabbard, 2005, p. 560). Sublimation by definition involves a socially approved result that is gratifying, supple and judged to be personally and socially beneficial. For example, an actor may have had a childhood in which he was rarely genuinely listened to, appreciated or otherwise validated by his parents; his need to be heard and admired gets sublimated in his choice of an acting career, of playing to an adoring audience. In the context of baseball, the player and spectator's involvement in the game is often enmeshed in his childhood experiences, and not only in terms of the father/son bonding and the Oedipal drama I have earlier described. Baseball is often a child's first introduction to the adult world, and its heroes are great men whose remarkable accomplishments can be grasped and internalized (Robson, 1998, p. x). Such identification with a hero evokes in the child, and for that matter in the adult fan, the fantasy that they too can have their transcendent moment of astonishing achievement (Gould, 2003, p. 101). In authentic sublimation, the original strong desire always comes through in the substitute activity. Meryl Streep and Marlon Brando have superbly described sublimation, the former with a pinch of humor, the latter acerbically: "Let's face it, we were all once 3-year-olds who stood in the middle of the living room and everybody thought we were so adorable. Only some of us grow up and get paid for it"; "Acting is the expression of a neurotic impulse. It is a bum's life. The principal benefit acting has afforded me is the money to pay for my psychoanalysis." Paul Newman and Al Pacino, respectively, have also regarded their acting careers as a kind of sublimation: "To be an actor you have to be a child"; "My first language was shy. It's only by having been thrust into the limelight that I have learned to cope." And finally, Stanislavski perceptively noted in his autobiography, "Actors often use the stage to receive what they cannot get in real life" (Marcus & Marcus, 2011, p. 239).

In baseball we also hear sentiments that call to mind childhood longings and urges: One of the greatest catchers of all time, Roy Campanella, made this exact point, "There has to be a lot of little boy in a man who plays baseball" (Will, 1990, p. 5). Former first baseman Wes Parker captures the childhood wish to be big and powerful in a larger than life way, "Players believe the mystique about big league baseball probably more than kids or fans do. It's those two words that are not applied to any other sport—big league" (Dickson, 2008, p. 150). With amusing, ironic distance, third baseman Graig Nettles expresses exhibitionistic wishes that are common in childhood: "When I was a little boy, I wanted to be a baseball player and join a circus. With the Yankees I've accomplished both" (ibid., p. 379). Pitcher John "Blue Moon" Odom captures the wish to remain embedded in the ambivalent comfort and protection of a nuclear family, "We liked the idea that we were a family. We could fight each other in the clubhouse and fight together outside the clubhouse. That's what made us good. You went to the ballpark never knowing what was going to happen" (ibid., p. 403). Joe DiMaggio captures the pure magic of childhood play in saying, "You always get a special kick on opening day, no matter how many you go through. You look forward to it like a birthday party when you're a kid. You think something wonderful is going to happen" (ibid., p. 144). And finally, Willie Mays and Ty Cobb speak to baseball as a venue for childhood-originating, sublimated aggression,[13] such as sibling rivalry and/or father/son competition: "Baseball is a game, yes. It is also a business. But what it most truly is, is disguised combat. For all its gentility, its almost leisurely pace, baseball is violence under wraps" (Dickson, 2008, p. 356); "Baseball is a red-blooded sport for red-blooded men. It's no pink tea, and mollycoddles had better stay out. It's a struggle for supremacy, a survival of the fittest" (ibid., p. 111). Thus, baseball players, like actors and others, come to their career choice by way of a highly idiosyncratic trajectory that has its psychological roots in childhood wishes, conflicts and deficits.

13 As Will notes, "Games are won by a combination of informed aggression and prudence based on information" (1998, p. 150).

Idealization

The experience and creation of beauty always involves the capacity to idealize. Idealization, a life-long process, especially observed when one is in love, is an unrealistic overstatement of a person's qualities. It involves the capacity for illusion; the other person or activity, like acting on a stage, is regarded as living perfection and magnificence. It goes without saying that children and adults idealize their baseball heroes. Stephen Jay Gould wrote that a foul ball that Joe DiMaggio hit and autographed "remains my proudest possession to this day" (2003, p. 133). Idealization can be a defense against ambivalence ("I love and hate my wife," "I love and hate the profession of acting or baseball"), it is a way of warding off disenchantment, sadness, guilt and other negative emotions. However, idealization in the context of beauty can represent a "healthy need" to be connected to someone or something that is experienced as perfect or ideal. As Babe Ruth said, "Baseball was, is and always will be to me the best game in the world" (Dickson, 2008, p. 473). Pete Rose quipped, "I'd walk through hell in a gasoline suit to play baseball" (ibid., p. 463). And Mickey Mantle said, "Well, baseball was my whole life. Nothing's ever been as fun as baseball" (Andrews, 2012, p. 43). This being said, idealization of the other, whether a beautiful person, thing or activity, like baseball, is a delicate and fleeting enterprise. Hagman states,

> the yearning that we experience before beauty is for an experience that is ultimately unattainable, which is already lost, perhaps forever. This is what makes beauty at times unbearable: the simultaneous sense of the ideal as both recovered and lost. (2005, pp. 95, 96)

Thus, the experience and creation of beauty is at times a painful and subjectively wounding process, something of which Stanislavski was acutely aware:

> Life [and the creative process] is an unremitting *struggle*, one overcomes or one is defeated. Likewise on the stage, side-by-side, with the through action there will be a series of *counter-through actions* on the part of other characters, other circumstances. The collision and conflict of these two opposing through actions constitute the dramatic situation.[14] (emphasis in original; 1989c, p. 80)

---

14 "Through-action/Counter-through-action" is "the logic of the sequence of actions, which bind together all the single actions and enables the character to reach his goal" (Benedetti, 1998, p. 154).

To be a great baseball player is also an "unremitting struggle" in that it fundamentally is a game of "failure"—just think of the odds of getting a hit. Moreover, there is a pronounced struggle between one team's desire to create opportunities to score, which often comes literally down to inches—"Baseball is a game of normal proportions and abnormally small margins" (Will, 1990, pp. 1, 34)—and the other team's utter commitment to stop them dead in their tracks.

Active Engagement

To experience and create beauty is not a passive undertaking; it requires marked involvement, energy and action. In acting and baseball, achieving excellence requires a total commitment of mind, body and soul. Only in this way, when the doer merges with the beautiful animate or inanimate other, is he liberated from his limited, subdued or truncated sense of himself. The experience of beauty and its creation involves an intellectual, emotional and spiritual engagement, an "interactive and intersubjective" process (Hagman, 2005, p. 96), one that tends to foster a sense of self-transcendence. In baseball, where fortune can change in a flash, especially disastrously, where memories of such disastrous moments are easily recollected by players and fans, victory is that much sweeter, for "hope builds slowly to success in a way that makes success more beautiful" (Sexton, 2013, p. 14). Perfect self and perfect world, creator and observer, loss/disappointment and abundance/satisfaction constitute, in part, the psychological landscape of the sense of beauty. In a way, as D. W. Winnicott pointed out, the experience of beauty, and for that matter all forms of art, takes place between the above mentioned dualities and polarities, in the overlapping "half way" space between subjective and objective, the psychic and the external worlds. Residing in this "betweenness" psychic space results in a wide range of emotions, such as "awe, joy, excitement, optimism and contentment" as well as "anger, sexual excitement and fear," as this range of emotions is embedded within the "formal structure" of the experience of beauty (Hagman, 2005, p. 97). Indeed, as insinuated earlier, baseball is chock full of dualities and polarities and emotional swings-and-roundabouts, and this is why when we observe a great player integrating these ambiguous if not conflicting forces, we are in awe. Giamatti notes, for example, that the great pitcher Tom Seaver "pitched as much with his head as with his legs and right arm, a remarkably compact, *concentrated* pitcher, brilliantly blending control and speed, those twin capacities for restraint and release that are the indispensable possession of the great artist" (Giamatti, 1998a, p. 17). Seaver claimed that at the height of his pitching control, "he could pitch within a quarter of an inch of a spot nine times out of ten" (Will, 1990, p. 149). To observe such professional craftsmanship, such excellence, is akin to experiencing a kind of "spiritual epiphany" (Sexton, 2013, p. 94), a sudden manifestation of the essence or meaning of athletic perfection.

Giving Way to the Healing and Self-Enhancing Experience of Beauty

In order to yield to the self-transcendent, transformative experience of beauty and its creation, one must be able to "let go," to hurl oneself into the invisible embrace. This "letting go" can be done in many different ways and intensities depending on the context, from passionately surrendering to the allure of a beautiful person or to the felt presence of God through prayer, to quietly admiring a lovely sunset or the elegance of a mathematical equation. This "letting go" is what separates the baseball fan from the observer who finds the game dull or boring. As Hagman noted, following Emmanuel Ghent, "Through this experience of surrender that we break out of the confines of our false selves and allow ourselves to be known, found, penetrated, and recognized—it is a vital, natural force toward psychological and spiritual growth" (2005, p. 98). This capacity to be open and responsive sounds easier than it actually is. As the great Roman lyric poet Horace wrote, "If you would have me weep, you must first of all feel grief yourself" (www.eng.aphorism.ru/author/horace, retrieved 6/15/14).[15] There are many people who are twisted up like pretzels, too inhibited, defended and in other ways internally restricted that they cannot appreciate beauty or creatively imagine and produce something beautiful. For them, life lacks the "presence and possibility" of a "real" encounter with the mysteriously beautiful, which is also always a striking

15 Acting, said Stanislavski, can be a "painful process," it "requires enormous self-mastery," "physical endurance" and "awareness," among other personal qualities difficult to cultivate (Stanislavski, 1989d, pp. 9, 70). Stella Adler also advocated that actors have to push themselves out of their comfort zone, which can cause anxiety: "You're here to learn to stretch yourself in life, and in so doing on stage as well" (2000, p. 207). This being said, "Acting is happy agony," said Sartre. So is baseball playing and spectatorship.

self-encounter. O'Donohue says, "Yet ultimately beauty is a profound illumination of presence, a stirring of the invisible in visible form and in order to receive this, we need to cultivate a new style of approaching the world" (2004b, p. 23). Thus, when beauty and its creation touches the "matrix of human selfhood" (ibid., p. 21), whether gently or disruptively, it always enlarges, expands and enriches consciousness—it is "an encounter of depth and spirit" (ibid., p. 23).

The encounter with the beautiful, whether as an observer or a creator, thus has a healing aspect to it. It is capable of facilitating a feeling of "harmony, balance, and wholeness" (Hagman, 2005, p. 99), better ways of experiencing and engaging the self and world. Moreover, it can "repair the feared fragmentation or damage done to internal objects by aggressive wishes." [Internal objects are "that towards which action or desire is directed; that which the subject requires in order to achieve" sexual or aggressive "satisfaction; that to which the subject relates himself" (Rycroft, 1995, p. 113).] Put more simply, beauty helps the person subdue, transform or undo the aggressive fantasies that we all consciously or unconsciously periodically have toward others (think of the anger the pitcher and batter feel toward each other; each sees the other as the "enemy"). It can also reduce the anxiety associated with death by putting the person "in touch" with a transcendent belief, value and self-experience that is regarded as definitively, overwhelmingly and eternally truthful and good.[16] As Hagman notes, "Beauty is not illusory, nor does it stand in or cover up something else" (though it can). Rather, beauty may express "man's search for perfection, transcendence and hope..." It is "one of the most exquisite forms of human meaning that exists" (2005, p. 101). In the context of baseball playing and/or spectatorship, Hagman has it exactly right. Giamatti's title to his scholarly baseball book, *Take Time for Paradise*, and John Sexton's title to his, *Baseball as a Road to God*, superbly capture Hagman's important observation about the nature of beauty. First baseman and manager Buck O'Neil made the same point, though using rather earthier language: "Baseball is better than sex. It is better than music,

16 As Gabriel Marcel has indicated, the denial of the transcendent reflects the "brokenness" of the self (e.g., the incapability or unwillingness to imagine and to wonder) and the world (e.g., the overvaluation of functionality, technical reasoning and so-called objectivity in everyday life). See Treanor, *Stanford Encyclopedia of Philosophy*, retrieved 10/29/13.

although I do believe jazz comes in a close second. It does fill you up" (1996, p. 63).

III. BASEBALL AS MORAL INSTRUCTION

"Baseball," said former catcher and announcer Joe Garagiola, "gives you every chance to be great. Then it puts every pressure on you to prove you haven't got what it takes" (Dickson, 2008, p. 192). The all-time greatest no-hitter pitcher who regularly threw pitches at 100 mph, Nolan Ryan, said something very similar, "One of the beautiful things about baseball is that every once in a while you come into a situation where you want to, and where you have to, reach down and prove something" (Stewart, 2012, p. 39). Proving yourself, especially to oneself, perhaps even more than to real and imagined others, is mainly a question of character, that is, moral and ethical excellence. As sports columnist Thomas Boswell wrote, "We are drawn to baseball because, while it may not always teach character, it usually reveals it" (Will, 1998, p. 48). Indeed, baseball is a game that brings out the best, and sometimes the worst, in its players, managers and spectators. For example, think of the tragic grandeur of Lou Gehrig's "farewell speech" at Yankee Stadium after he was diagnosed with the fatal disease named after him—"Yet today I consider myself the luckiest man on the face of the earth," versus the nastiness, if not sadism, of Ty Cobb, whom baseball scholar Stephen Jay Gould calls both the "finest player in the history of baseball" and "the meanest star in the history of American sport" (Gould, 2003, pp. 328, 329).[17] As pitcher great Jim Bouton wrote in *Ball Four Plus Ball Five*, "There's pettiness in baseball, and meanness and stupidity beyond belief, and everything bad that you'll find outside of baseball" (1984, p. xix). Most importantly for this chapter, baseball is a venue of moral insight, for it articulates and instantiates life-affirming values and commitments that point to what really matters in life; that is, to the importance of embracing transcendent valuative attachments that can enhance one's autonomy, integration

17 Ruth had a similar impression of Cobb: "Cobb is a prick. But he sure can hit. God Almighty, that man can hit" (Dickson, 2008, p. 473). Cobb was also a racist; he refused to sleep in the same hunting lodge as Babe Ruth, whom he and others believed was a Black American (he was often teased, being called "nigger lips"): "I never slept under the same roof with a nigger, and I'm not going to start here in my own native state of Georgia" (ibid., p. 109).

and humanity. Such valuative attachments often reflect rather finely nuanced moral reasoning: As one batter who was brushed back by a pitcher's fastball quipped, "They shouldn't throw at me. I'm the father of five or six kids!" (Will, 1998, p. 68).

What existential philosopher Albert Camus (who was an impressive goalkeeper for his university until he was stricken at age 18 with tuberculosis) said about sports readily applies to baseball: From "sports…I learned all I know about ethics" (1960, p. 242). Camus was emphasizing that from the moral perspective, baseball, like all sports that are played fairly, should have the same purpose as great artistic creations, namely, to expand and deepen the individual's totality of freedom and responsibility (ibid., p. 240).

Like with Adam and Eve before their fall, unrestricted, unrestrained freedom is as close to "paradise" as one can get. Baseball, says Giamatti, speaks to American moral identity like no other sport, for it "best mirrors the condition of freedom," that amalgamation of intense energy and complex order, "that Americans ever guard and aspire to" (1989b, p. 83). Similar to all sports, baseball assumes equality for the reason of creating inequality, a level playing field on which the best will assert their superiority (Will, 1998, p. 220). It teaches us how to win based on excellence.[18] However, like in everyday life, there can be a rough justice in baseball. Sometimes "good guys" come in last, reminding us that life often feels grossly unjust. Baseball also teaches us how to lose graciously. Moreover, Giamatti claims, "Our national plot is to be free enough to consent to an order that will enhance and compound—as it constrains—our freedom. That is our grounding, our national story, the tale America tells the world" and itself (1998b, p. 83). Commenting on Giamatti's important point, Will notes that baseball perfectly duplicates the challenge of freedom that Americans so cherish, especially through those who impartially protect the rule of law and dispense justice—the quintessential constrainers of baseball freedom, the umpires (Will, 1998, p. 220). As an angry Babe Ruth told hard-nosed umpire Babe Pinelli who called him out on strikes, "There's 40,000 people here who know that last one was a ball, tomato head." Pinelli

18 As Hamilton notes, baseball has had its fair amount of cheating over the years, like "using corked bats, pitches who doctor baseballs, or coaches who teach players break the rules," and of course, most recently, the use of performance-enhancing drugs. Many believe that it has been institutionally tolerant of a degree of cheating (Hamilton, 2004, p. 127).

famously replied, "Maybe so, but mine is the only opinion that counts" (Will, 1990, p. 64). The point is that truth may be inflexible and inviolable, but ironically, it is also context-dependent and setting-specific, that is, "truth is a circumstance, not a spot" (Gould, 2003, pp. 49, 48).

As in real life, in baseball, freedom is knotted to responsibility, for it is not only a matter of individual self-affirmation and personal accountability, but it centrally includes actions that strengthen and deepen moral community.[19] Baseball values individual achievement but never at the expense of the common good and the team's overarching goal of a fair win. That is, baseball values actions that are, to paraphrase ethical philosopher Emmanuel Levinas, firstly "for the other" rather than "for oneself." These are the instances where one's crude narcissism, the egotistical search for individual immortality, must give way to the more commanding needs of the team. In baseball, this being for the other before oneself is manifested in many ways, but most obviously it is personified in the notion of "sacrifice," especially the "sacrifice bunt" or "sacrifice hit." A sacrifice bunt is when a batter purposely bunts the ball (that is, the batter loosely holds the bat in front of home plate and intentionally lightly taps the ball into play) before there are two men out to permit a runner on base to proceed to another base. The batter is usually sacrificed, which is the purpose of the bunt, though occasionally he gets to first base because of a fielder's error or strategic decision. Young further elaborates other instances of baseball sacrifice:

> a sacrifice fly, advancing to draw a throw so a runner may score, or pitching deep into a ball game to let the bullpen rest. A batter may let himself be hit by a pitch, to give his team a base runner; or, if an opposing team pitches the batter's inside, a pitcher may throw at the opposing team, risking ejection or retaliation to protect the other players. (2004, p. 61)[20]

Indeed, baseball's notion of sacrifice is so compelling that it has become a metaphorical way of affirming the personal meaning of this moral virtue in other critical contexts. As the Admiral said to Lt. Brickley in John Ford's 1945 film classic, *They Were Expendable*, "Listen, son, you

---

19 In his book *God is Round* (2010), Mexican writer Juan Antonio Villoro Ruiz has discussed soccer as representing the wish to form an emotional community, one that both celebrates the game and themselves.

20 I am indebted to Young for drawing my attention to the philosophical notion of sacrifice and its relationship to baseball.

and I are professionals. If the manager says, 'Sacrifice,' we lay down a bunt and let somebody else hit the home runs...Our job is to lay down that sacrifice. That's what we were trained for, and that's what we will do" (TCM, "They Were Expendable," retrieved 9/13/13).

While the notion of "sacrifice" is a hugely complex and multi-faceted philosophical and psychological notion, I want to briefly focus on the most obvious, though often underappreciated, aspect of sacrifice in baseball, namely, that the game has evolved so that the very notion of "sacrifice" is central to its play. As the saying goes, baseball is "almost the only place in life where a sacrifice is really appreciated."

What a "sacrifice bunt" in baseball puts into sharp focus is the importance of committing yourself to something beyond yourself, beyond what psychoanalyst Karen Horney called the narcissistically-driven individual "search for glory." Whether player, manager or fan, baseball at its best should be about fashioning a close tie with others who share similar transcendent-pointing values (Senor, 2004, p. 55), like the importance of teamwork. As Yogi Berra allegedly said, "When you sacrifice, you stand beside your teammates, by putting them in front of yourself" (Young, 2004, p. 57). Cal Ripken noted, "I was raised to play for the team, not for yourself" (Will, 1990, p. 233). It is precisely this being for the other, or "being-for-us," that is foundational to the important narrative role that baseball has in American life, and to all others who love the game, including because of "the moral community it inspires" (Morgan, 2004, p. 167). The power of baseball is that it draws "people together for something more than merely baseball" (Sexton, 2013, p. 192), something beyond one's self-serving, selfish needs.[21] Morgan further elaborates this point just right: "the goods [that is, the moral standards and sensibility] of baseball are very much like those of friendship, in which an important part of what is valued is the very fact that they are shared." In a similar manner, Morgan says, "becoming a member of the baseball fraternity also requires us

21 I am aware that being for the other before oneself, which is often discussed in terms of altruism in psychological literature, always has a narcissistic motive to it. Such behavior engenders the narcissistic gratification associated with behaving in a manner that is congruent with one's "higher" valuative attachments that are self-esteem boosting and self-concept enhancing. This being said, what makes radically altruistic behavior so unusual, if not compelling, is that the narcissistic gratification appears to be deep in the individual's unconscious motivational background as opposed to being in the conscious foreground.

to transform our own desires for the sake of the common good of the game" (2004, pp. 163–164). It is from a caste of mind that regards being for the other and "being-for-us" as paramount that other related moral values such as accountability to one's teammates, like not letting them down, and to opposing players the importance of fair play, and generating "courage in the clinch" and "strength in adversity" (Gould, 2003, p. 177) probably emanate. As Will notes, to play baseball skillfully, "a remarkable degree of mental and moral discipline is required" (1990, p. 226). Indeed, this other-directed, other-regarding, other-serving moral vision that baseball personifies at its best has been suggested by some of baseball's heroes, Joe DiMaggio and Tom Seaver. Tellingly, both of these greats refer to one of the paradigms of selfless giving, namely, the love a parent gives their child. Moreover, both express a wish for symbolic immortality in terms of one's legacy of excellence that is passed on to the next generation. Joe DiMaggio says, "There is always some kid who may be seeing me for the first time. I owe him my best" (Rosen, with Bruton, 2012, p. 125); Tom Seaver quotes, "My children will be able to take their children to the Hall of Fame and say, 'There's your grandfather. He was pretty good at what he did.' It's something that solidifies a family" (Dickson, 2008, p. 486). Finally, there are the uplifting words from the master of the "cutter" pitch, the extraordinary Mariano Rivera, a fervent religious believer, who said, "Everything I have and everything I became is because of the strength of the Lord, and through him I have accomplished everything. Not because of my strength. Only by his love, his mercy and his truth." Most importantly for this chapter, Rivera says, "He put it in me, for me to use it. To bring glory, not to Mariano Rivera, but to the Lord" (Miller, 2013, p. 22). Sometimes when a person is being for the other before oneself, the "other" is highly abstract, that is, unthematizeable and unrepresentable using ordinary language. That "other" is literally and metaphorically beyond oneself, or at least it feels that way, and yet the "other" positively animates one's everyday outlook and behavior. The "other" is thus both transcendent and immanent. In religious parlance, this feeling of being "beyond oneself," a feeling that points to an inexplicable "something more," has been described by theologians and others as "calling to mind" God, the Ineffable, the Eternal, the Infinite, or as I have called it, the sense that one is glimpsing immortality. It is on this topic that I will conclude this chapter.

IV. BASEBALL AND IMMORTALITY

Robert Jay Lifton has described the personal encounter of glimpsing immortality in everyday life as a form of experiential transcendence, a moment when time and death seem to vanish (Lifton, 1976, pp. 33–34). Such profoundly transformational and pleasing moments reflect what psychoanalyst Margaret Mahler characterized as emblematic for the well taken care of child beginning to walk, a toddler's "love affair with the world." Such adult analogues of being charmed, if not in love with life, always involve an "unselving" or self-emptying, that is, a "losing oneself" and entering into what feels like a different dimension of the spirit, a "higher" plane of existence. In baseball, there are at least two modes of glimpsing immortality. The first is a more familiar and accessible experience, those moments when one witnesses a brilliant flash of astonishing excellence in baseball craftsmanship, like Willie Mays's famous on-the-run, over-the-shoulder catch on the warning track during the first game of the 1954 World Series between the Cleveland Indians and the New York Giants at New York's Polo Grounds. The second mode of glimpsing immortality is less brilliant but no less elevating and transformational—the dreamy, mystical-like experience of going to a ball game, that sacred place where freedom is the condition of possibility for an upsurge of faith and hope as it longs for fulfillment.

"Peak" Moments in Baseball

Like any sport, baseball loves its moments of pure perfection, when an individual player or team achieves something so extraordinary that it feels nearly god-like or divine. These perfect moments become the stuff of legend, "canonical stories" (Gould, 2003, p. 237) that are told and retold and provide the meaning and pleasure associated with a retrospective consciousness. Such memories are often textured with nostalgia, reminding us of "the most poignant fact" about the game, and indeed of any sport—the fleeting nature of an accomplishment (Sexton, 2013, p. 39). Nostalgia is one of baseball's most distinctive aspects. "The game's past shadows its present, to prod memories, and to revive dormant emotions. Nostalgia is the tribute the present pays to the past" (ibid., p. 198). As Gould reflects:

> As a pure contingency of my own life, I happened to come of baseball fandom's age in the greatest conjunction of time and place that

> the game has ever known: in New York City during the late 1940s and early 1950s [Gould was born in 1941]. The situation was entirely unfair to the rest of the country—hey—you can't possibly cast any blame on me, so I owe no one any apology. From 1947 to 1957 New York City had the three greatest teams in major league baseball [the Dodgers, the Yankees and the Giants]...All New York City boys of the late 1940s and early 1950s were baseball nuts, barring mental deficiency or incomprehensible idiosyncrasy. How could one not be? (2013, p. 32)

Central to this part of baseball history was the 100-year Brooklyn Dodgers rivalry with the Manhattan-based New York Giants, what many baseball scholars have called the greatest rivalry in baseball history. Most noteworthy was the 1951 legendary game-winning ninth inning homerun—"the Shot Heard 'Round the World"—hit by Giants outfielder Bobby Thomson off the Dodgers pitcher Ralph Branca at the Polo Grounds, a celebrated hit that led the Giants to win the National League pennant and go to the World Series against the Yankees (the Yankees won). Thomson's remarkable homerun, and the Giants' win after surmounting a double-digit deficit in the standings during the weeks before the showdown, made the Giants' victory that much more magnificent. Thomson described the exhilaration of that moment that was shared with thousands of fans and spectators:

> Cloud nine. How else can I describe the feeling? We beat the Dodgers. We won the pennant. I hit a home run. Everybody went nuts. Storybook stuff, the whole thing. I still don't know why I was hyperventilating as I ran around the bases. It must have been the excitement, the pure joy, all those amazing feelings just coming together...I didn't run around the bases—I rode around 'em on a cloud. Wow, I still don't know what time it is or where I am. Frankly, I don't care. (Dickson, 2008, p. 553)

The great sportswriter for the *New York Herald Tribune*, Red Smith, famously wrote about the Giants victory: "Now it is done. Now the story ends. And there is no way to tell it. The art of fiction is dead. Reality has strangled invention. Only the utterly impossible, the inexpressibly fantastic, can ever be plausible again" (1951, n.p.).

As Sexton correctly pointed out, Thomson's homerun and the Giants victory has become part of baseball mythology. Similar to liturgical stories, such moments are "forever remembered and repeated with the solemnity of the most beloved sacred stories." In baseball there are hundreds of such stories, and as the quotation from Thomson indicates, such moments involve "heightened awareness—divergent from ordinary time and place—in which some discover a connection to something deeper than the ordinary." Such moments are not only remembered for what they were, but more importantly, "what they have evoked in those who experienced them" (Sexton, 2013, pp. 15, 195), namely, a sense of wonder and awe, of the miraculous. And like observing a miracle, they are thoroughly elevating and inspiring to those who engage the experience with the fullness of their being. As Gould notes about the Thomson homerun,

> Nothing can explain the meaning and excitement of all this to nonfans. No sensible person would even try. This is church—and nonbelievers cannot know the spirit. One can only recall Louis Armstrong's famous statement about the nature of jazz: "Man, if you gotta ask, you'll never know." (2003, p. 74)

My point is simple: To glimpse immortality in everyday life, one must be radically welcoming of the transcendent, the willingness and ability to be receptive and responsive to the "other." This includes embracing the otherness of the subtle, nuanced and complex game of baseball that skillful and heartfelt spectatorship at its best demands. To fully engage the tapestry of life-affirming, numinous presences, events of "pure disclosure," like the "sudden epiphany" (O'Donohue, 2004b, p. 12) of Thomson's homerun and the Giants' victory, is to be actively receptive to what can be described as a moment of "grace." Indeed, the sublime, spontaneous baseball moments have the hallmarks of a grace experience, including the gratitude that one feels for having been given a "gift" of witnessing baseball perfection, and of course, of one's beloved team achieving victory. Moreover, in a game that involves so many inexplicable changes of fortune, accident and lucky breaks, like in all grace experiences, there is a felt sense of the "gift" being unmerited, an aspect of the grace experience that makes it feel that much more uplifting and gratitude-inducing. As Joe DiMaggio famously said in 1949 at Yankee Stadium, "I'd like to thank the Good Lord for making me a Yankee" (Dickson, 2008, p. 142).

THE "BEAUTIFUL INFINITUDE" OF BASEBALL

Glimpsing immortality can also take place amidst less dramatic moments than witnessing, say, a clutch home run by Bobby Thomson, a triple play, or a runner stealing home (a lost art these days). Unlike football, basketball and soccer, baseball is a game that has no time limitations, and this is perhaps one of the reasons why it tends to display a more subtle "beautiful infinitude" (Sexton, 2013, p. 217), at least to those who can appreciate not only the nuances of the game, but the overall ambiance of the stadium, the place that holds "paradise, the public place for public pleasure" (Giamatti, 1998b, p. 78), and spiritual enlightenment within the context of a community. Baseball has no clock; it moves counterclockwise and therefore has its own unique rhythms, tempos and patterns (Will, 1998, p. 219),[22] most notably, the long season that begins in spring and gradually builds up to its thrilling culmination points in autumn, playing for the pennant and in the World Series. Thus, baseball beckons us to live more slowly, mindfully and seasonally, to view the world "differently and more intensely" (Sexton, 2013, p. 217)[23] than we usually do. When we take time to notice, we are able to perceive and appreciate some of the quieter lovely moments, the "fragile intangibles" (Will, 1998, p. 47)[24] that are taking place throughout the typical baseball experience, moments of perception that constitute some of its more subtle "ineffable joys" (Sexton, 2013, p. 220).

To begin with, there is the zany world of baseball fandom, a world that is forever amusing in its extremism about something that has no serious implication for everyday life. Indeed, as Will aptly notes, "Americans, myself emphatically included, are prone to forget that sports are only serious in a funny way. Part of the fun of having flaming passions about our favorite teams—the fun of being a 'fan,' short for *fanatic*—is the comic lack of proportion in it" (1998, p. 25). As

22 Unlike most other sports, baseball has a frequent sense of stillness, such as when the pitcher winds up before he releases the ball. During those few seconds, the batter, fielders and umpire are all poised like cats ready to pounce.

23 Baseball, says Gould, satisfies our need for cyclical repetition, that is, "to forge time into stories" and to "grant stability, predictability and place." To the baseball fan, "opening day marks our annual renewal after a winter of discontent," it both calls to the mind the bittersweet past and the passage of time, and the promises of the beckoning future (2003, p. 55). These are the "seasonal ceremonies of birth and renewal" that humans seem to need (Sexton, 2013, p. xii).

24 Will is paraphrasing Giamatti.

the anonymous saying goes, "A baseball fan is a spectator sitting 500 feet from home plate who [actually believes he] can see better than an umpire standing five feet away!"

Baseball's zany fans are also uniquely obsessed with statistics. I am reminded of a billionaire (not millionaire, a billionaire) businessman patient I saw in psychotherapy who told me that the first thing he does when he comes down for breakfast is check the baseball statistics from the previous night. Only after digesting these numbers does he then review what happened in the European and Asian financial markets! The charm of baseball, especially for us ordinary beleaguered adults, is the illusion it provides that life can be controlled, if not mastered, if it is reduced to numbers. That is, just as managers and coaches rely on performance averages, like batting averages, sacrifices, stolen bases and the like, to try to predict future player performance, the typical fan unconsciously believes that if he studies the numbers associated with baseball, and this becomes a caste of mind that he applies to everyday life, he will never get surprised, let alone overwhelmed or defeated. Of course, this is pure nonsense because like baseball, says Will, life is a "magical mix of science and serendipity." There is an "irreducible indeterminacy" to baseball statistics that make the quest for perfect control an absurd undertaking (1990, p. 298). Listening to two baseball fans talk baseball statistics and what they allegedly mean for the future, especially if they root for different teams, is almost as much fun as watching a lively presidential debate. As Will further notes, fans' love of statistics has childhood origins—"baseball statistics gave many of us our first sense of mastery, our first (and for some of us our last) sense of what it feels like to really understand something, and to know more about something than our parents do" (1998, pp. 55, 66).

The fan's obsession with baseball statistics often also involves the accumulation of other interesting information about the game, anecdotes that demonstrate that deeply "caring" about the game for its own sake is a worthwhile endeavor. This "caring" mirrors baseball players at their best. Baseball heroism, John Updike wrote, "comes not from flashes of brilliance, but...from 'the players who always care' about themselves and their craft" (ibid., pp. 159–160). Thus, fans have a great sense of baseball history and tradition involving comparisons between current and past players, teams and eras. In fact, as Giamatti pointed out, "baseball is in a sense, the conversation about it" (ibid., p. 192). It is such baseball talk that provides a sense of historical continuity, a form of "institutional memory," that strengthens a fan's (and player's) attachment and loyalty to the national pastime. Will makes this point just right: Baseball "has had an ambience of ritual matured through long, steady seasons. It has conveyed a marvelous sense of cumulativeness of life, captured in the richness of baseball statistics" and conversation (ibid., p. 48).

Baseball players and fans also provide a powerful context for observing the dynamics of faith and hope (and their opposites),[25] which can be uplifting to observe. One only has to recall the great relief pitcher Tug McGraw's immortal words spoken in late July 1973, words that became the motto and exhortation that was used by the underdog New York Mets as they advanced from sixth place to the National League pennant, "Ya gotta believe" (Dickson, 2008, p. 363). McGraw's motto personifies the faith that the improbable is possible, if one is hugely motivated to prevail. In this sense, baseball provided what faith at its best does, the consolation, incentive, comprehension, and most of all, a "meaning and ultimate purpose" that transports a player and fan to a different dimension of the spirit, to what feels like a "higher" plane of existence (Sexton, 2013, pp. 36, 45). Even when one's team loses, when one's aspirations have been crushed, hope springs eternal. Just think of the vanquished fan's heartfelt cry, "Wait 'til next year!"

Likewise, every time a batter comes to the plate, it evokes an upsurge of hope in the spectator. When the batter gets a hit, especially in the clutch, the experience becomes etched in our memory, "memories of our best hopes." Giamatti further clarifies,

> They are memories of a time when all that would be better was before us, as a hope, and the hope was fastened to a game. One hoped not so much to be the best who ever played as simply to stay in the game and ride it wherever it would go, culling its rhythms and realizing its promises. That is, I think, what it means to remember one's best hopes, and to remember them in a game, and revive them whenever one sees the game played, long after playing is over. (1998a, p. 88)

What is noteworthy about this hope/memory dynamic is that it is linked to our deepest individual and collective aspirations for self-transformation, the wish to be all we can be as we honorably strive

25 Doubt, says Sexton, "is at the core of baseball," and I would add, of life; it is what Freud called ambivalence, a feeling that is often evoked when one is faced with ambiguous circumstances that require a decision (2013, p. 55).

for real or imagined excellence. This emotional cluster is part of what makes baseball so lovely and lovable. As Morgan aptly notes, baseball invokes a moral image of America at its best, one that as individuals and a nation we want to passionately identify with: "a nation of strivers moved not so much by greed and crass self-interest as by a larger vision of excellence, one obtained by arduous effort, social cooperation, and an abiding sense of fair play" (Morgan, 2004, p. 157). For those fans who love the game around the world, the universal spirit of this moral image also deeply resonates.

V. FINAL REFLECTION

I have argued that baseball, when skillfully and passionately played and observed, is "a form and object of love," and because it is, it touches, sometimes only marginally, on many of "life's great themes" (Will, 1998, p. 100). Most importantly, baseball teaches us something about what is a critical psychological achievement in terms of human growth and development, and what it takes to live the "good life." A flourishing life requires effectively negotiating separation and individuation, that daunting process that begins in childhood, of "becoming a person," of actualizing inner autonomy, integration and humanity. Giamatti has noted that in baseball the batter's Odysseus-like goal is "to arrive at the same place, which is where they start," home plate, though reaching home is less a place than a state of mind. As I have emphasized, this state of mind is very different from when one began one's odyssey, whether on or off the baseball field. Such an altered state of mind personifies the actualization of inner freedom and responsibility as one confronts the challenges that leaving one's home entails. As Ted Williams said, "God gets you to the plate, but from then on, you're on your own" (Gould, 2003, p. 17).[26] Most importantly, unlike Odysseus, who nostalgically longs for the return to an existence that he has always lived, baseball also calls to mind the biblical image of Abraham, who is uprooted from his country and never looks back, having no hope of

26 Baseball wisdom, like in real life, asserts that while "natural" talent is important, it is how hard you work at the game of mastering the skills of this most challenging of games, that ultimately distinguishes the great player from the good one. Though there have been exceptions, such as Babe Ruth, who was hardly a disciplined athlete, he did "more than his share of drinking and whoring," though "his play didn't seem to suffer" (Gould, 2003, p. 139).

returning home. That is, as Levinas has noted, it is the estrangement of the uprooted, the engagement with the unfamiliar and foreign, both externally and internally, on and off the baseball field, which brings about one's individuation, integrity and humanity (Marcus, 2008, p. 200). Indeed, this is one of the important insights that baseball teaches us—there is no such thing as "going home again" in an absolute way. By resigning oneself without despair to this existential truth, by never making your home in a place, one learns to reside in the imaginative realm of the mind, in that "internal stadium"[27] of cherished memories and dreamy hopes. It is these inspiring and nurturing memories and hopes that we safely preserve deep within us that provide the emotional staging ground for appreciating, if not celebrating, the loveliness and profundity of baseball. Such a "reverential mind" allows the possibility for transcendence, for we graciously let a thing simply be, and celebrate its beauty without wanting something tangible from it (O'Donohue, 1998, p. 111). As the immortal "Sultan of Swat," Babe Ruth, said on Babe Ruth Day at Yankee Stadium in 1947, "I thank heaven we have had baseball in this world" (Dickson, 2008, p. 475).[28]

27 Roger Angell used the phrase, "the interior stadium" (Will, 1998, p. 311).

28 Former Vice President Al Gore is probably right when he noted that at least three baseball players have transcended the game to become a constituent part of American legend: "Where Babe Ruth was known for his power and Jackie Robinson was known for his courage, Joe DiMaggio was known for dignity and grace" (ibid., p. 215).

CHAPTER 4

CHESS: THE ROYAL GAME

> "For Life is a kind of Chess...Several very valuable qualities of the mind, useful in the course of human life, are to be acquired or strengthened by it..."
>
> Benjamin Franklin (Shenk, 2006, p. 281)

"The human element, the human flaw and the human nobility," said Russian grandmaster Viktor Korchnoi, "those are the reasons that chess matches are won or lost" (www.chess-games.com, retrieved 4/8/14).[1] Indeed, there is no game or sport that has been written about more than chess as a metaphor for life. Even Freud used a chess metaphor in his discussion of human attitudes toward death: "For it is really too sad that in life it should be as it is in chess, where one false move may force us to resign the game, but with the difference that we can start no second game, no return-match" (Freud, 1915, p. 291).[2] The author David Schifrin has aptly summarized some of the larger psychological themes that infuse chess with its metaphorical power: "The game of chess—with its rich-

1 The legendary Borris Spassky made a similar observation: "Chess, with all its philosophical depth, its aesthetic appeal, is first of all a game in the best sense of the word, a game in which are revealed your intellect, character and will" (Saidy, 1994, p. 198).

2 Freud noted elsewhere a connection between chess and psychoanalysis: "Anyone who hopes to learn the noble game of chess from books will soon discover that only the openings and end-games admit of an exhaustive systematic presentation and that the infinite variety of moves which develop after the opening defy any such descriptions. This gap in instruction can only be filled by a diligent study of games fought out by masters. The rules which can be laid down for the practice of psycho-analytic treatment are subject to similar limitations" (1958, p. 123).

ness, complexity and barely suppressed violence—is an extraordinary metaphor for the human condition. Some of the most important fiction writers and poets of the last two centuries—Nabokov, Borges, Tolstoy, Canetti, Aleichem, Elliot, and others—have fully recognized the uncanny ability of a chess game to represent the contradictions, struggles, and hopes of human society" (Shenk, 2006, p. 241).[3] It is, in part, for this reason that since chess was first invented in India in about A.D. 600, this strategic board game that exquisitely blends reason and beauty has been played in nearly every part of the world, capturing the fancy of millions of devotees.

In this chapter I discuss some of the intellectual, aesthetic and emotional elements that make chess so compelling to play and watch and what this suggests beyond the chess match about the art of living the "good life." While the intellectual and aesthetic aspects of chess are more familiar than the emotional ones, it is the fact that chess is suffused with intense emotion that most accounts for its sway on the player and spectator imagination.[4] Three illustrative quotations from grandmasters support this notion: Borris Spassky noted, "In a long match, a player goes very deep into himself, like a diver. Then very fast he comes up. Every time, win or lose, I am so depressed. I want to die" (Shenk, 2006, p. 150)[5]; "The work of a chess," said Alexander Suetin, "is similar to a blast furnace process; it is continuous and demands a heated passion for chess" (www.chessgames.com, retrieved 4/10/14); and finally, John van der Wiel quipped, "When you absolutely don't know what to do anymore, it is time to panic" (www.chessquotes.com, retrieved 4/10/14). [6] Thus, while in a certain sense those who

3 For a very good anthology on chess and world literature, see Hochberg, 1993.

4 One should remember that intellect (thought), emotion (including the perception of beauty) and action are always operative together, that the human being resides in the world as an integrated being. Treating these faculties separately is only useful for pedagogic purposes.

5 Spassky further noted, "Actually I feel very nervous inside during a game, as if there was an explosion in progress" (Fine, 1973, p. 60).

6 Russian grandmaster Vladmir Kramnik noted, "Chess is an incredibly emotional game. If everything around is harmonious, when you are feeling good, you are in a creative mood. If something is disturbing you and you are in a bad mood, then it is difficult to be creative. So you have to create the right atmosphere" (www.en.chessbase.com, retrieved 4/19/14).

claim that chess is a game where the randomness of life is absent and replaced by a "pure" intellectual acuity (Zweig, 1976)—"Chess is the touchstone of human intellect," said Goethe (www.chessgames.com, retrieved 4/8/14)—to the psychoanalyst there is a lot more going on, including the enactment of love and aggression within the context of an erotically-tinged family romance. It is to this subject that I now turn.

I. THE EROTICIZATION OF THOUGHT

As the great German chess champion player, mathematician and philosopher Emanuel Lasker said, chess "gives us a satisfaction that life denies us." He further explains, "And for the chess player, the success which crowns his work, the great dispeller of sorrows, is named 'combination'" (1960, p. 114). A combination is a tactically motivated sequence of forcing an opponent's moves with a particular objective in mind, usually involving an initial sacrifice of one piece and the element of surprise. The goal of a combination may be defensive in nature or to attain positional advantage, though at its best it is a mating attack meant to win the game (Hooper & Whyld, 1991, p. 86). According to Lasker, "lies and hypocrisy do not survive long" on the chessboard. "The creative combination lays bare the presumption of a lie; the merciless fact, culminating in a checkmate, contradicts the hypocrite" (www.chessgames.com, retrieved 4/8/14). When we understand the word "combination" not merely as a technical chess term but more psychologically, as possibly pointing to unconscious sexual and aggressive desires rooted in repressed family dynamics—we enter a world of intriguing motivations that may animate chess playing and spectatorship, motivations that psychoanalysts have discussed in depth. For whether one is hitting a baseball or kicking a soccer ball, like with all sports and games played, especially at their professional level, chess represents an ability and a beauty that have no import or significance beyond the limits of the game itself, and yet so many people have become interested in, if not addicted to, the game (Cockburn, 1974, pp. 12, 13).[7] After all, why would an adult person want to dedicate all of his psychic energy for, say, forty years to the absurd enterprise of cornering a wooden King on a wooden board trying to best another man

7 Albert Einstein noted, "Chess holds its master in its own bonds, shackling the mind and brain so that the inner freedom of the very strongest must suffer" (Shenk, 2006, p. xvi).

(ibid., p. 77)?![8] As science fiction writer H.G. Wells famously said, "The passion for playing chess is one of the most unaccountable in the world. It slaps the theory of natural selection in the face. It is the most absorbing of occupations, the least satisfying of [normative] desires, an aimless excrescence [an ugly addition to something] upon life." What made chess such an excrescence, though an extremely appealing one, according to Wells, was its strategic and tactical violence potential: "It annihilates a man. You have, let us say a promising politician, a rising artist that you wish to destroy. Dagger or bomb are archaic and unreliable, but teach him, inculcate him with chess" (1901, p. 140).

Indeed, the key word in Wells's observation is "passion," and as Freud has taught us, passion is another way of saying that an activity like chess stirs up "primal forces," strong emotions that are usually beyond our conscious control (Shenk, 2006, p. 148). Indeed, many boys and men who play chess (and more recently, women),[9] and certainly "chess junkies" relate to the game as if it had ultimate significance in their lives. While it may appear to the casual onlooker that the grandmaster plays his game dispassionately, like some kind of emotionless "thinking machine," to insiders it is clear that they do not play in a psychologically pristine and pure manner as the previous quotations about chess emotionality from grandmasters indicated (Selinger, 2008, p. 83). Indeed, as psychiatrist Karl Menninger noted, there are "waves of emotion" involved in playing chess, such as modulated composure and carefulness at the start of the game to razor-sharp concentration on plotting, excitement by the discovery of a weak spot, fear and anxiety on the part of the threatened player, ecstasy of success in the devastation of the

8 Cockburn is quoting from Stephan Zweig. George Bernard Shaw viewed chess similarly: "[Chess] is a foolish expedient for making idle people believe they are doing something very clever, when they are only wasting their time" (www.chess.com, retrieved 5/5/14).

9 In 2005 in the United States only about 3% of competitive adult-rated players were women and this number has remained steady between 2000 and 2005. Worldwide, the statistics are somewhat better—about 6% of women are active adult players. There is only one woman, Judit Polgar, who was rated in the top 20 players worldwide (in 2004 she was rated number eight), and about 5 women in the top 100 players in the United States. By far there are fewer women who play chess than men (Shahade, 2005, pp. 3, 91). Active worldwide in 2014 there are 1,389 grandmasters, 1,362 of which are men and 27 of which are women (1.9%) (www.chessmaniac.com, retrieved 4/29/14).

opponent, admiration and envy of the opponent's skillfulness, and a desire for revenge in a future game (Menninger, 1942, pp. 399–416).[10] Most importantly for this chapter, there is considerable "erotic symbolism" in chess if one is attuned to noticing it (Hochberg, 1993, p. 243). If the claim that there are "erotic connotations" to chess, as grandmaster Jennifer Shahade has described it, seems like Freudian overreach, consider that American champion grandmaster Alexander Shabalov said that during the majority of games he thinks "about girls for about fifty to seventy-five percent of the time." Moreover, said Shabalov, "most men, regardless of their strength, are thinking about sex for most of the game." In one rather far-fetched instance an Australian player lost to a young woman and complained to authorities that the woman's sexy, low-cut blouse had distracted him and was the reason he lost the match (Shahade, 2005, pp. 6, 71).[11] While Shabalov may be speaking only for himself, Shahade believes that "the sexual symbolism in chess is a rich topic" (ibid., p. 70). One must always remember that the meanings of symbols are never obliging to precise transliteration (Cockburn, 1974, p. 161). What, then, are some of the erotically charged psychological themes that infuse chess that may explain the powerful traction that the game has on the minds and hearts of players and spectators? And what does this teach us about the art of living the "good life"?

The late Reuben Fine, himself a grandmaster and psychoanalyst, aptly summarized the main unconscious psychological themes that animate chess playing. Chess is a sublimation of conflicts relating to

---

10 Menninger is paraphrasing the findings of Fleming & Strong, 1943, pp. 399–416.

11 It is not clear how Shabalov knows that the majority of male players are thinking about sex during most of the game. I assume this is simply his impression. Shahade does not quote Shabalov, she only claims he said what she paraphrases. One also wonders what, in the minds of men (and women), an intellectually powerful and sexy woman conjures up. Alexandra Kosteniuk, a Russian grandmaster, has taken commercial advantage of her good looks and has created a frequently updated website that includes "photo-shoots, game scores, and future tournament and travel schedules" that, says Shahade, "at times verges on pornographic" (like a photo of her wearing a "pink thong bikini" that is seductively and simply described as "Alexandra is now in Miami!"). As one journalist said about Bulgarian grandmaster Antoaneta Stefanova, "Sexy, self-confidant, sociable…can we be talking about a professional chess player" (Shahade, 2005, pp. 174, 159).

"aggression, homosexuality, masturbation and narcissism which become particularly prominent in the anal-phallic phases of development." Moreover, given that it is typically a game taught to a son by his father or a father replacement, it becomes a way of resolving son-father rivalry (Fine, 1965, p. 10).[12]

Aggression

"Chess is ruthless," said English grandmaster Nigel Short, "you've got to be prepared to kill people" (www.chesscorner.com, retrieved 4/18/14). Indeed, chess can be viewed as a game in which players are silently scheming, endeavoring to carry out murderous cabals of patricide, matricide, fratricide, regicide and severe chaos and disruption (Menninger, 1942, p. 83). The great French-American painter and sculptor Marcel Duchamp, who in his thirties gave up his artistic work and became utterly obsessed with chess and a "master" level player, depicted the game similarly: "Chess can be described as the movement of pieces eating one another" (www.saidwhat.co.uk, retrieved 4/18/14). The bellicose if not sadistic Bobby Fischer noted, "Chess is war over the board. The object is to crush the opponent's mind....I like the moment when I break a man's ego....I like to make them squirm" (www.chessquotes.com, retrieved 4/18/14; www.chessquotes.com, retrieved 5/2/14). [13] Many more quotations can be cited to make the point that while the main focus in chess is on imposing a better strategy that leads to victory, as Fischer fiercely notes, the game is also about destroying your opponent's will and self-esteem (Shenk, 2006, p. 6). Chess, says the American poet Alfred Kreymborg, is thus a sublimation of a wide range of aggressive wishes: it "is nothing less than a silent duel between two human engines using and abusing all the faculties of the mind....It is warfare in the most mysterious jungles of the human character" (ibid.). Indeed, you don't have to be a Freudian analyst to sense that chess is a war game, and for male adults it is a highly intellectualized substitute that calls to mind the maneuvers enacted by little boys playing with toy soldiers (Cant, www.chess.com, retrieved 4/19/14) while engaging in make-believe battles. It is worth noting, however, that while chess may be a violent war game substitute for

12 See also Fine's *Bobby Fischer's Conquest of the World's Chess Championship*.

13 Fischer was known to say "*smash, crunch* and *bam*" during competitions (Waterman, 1993, p. 15).

men, for women the nature of the war metaphor may have a more benign feel to it. For example, Women's World Champion Susan Polgar noted that when she was at the height of the Oedipal phase, age four, she fantasized chess as a "fairy tale" mainly because her father had told her wonderfully dramatic stories that included Kings, Queens, castles and romance. In other words, if chess is indeed a war metaphor, it need not be a typically aggressive one as adult men conceive it, "it is not war as hell, but war where fairness, females, and rules matter above all" (Shahade, 2005, p. 11).

Much of the psychoanalytic literature on chess locates the main unconscious motives in players and spectators in an unresolved Oedipus Complex. In this context the main aggressive wish that is sublimated is hostility to the father, symbolized by the King. As Latvian chess master Alexander Koblencs noted, "No price is too great for the scalp of the enemy King" (www.chessquotes.com, retrieved 4/30/14). This claim is based on the fact that most professional chess players, and for that matter, most ordinary players, are male and they have often learned the game from their father or father substitute prior to puberty, about age twelve (sometimes a bit earlier), when there is a resurgence of Oedipal issues, what Freud described as the struggle against helplessness. This is when a boy typically begins to compare himself with his grown-up father as he tries to figure out where he wants to go in his life. Moreover, as he enters adolescence proper, the boy is geared toward making constant efforts to exceed his father (Fine, 1973, p. 75). Often, the child prodigy defeats his father/teacher soon after he learns the game, this being a memorable psychological moment in the boy's masculine development, though often not without paying an unconscious price in terms of guilt and the fear of punishment. That is, given that the objective of the game is to topple the King, to render him helpless, hopeless and hapless, in short to "castrate" him (though tellingly perhaps, not to murder him, while protecting one's own King), then the main pleasure associated with playing chess is that it is equated with childhood rebellion against the powerful father/King, a form of "castration revenge" (Coriat, 1941, p. 1). While the etymology of the word "checkmate" has been debated, many scholars believe that it comes from Persian "shah maat," which has been translated as "the

King is dead." It has been debated in psychoanalytic circles whether capturing the King and murdering him are unconsciously the same.[14]

Psychoanalysts have further pointed out that while the King is the most important piece on the board, though weak in terms of his mobility, it is the Queen, the symbolic mother, which is the most powerful, perhaps, as some analysts have surmised, her empowerment being a revenge against her imagined castration. It is worth noting that historically the Queen was a weak masculine piece. In the Persian version of the game, she was the adviser, and via displacement and identification with the King/father, in about A.D. 1000 she became the King's female sexual partner, though also a powerful woman who was often instrumental in murdering the King.[15] Thus, for the adult man playing and watching chess, the ambivalent wish to murder and protect the King/father is expressed, as is the wish to be allied with the powerful mother who assists in the patricide and leaves the son and mother to celebrate their victory in joyful togetherness. As Dutch grandmaster Jørgen Bent Larsen noted, and he may have unconsciously had the Queen piece in mind, "Chess is a beautiful mistress to whom we keep coming back, no matter how many times she rejects us" (Saidy, 1994, p. 175).

Homosexuality

The claim that in men there is a homosexual aspect to chess playing and spectatorship is based in part on its connection to the anal-sadistic aspects of the game. By anal-sadistic I mean the sadistic fantasies that are believed to emanate in the anal stage of child development, when libidinal gratification is gained through sphincter control, that is, expulsion and retention of feces. The anal phase also has anal-erotic aspects related to actual fecal matter. Children unconsciously fantasize by aggressively playing with and using their excrement for violent purposes. In the chess context this becomes the wish to make the opponent "into shit" and/or feel "like shit" by defeating him. It was Ernest Jones in his famous essay, "The Problem of Paul Morphy:

---

14 Karl Menninger, for example, believes that Ernest Jones in his study of Paul Morphy has mistakenly equated them (1943, p. 82).

15 According to H. J. R. Murray, the author of the magisterial *A History of Chess*, the Queen was made a feminine piece due to the needs of the "general symmetry of the arrangement of the pieces, which pointed to the pairing of the two central pieces" (2012, p. 423).

A Contribution to the Psychology of Chess"[16] who probably first discussed in depth the homosexual aspects of chess:

> It is perhaps worth remarking further that the mathematical quality of the game gives it a peculiar anal-sadistic nature. The exquisite purity and exactness of the right moves, particularly in problem work, combine here with the unrelenting pressure exercised in the later states which culminates in the merciless *denoument*. The sense of overwhelming mastery on the one side matches that of unescapable helplessness on the other. It is doubtless this anal-sadistic feature that makes the game so well adapted to gratify at the same time both the homosexual [i.e., the wish to sexually assault the father in order to humiliate/defeat him and/or extract his masculine power] and the antagonistic aspect of the son-father context. (Jones, 1974, pp. 169–170)

Jones supports his claim by referring to the unconscious sexual symbolism of chess, such as mentioning that Morphy had great "skill…in attacking the King [father] from behind or in separating the opposing King and Queen." Moreover, said Jones, these assumed "parricidal impulses" were "bound" by an erotic cathexis (investment of psychic energy), actually a homosexual one (i.e., a sexual aggressivity towards the father), and that this in its turn was sublimated (ibid., pp. 176, 195) in his chess passion.

While Jones's classical Freudian application to chess may seem a bit of a stretch to the non-Freudian, others have suggested that there is a subtle homosexual aspect being played out in the chess encounter, in that typically two men sit together a few feet away from each other for five or six hours with no women present in which their minds passionately interpenetrate (Fleming & Strong, 1943, p. 405), albeit, in the most beautifully violent manner. While men may be consciously

16 Paul Morphy (1837–1884) was an American chess prodigy who, in 1858, beat three of Europe's leading masters when he was only age 21, becoming the best player in the world. Inexplicitly, Morphy then quit playing the game. After 1859 he became more and more reclusive and was plagued with paranoid delusions. He died of a stroke while taking a bath at age 47, having been looked after by his mother and sister. It is said of Morphy that he was "the pride and sorrow of chess." Jones's essay tries to account for why Morphy quit playing chess when he was at the zenith of his achievement by suggesting that Morphy felt intense guilt for his unconscious wish to sexually assault his father and kill him, this leading to his obligatory self-punishment via his paranoid delusions.

thinking about women, as the earlier Shabalov quote suggests, on an unconscious level they are somewhere else.[17] That is, chess involves each player getting deeply into the mind of his opponent to exploit his weaknesses, to wreak havoc and to ultimately destroy him, but this is still a form of intimacy, of sexualized aggressivity, that calls to mind a form of male-to-male, so called "homosexual" connectedness. More generally, it is perhaps in chess more than in any other sport or game that a player needs to acknowledge the "otherness" of the other, such as in the warding-off of moves, the swapping of roles, the mindfulness of the opponent's strategy and tactics, the upsurge of powerful emotions, the desire to triumph over the opponent and the coming to terms with defeat. All of this emphasizes the incredible intimacy that constitutes the clash between two opponents (ibid., p. 406), what I would call a "dance of death," playing off of August Strindberg's play about a marriage that has gone macabre but one in which the couple can't live with or without each other.[18]

Masturbation

Psychoanalytically speaking, the homosexual aspects of chess are often connected to masturbatory wishes, especially when one remembers the phallic symbolism of the King, the piece on the board that is "indispensable, all-important, irreplaceable, yet weak and requiring protection." As I have suggested, not only does the King symbolize the father but it can also symbolize (1) the boy's penis in the phallic phase when he is prone to castration anxiety; (2) the important aspects of the masculine self-image, hence it resonates in the men who view themselves (or would like to view themselves) as indispensable, all-important and irreplaceable, this being a way of working out narcissistic conflicts; and (3) "the father pulled down to the boy's size" (Fine, 1965, p. 12). Chess etiquette allows for derivative, partial enactment and gratification of these psychological concerns clustered around the King/father/penis symbolism.

---

17 One could argue that the male chess player's conscious thoughts of women are a defense against homoerotic wishes.

18 Overt homosexuality is almost non-existent among grandmasters. Interestingly, as Fine points out, while many chess masters compare themselves to artists, unlike the artistic community which has many overt homosexuals, the chess community does not (Fine, 1965, p. 22).

So, for example, except for when one is making a move, chess etiquette prohibits touching one's own and the opponent's piece, which is suggestive of the deeply repressed wish to make a homosexual advance on one's opponent, to masturbate with, and/or in front of him (Krauthammer, 1993, p. 10). Many serious chess players become interested with the game when they are in adolescence during their budding sexuality and prowess that often includes conscious and/or unconscious homosexual yearnings. Chess etiquette mirrors the rule of sexual engagement of that period: "Don't touch your piece until you are ready to move it," which unconsciously means, "Don't masturbate" (Shahade, 2005, p. 4). Indeed, chess satisfies the voyeuristic and exhibitionistic fantasies (think of the hero worship in chess) in players and spectators.

Finally, in a certain sense the whole enterprise of chess playing is about asserting intellectual power and superiority over another man, a way of declaring "my penis is bigger and stronger than yours," this being a reflection of the wishes that most men unconsciously have, especially toward one's childhood father who represents the powerful man, the "King of the castle" one might say, that he has to submit to within the Oedipal drama. It is perhaps telling that Bobby Fischer said in an interview that one of his deepest longings, actually a fantasy, was to build a special kind of house: "I'm going to hire the best architect and have him build it in the shape of a rook. Yeh, that's for me. Class. Spiral staircases, parapets, everything. I want to live the rest of my life in a house built exactly like a rook." Fischer's fantasy has two likely meanings—firstly, it represents the wish for a strong penis, a noteworthy compensation for a man who had a legendary aversion to women (he called them "weakies"), and secondly, it is a castle, a fortress in which he can live in grandiose fantasy, similar to the Kings of Medieval times, secluded from the real world and shielded by moats and soldiers from threat of attack (Fine, 1973, pp. 39, 85).

Narcissism

I have already mentioned in passing that chess playing and spectatorship involves a tremendous narcissistic investment, that is, it is a way of enhancing one's self-esteem and improving one's self-concept. Most importantly, chess is an expression of phallic narcissism, an overinvestment in the penis, symbolically the King and other pieces, as a way of enhancing self-esteem. As chess champion Charles Warburton noted, "Chess is an egotistical game, and all its protagonists hold conceits of some kind or other, else there would be no point in playing" (www.correspondencechess.com, retrieved 4/29/14). French grandmaster Joel Lautier concurred, "Most strong players are completely self-centered....They are blind to how other people feel or else simply don't care" (www.chessquotes.com, retrieved 5/2/14). Fischer's "colossal egotism" was well-known (Fine, 1973, p. 25). There are a number of aspects of chess that point to its narcissistic importance to players and spectators. For example, in one sense chess is a completely individual gladiatorial fight, though rather importantly there is a kind of interdependency and interpenetration of thought between players that even the most schizoid chess player can't obliterate. One of the greatest chess players of all time, Alexander Alekhine, the "sadist of the chess world" as Fine has correctly called him (he was a Nazi collaborator and openly sadistic toward his fifth wife), noted that chess is not entirely self-contained. That is, even a sadistic grandmaster must come to terms with the otherness of the other: "Oh! This opponent, this collaborator against his will, whose notion of Beauty always differs from yours and whose means (strength, imagination, technique) are often too limited to help you effectively! What torment, to have your thinking and your phantasy tied down by another person" (www.chessquotes.com, retrieved 4/25/14).

Chess also taps into individual narcissism in terms of players identifying with pieces, like the King, which symbolize phallic strivings and grandiose aspects of the self, especially when victorious. However, identification with the King may also expose the player to feelings of weakness and depletion when defeated in a game. Ukrainian grandmaster who defected to the United States, Lev Alburt, put the matter just right: "Nothing is dearer to a chess player's heart than his rating. Well, of course everyone knows he's under-rated, but his rating, its ups and downs, however miniscule, are his ego's stock market report" (www.chessgames.com, retrieved 4/29/14).

"The essence of chess," said grandmaster David Bronstein, "is thinking about what chess is" (Shahade, 2005, p. 267). Psychoanalytically understanding chess in terms of metaphor, in particular its unique storylines of sexual symbolism, reflects the classical Freudian angle that I have been using to discuss the game. Other psychoanalytic perspectives, like a Jungian one, might understand chess playing in terms of different sets of controlling metaphors such as a "system of opposites, from the black and white colors of the pieces and squares to knowing when it is time to attack and when to defend" (ibid., p. 5). In this view, styles of play can reflect the "yin and yang," the dualism of feminine (e.g., passivity and depth) and masculine (e.g., activity and height) principles that exist in both women and men (Saidy, 1994, p. 7). This being said, the important question that needs to be addressed is what insights can we gain about the art of living the "good life" from our classical Freudian metaphoric gloss on "the best of all games" (Menninger, 1942, p. 80)?

As with any metaphor, dictionary defined as a figure of speech in which a word or phrase is applied to an object or action to which it is not literally applicable, Freudian metaphors assists us in clarifying, simplifying and organizing our thoughts while at the same time liberating us from former context-dependent and setting-specific limitations. Such a way of construing the world moves against the literalizing propensity that humans seem to have that deadens our perceptions and blunts the range and depth of our experience. Rather, Freud understood that imagination has a reparative ripple effect in the human psyche, thus it is not surprising that Bronstein said, "Chess is imagination" (Saidy, 1994, p. 100). Calling to mind the connection between eroticism and the imagination, grandmaster Mikhail Tal, perhaps the greatest tactician in chess history (nicknamed the "The Wizard from Riga") noted, "Just as one's imagination is stirred by a girl's smile, so is one's imagination stirred by the possibilities of chess" (ibid., p. 127). Since much of life is elusive and intangible, that is, ambiguous and ambivalent, skillfully crafted and placed symbolic comparisons help to expand and deepen our angle of vision as we try to make greater sense of our experience and what we transmit to others (Shenk, 2006, p. 56). Most importantly, perhaps, Freudian metaphors are powerful forms of visual imagery that are saturated with strong sexual and aggressive feeling as they transfer the qualities of one familiar and understandable object, say the penis, onto another, say the King piece, and thus enhance the King's emotional significance and impact. For example, the capacity to experience chess as the "royal game" provides an opportunity for the "higher" expression of fundamental sexual and aggressive drives: "It is as if in the enjoyment of the game one experiences a kind of *unio mystica* [communion and identification] with Kings and Queens, with their family romance, and in participating in its royal richness, a part of lost omnipotence is recaptured" (Reider, 1960, p. 79). Such "magic realism," as the literary genre is called in which the fantastical and the real merge, can deepen and enliven our understanding of reality. Thus, by skillfully embracing a Freudian way of metaphorically construing the world—man as pleasure-seeking in an erotically tinged universe[19]—we implement a kind of erotically charged visual thinking, what I have called the "eroticization of thought"—thinking as an aphrodisiac, that permits you to connect the new with the old, the strange with the familiar, the dream-like with the real, in a creative, enlivening and life-affirming manner. By directly impacting our senses and honing our imaginations to understand what is being communicated, Freudian metaphors provide a life-like feel to our way of experiencing the world and communicating to others, one that is a fertile breeding ground for the development of an aesthetically pleasing affect-integrating, meaning-giving and action-guiding way of being. Imagine what life would feel like if one could engage the business of everyday living the way the grandmaster Shahade engages the chess match: "Great chess moves can pierce me with momentary but intense pleasure like a smile in a dream" (Shahade, 2005, p. 285).

II. THE BEAUTY OF CHESS

"I try to play, always beautiful games," said chess great Garry Kasparov, "always I wanted to create masterpieces" (Saidy, 1994, p. 280). Indeed, what distinguishes the chess genius from the amateur and the expert has been aptly described by American Pulitzer Prize-winning syndicated columnist, Charles Krauthammer, himself a serious chess devotee:

> The amateur sees pieces and movement; the expert, additionally, sees sixty-four squares with holes and lines and spheres of influence; the genius apprehends a unified field within which space and force and mass are interacting valences—a bishop tears the board in

19 While I am emphasizing the man as pleasure-seeking master narrative, I believe that humans are best viewed as simultaneously and indivisibly object and meaning-seeking. Freud, for example, always maintained that instinctual drives express themselves "in and through relationships," and his clinical approach personified this. Hence the object relational critique of Freud is something of a "straw dog" argument (Aragno, 2014, p. 287).

> half and a Pawn bends the space around it the way mass can reshape space in the Einsteinian universe. (Krauthammer, 1993, p. 12)[20]

Krauthammer is, of course, confirming what any serious chess player knows and has been succinctly defined in the Great Soviet Encyclopedia, chess is "an art appearing in the form of a game" (ibid., p. 5). What exactly makes chess beautiful to play and watch?

The beautiful aspects of chess can be appreciated by looking at the game as a totality. First, the game displays the perfect implementation of a strategy and tactics.[21] Consider, for example, the difference between positional and combinative play. Positional play refers to the long-term maneuvering that constitutes strategy, that is, moves are made with an eye to improving the player's position that are mainly focused on the end game. This differs from the more tactically-oriented short-term attacks of combinative play in which the aim is to checkmate the opponent or gain pieces and Pawns ("material" in chess lingo). The difference between strategy and tactics, positional and combinative play is always murky, since as in military strategy, every strategy has a tactical significance and vice versa. As national master Dan Heisman noted, "Chess isn't 99% tactics, it's just that tactics takes up 99% of your time" (www.exeterchessclub.org.uk, retrieved 4/30/14).[22] All great chess players use positional play with the ultimate goal of prosecuting a decisive attack, or achieving a victorious Endgame (Hooper & Whyld, 1991, p. 316). As former U.S. Chess Champion Stuart Rachels points out, great chess games amalgamate superb strategy and tactics into the "flawless execution of a plan," one that can be described as "breathtaking works of art." Consider the Queen's Gambit Declined: "White launches a minority attack on the Queenside, creates a weak black Pawn on c6, organizes his forces around that Pawn, wins it, and displays good endgame technique"

---

20 Krauthammer recognizes the addictive quality to chess: "It's like alcohol. It's a drug. I have to control it, or it could overwhelm me. I have a regular Monday night game at my home, and I do play a little online" (www.newsmax.com, retrieved 4/29/14).

21 Of interest is that one of the greatest military strategists of all time, Napoleon Bonaparte, was not a very good chess player. Apparently chess may not be a transferable talent to other strategic/tactical endeavors.

22 I have not taken up the interesting problem of timing in chess, nor the issue of time limits to move a piece. Nabokov noted that "Time is merciless in the universe of chess" (Cockburn, 1974, p. 36).

(Rachels, 2008, p. 213). In other scenarios where there is a long, drawn-out battle we can appreciate the aesthetically appealing "agonistic" nature of chess. "Agonism," from the Greek meaning "combat," captures chess's reciprocal incitation and struggle, its mutual taunting and strategy of reaction, and its confrontational strategies and strategic reversals, similar to watching a great wrestling match. Such a dynamic intellectual struggle that characterizes chess, especially its continuously surprising nature and its unpredictable results, makes it a "highly ritualized aesthetic event" (Shenk, 2006, p. 188), one of "true beauty and grace" (ibid., p. 39). It should also be emphasized that a perfect strategic and tactical game is not in itself said to be beautiful unless one's opponent is formidable (Rachels, 2008, p. 214). Defeating an inferior player, a "woodpusher," is hardly notable or memorable. "The development of beauty in chess never depends on you alone," grandmaster Vladmir Kramnik noted, "No matter how much imagination and creativity you invest, you still do not create beauty. Your opponent must react at the same highest level" (www.kramnik.com, retrieved 4/29/14). It is for this reason that it is an absurd exercise to play against oneself.

The beauty of chess is also evident in the styles of play, reflecting the character and outlook of the player, both his idiosyncratic psychological trajectory and socio-cultural context. As grandmaster Kramnik noted, "I am convinced, the way one plays chess always reflects the player's personality. If something defines his character, then it will also define his way of playing" (ibid.). This being said, there are certain "schools" of chess that are more or less in sync with a particular player's personality. There is, for example, the Romantic school, running from about the same time as the Romantic period in the arts, the mid 1800s, which was characterized by bold sacrifices, such as of the Queen leading to a checkmate, and a fluid, open,[23] adventurous, tactically-oriented style as opposed to strategically conceived one. The King's flank was often viewed as most critical. As Shenk further notes, the Romantic style was characterized by "swashbuckling attacks, clever combinations, and a relative lack of long-term planning" (Shenk, 2006, p. 100), as if playing in style mattered more than winning. The

23 An open game is one "in which Pawn exchanges open diagonals, files, and perhaps ranks for use by the line-pieces, as distinct from a close game, when the range of these pieces is restricted" (Hooper & Whyld, 1991, p. 279).

"Immortal Game" as it has been called, between Adolf Anderssen and Lionel Kieseritzky (an extreme narcissist, he called himself the "Chess Messiah") that took place during the break of the first international tournament in London in 1851, a so-called "friendly game," was the best example of the Romantic style of play. Anderssen, a "modest" German instructor of German and mathematics at the gymnasium, checkmated Kieseritzky with minor pieces after sacrificing both of his rooks, a bishop and the Queen (Saidy, 1994, p. 10).

A more "Classical" or "Scientific" style of chess playing was manifested in the systematically approached games of Wilhelm Steinitz, "the founder of modern chess," who developed positional thinking, emphasizing the importance of the center as well as classifying the Openings. Prior to Steinitz, chess principles were hardly comprehended (Fine, 1973, p. 5). As Saidy notes, "While the Romantics sought constantly to unveil the lovely flower of combination, Steinitz built up the mighty tree of position. He was not a poet but a thinker." Reflecting Steinitz's so-called "naturalism," "He approached the structure and dynamics of the game of chess as a geologist might analyze a stratum of earth" (ibid., pp. 14–15). It is not surprising that Steinitz personified the intellectual aggression that is common among chess players, "Chess is not for timid souls" he said (Fine, 1965, p. 39).

A revolution against Steinitz's chess style, the "Hypermodern" school of chess emerged in the 1920s. A number of players from Central Europe such as Richard Reti (the "poet of the chessboard," Saidy called him), Aaron Nimzowitsch and Ernst Gruenfeld suddenly dominated chess during the next twenty or so years. Their main gripe with Steinitz and, most importantly, with the formalism, fastidiousness and rigidity of the "father of classical thought," Siegbert Tarrasch, was focused around the problems of the Opening and control of the center. That is, their concern "was that a large Pawn center would eventually overextend itself and become a target." Nimzowitsch, for example, especially asserted "the importance of piece play against the center." The Nimzo-Indian Defense, which focuses on restraining the central Pawns with pieces, is a widely used one with the world's strongest grandmasters (www.chess.com, retrieved 4/29/14).

While Hypermodernism and Classical dogma often competed for influence and control during the 1930s, Classical style won out as exemplified by two Openings dominating international chess: the "Queen's Gambit Declined" and the "Ruy Lopez." However, after the great surprise attacker, Alekhine, died, a new generation of Soviet masters began to dominate the game and brought in a new center approach. Russian Dynamism has been characterized as merging Hypermodernism, which emphasizes piece play, and Classicalism, which stressed the Pawn center, such as in the Indian Defenses and the Sicilian Defense. In effect, Russian Dynamism asserted that it was acceptable to permit "central Pawn weaknesses for dynamic piece play" (ibid.).

It was Bobby Fischer, called the "greatest genius to descend from the chess heavens" by grandmaster Tal, who is most associated with the "Modern" approach to chess. Fischer believed that an approach to chess that included the maneuvers from all of the above-described schools was the best approach to winning. In a certain sense the megalomaniacal Fischer's eclectic approach to chess was not only an intellectually sound practice, for eclecticism is a respectable philosophical outlook, it also dovetailed with his sadistic personality: that is, his style of playing was direct and vigorous, but most importantly, "relentlessly aggressive" (Hooper & Whyld, 1991, p. 138). Fischer was thus not inhibited from taking the best strategic and tactical insights from wherever they came; he was not overwhelmed by the process of selection that eclecticism demands or ambivalent about doing so because he was not loyal to one school of thought. As Garry Kasparov noted about Mikhail Chigorin, "Once he fixated on an idea, his theoretical point became more important to him than winning, and this lack of competitive pragmatism prevented him from making it to the top" (www.chessquotes.com, retrieved 5/2/14). In Fischer's case, when all that matters is to win by the greatest possible margin, to "crush the opponent's mind" as Fischer said, the predatory mind is unleashed with terrifying efficiency and violent beauty.

Regardless of what school of chess one is lodged in, there are at least four important aspects of intellectual acuity that are in play in the strong player, aspects of intelligence which are helpful in terms of living the "good life": memory, especially pattern recognition; visualization; organization and imagination (Fine, 1965, pp. 18, 19). To be great at chess one must be able to remember thousands of former positions.[24] For example, a grandmaster can play sixty boards at the same

24 This being said, the word "remember" might be misleading without some clarification: "In the middle of playing a simul, I could probably reproduce a few of the games, or at least only half or something like that. However,

time, moving from one board to another, recognizing even the minutest change of a Pawn. Visualization skills are also vital, for the player must be able to abstractly imagine a move as it is against the rules to move the pieces as one is figuring out one's move. Playing chess while blindfolded personifies the master's amazing visualization and memory skills, with some players being able to play multiple games at the same time. The chess master is also extremely adept at organization, that is, he has the ability to coordinate and integrate the actions of the various pieces so that they are maximally effective. Imagination, especially combinative imagination, as we have already discussed, is the lynchpin of great chess playing. As Rachels points out, when Fischer was preparing to compete in a match against Spassky in 1972, including the "Game of the Century," he poured over Spassky's games as compiled in a German "red book" (named thusly due to its red cover) that contained 353 of Spassky's games (there were no computer-based databases in those days). Apparently, one could give Fischer any number between 1 and 353, and he could recite verbatim all the moves to the game, the analysis of the game provided in the "red book," and his own, better analysis of the game. While this is a superhuman feat of memory and intellectual prowess, many chess players have an extraordinary intellectual capacity along these lines (Rachels, 2008, p. 216).

As the great painter and chess player Marcel Duchamp noted, when all of these intellectual capacities are unified and operating at the highest level of clarity and skillfulness, the master experiences two aesthetic pleasures: "First, the abstract imagery akin to the poetic idea of writing; secondly, the sensuous pleasure of that ideographic execution on the chess board." Moreover, says Duchamp, "From my close contact with artists and chess players I have come to the conclusion that while all artists are not chess players, all chess players are artists" (Cockburn, 1974, p. 190).

Perhaps the best expression of the artistic nature of chess is the so-called "composed problem," roughly analogous to an intellectual puzzle, one that is mathematically informed in a manner that calls to mind the way mathematics is used in music composition. A chess composition includes "a position, a task, and a solution." As Rachels

---

upon seeing a position, I can tell if a Pawn has been moved because the rest of the position helps me recall where the Pawn was." Thus, the role of memory is rather complex in chess (Rachels, personal communication, 7/20/14).

further notes, most often the task "is for White to force checkmate, or to arrive at an obviously winning position, or to force a draw from a starting point that appears hopeless" (2008, p. 218). The Armenian international grandmaster for chess compositions Henrikh Kasparyan, who began composing at age 15, was one of the greatest composers of his time, particularly of Endgames. Sam Loyd and Alexi Troitsky are other well-known composers, all of whom put in incredible amounts of time, effort and cost to create their problems. As Einstein noted, himself a chess player and good friend of the legendary grandmaster Emanuel Lasker, "If I had an hour to solve a problem I'd spend 55 minutes thinking about the problem and 5 minutes thinking about solutions" (www.psychologytoday.com, retrieved 4/30/14).

Chess composition has its own specialized vocabulary and guidelines; it does not follow that a great composer is also a great player. The writer Vladimir Nabokov, himself a chess composer, captured the aesthetic nature of composition when he said, "Chess problems demand from the composer the same virtues that characterize all worthwhile art: originality, invention, consciousness, harmony, complexity, and splendid insincerity" (www.chessquotes.com, retrieved 4/30/14). While Nabokov appreciates the "quasi-musical, quasi-poetical" inspiration (Nabokov, 1993, p. 25) of chess composition, the great English pure mathematician, G.H. Hardy, perhaps best known outside of his field for his essay on the aesthetics of mathematics, noted the important difference between chess composition and mathematics: "A chess problem is genuine mathematics, but it is in some way 'trivial' mathematics. However ingenious and intricate, however original and surprising the moves, there is something essential lacking. Chess problems are unimportant. The best mathematics is serious as well as beautiful—'important' if you like..." (www.vigyanprasar.gov.in, retrieved 4/30/14). No doubt Hardy is right that the ideas that constitute chess problems are not as "high order," finely nuanced, and elegant as those generated in pure mathematics. Moreover, the emotional impact of chess problems is hardly as evocative as music, which also draws from mathematics. This being said, there is something utterly compelling about chess compositions that perhaps speaks to the human need to formulate challenging problems for their own sake. Many chess composers have noted that the solution to a problem is not nearly as satisfying as formulating it. Indeed, to the psychoanalyst who listens with the "third ear," who intuitively perceives unconscious wishes and fantasies, chess composition seems to have an erotically tinged appeal that may in part account for its powerful hold on composers, players and spectators. As chess champion Rachels has noted: "I cannot exaggerate how marvelous chess problems are. There are *thousands upon thousands* of gloriously beautiful problems. They are awesome, fantastic, stunning" (emphasis in original; Rachels, 2008, p. 210).

In terms of living the "good life," there is a lot one can benefit from by embracing many of the intellectual values that chess wonderfully personifies, what has been described by Soviet grandmaster Eduard Gufeld as "the search for the chess Mona Lisa," or "chess beauty" (Martin, 2008, pp. 92–93). A few examples would be helpful to drive this point home. As Russian grandmaster Mikhail Botvinnik noted, "Chess is the art of analysis." Indeed, there is probably no game or sport in which the imagination so marvelously synergistically merges with the logical, mathematical and in other ways calculative working through of technical theorems (Saidy, 1994, pp. 49, 50). Though chess recognizes that knowledge is not absolute but is context-dependent and setting-specific since the game is always changing, it advocates a kind of cognitive optimism. That is, it expresses the belief that one can usually successfully navigate this challenging world if one has perfected the intellectual faculties like memory, visualization, organization and imagination. Chess, like life, is an intellectual and, in other ways, individual struggle in which one is on one's own, particularly in terms of motivation, will and ability. Moreover, the game's intellectual values also honor the fact that, on and off the wooden board, there is an unpredictable and surprising quality to chess and life since it can be played and lived in infinitely numerous and diverse ways, and therefore continuous creative adaptation is necessary. As American grandmaster Samuel Reshevsky noted, "In this position…I had to survive," and this requires the capacity for inventive improvisation that is lodged in a "purity of vision," one that values prevailing at all costs (ibid., pp. 68, 70). Chess understands that intellectual acuity is not enough to survive, let alone flourish, on and off the wooden board. One also needs a high level of self-awareness and self-understanding. That is, chess players are not simply "fine tuned camera-computers," superbly able to acquire and process visual data with terrifying efficiency. Rather, being great in chess and living requires "a combination of resonant feelings, meaningful experiences, and rich memories" that are completely infused with "human feeling" (Shenk, 2006, p. 126). One only has to recall, for instance, that Spassky, known to be a "nice guy," a competitor who always displayed an elegant demeanor and who maintained perfect manners and restrained comportment in his famous match with the provocatively obnoxious and mean-spirited Fischer, "confided to a writer that he would like to kick Fischer in the behind" (Cockburn, 1974, p. 152). Whether Spassky's anger at Fischer negatively influenced his playing is hard to know for sure, but what is important to emphasize is that such distracting anger could not have been helpful in his gladiatorial contest where concentration and attention are so important. Self-mastery is necessary in both chess and life. It is to this subject, what chess has to teach us about the moral life, that I now turn.

III. CHESS AS MORAL TEACHING

As had been insinuated earlier, there is more to chess than its psychoanalytically-glossed sexual symbolism and the poetico-mathematic beauty of chess composition and thinking (Nabokov, 1993, p. 25). Chess also has some important moral insights that are pertinent to the art of living the "good life."

Benjamin Franklin's famous "The Morals of Chess" described some of the salient themes of chess's "effects on the mind" (2006, p. 281), a game, incidentally, that Freud called the "noble game" (Freud, 1958, p. 123), probably because of the Stoic comportment that chess etiquette requires. Franklin mentions foresight, the ability to imagine possible future problems or obstacles; circumspection, the quality of being wary and unwilling to take risks; caution, using care and thoughtfulness in decision-making; and maintaining confidence, not being discouraged by a bad situation, a kind of self-confidence in the face of adversity. Along with the other qualities mentioned above, these are extremely valuable qualities of mind and heart both on and off the wooden board. As Franklin notes, "Life is a kind of Chess...By playing chess...we may learn" (2006, p. 281) how to live better.

Chess is divided into three phases, the Opening, Middlegame and Endgame, that arguably have their real-life analogues in terms of living the "good life." While much can be written on this important subject, I will provide a few illustrative examples of these analogues. In these three phases of chess, as in life, psychology is a key factor in order to prevail. Players spend considerable time and advanced study trying to discern the personality, character and overall caste of mind of their opponent. As the great Garry Kasparov noted, "You can't overestimate the importance of psychology in chess, and as much as some players try to downplay it, I believe that winning requires a constant and strong psychology not just at the board but in every aspect of your life" (www.chessquotes.com, retrieved 5/2/14).

As Shahade describes it, the Opening is the first phase in which the pieces are developed. Strong amateur competitors have their fundamental ideas and moves of their planned Openings memorized, while grandmasters memorize multiple Openings and variations, and usually also have theoretical novelties that they are trying for the first time (Shahade, 2005, p. 291). There are literally over a thousand Openings, though most grandmasters are comfortable with only a few unless they are being innovative. As Kasparov noted, "By the time a player becomes a Grandmaster, almost all of his training time is dedicated to work on this first phase. The Opening is the only phase that holds out the potential for true creativity and doing something entirely new" (www.chessquotes.com, retrieved 5/2/14).

Given that the Opening is the beginning of the game, it follows that psychologically speaking it is crucial for establishing the power dynamics between the players and the tone of the game. Indeed, one should never underestimate the psychological importance of intimidating one's opponent from the beginning of a gladiatorial contest. The great boxing champion Mike Tyson put this point just right: "I don't try to intimidate anybody before a fight. That's nonsense. I intimidate people by hitting them" (www.quotes.lifehack.org, retrieved 5/2/14). The point is, whether on the chessboard, or in life, what matters most is to approach a competitive or in other ways challenging situation with a high degree of fearlessness. Most opponents give way in the face of fiercely demonstrated bravery. The great grandmaster Aaron Nimzowitsch was all too aware of the self-confidence-eroding nature of fear: "How vain are our fears! I thought to myself. Sometimes we fear that which our opponent (or fate) had never even considered! After this, then, is it any longer worthwhile to rack one's brain to find new ghosts to fear? No, indeed: All hail optimism!" (www.chessquotes.com, retrieved 5/2/14).

The Middlegame, the phase between the Opening and Endgame, is when a player must depend on his creativity, intuition, and calculative rationality (Shahade, 2005, p. 290). Many believe that it is the most important part of the game. As Russian master Eugene Znosko-Borovsky noted, "The middlegame I repeat is chess itself, chess with all its possibilities, its attacks, defences, sacrifices, etc." (www.chess-lessons4beginners.com, retrieved 5/2/14). The Middlegame is thus when the opening moves have laid the groundwork for play, this being when the battle of wits is most salient. Sometimes, as Borris Spassky pointed out, the Middlegame can make up for a weak Opening and Endgame: "My forte was the middlegame. I had a good feeling for the critical moments of the play. This undoubtedly compensated for my lack of opening preparation and, possibly, not altogether perfect play in the endgame. In my games things often did not reach the endgame!" (www.chessquotes.com, retrieved 5/2/14). Rather interestingly, as in life, where the Opening ends and the Middlegame begins, and where the Middlegame ends and the Endgame begins, has never been clearly delineated.

While there has been less written in the chess literature on the Middlegame compared to the Opening and Endgame, probably because every Middlegame is unique to the specific circumstances of a particular game, perhaps what is most important with regards to the Middlegame/life analogy is that the Middlegame puts into sharp focus a basic problem of human social life: Deciding whether to continue to escalate a threat or begin responding to it (Shenk, 2006, p. 118). That is, knowing when to go on the offensive and when to go on the defensive. Indeed, while the great philosopher of war Carl von Clausewitz noted, every offense is a defense and vice versa, there are still questions of judgment that are in play in terms of knowing when to attack and when to defend (and when to do nothing, to wait). Reuben Fine's classic *The Middlegame in Chess* emphasizes that every Middlegame must consider three elements: the safety of the King, force ("material," a pieces relative value) and mobility. When the King is under attack, the only thing that matters is preserving his safety; Force advantage is usually correlated with victory; Mobility refers to having a wide range of actionable moves and enemy pieces to attack (Fine, 1952). No doubt, complex psychological issues related to safety, power and freedom are subtly played out in the Middlegame. However, what links these three considerations in order to prevail both in chess and life, and especially in competitive situations like war is the willingness and ability to be audacious. As Clausewitz famously said, "Never forget that no military leader has ever become great without audacity." Indeed, Karparov has beautifully elaborated this point:

> Ultimately, what separates a winner from a loser at the grandmaster level is the willingness to do the unthinkable. A brilliant strategy is, certainly, a matter of intelligence, but intelligence without audaciousness is not enough. Given the opportunity, I must have the guts to explode the game, to upend my opponent's thinking and, in so doing, unnerve him. So it is in business: One does not succeed by sticking to convention. When your opponent can easily anticipate every move you make, your strategy deteriorates and becomes commoditized. (www.chessquotes.com, retrieved 5/2/14)

What makes audacity so important in chess and life is that it is intimately linked to other important qualities of mind and heart that are needed to survive and flourish, such as a well-developed imagination, tact, and trusting one's instincts and courage, these being the antidotes to the hesitation and fear that people feel when in competitive and challenging situations. What the Middlegame teaches, then, is that on and off the wooden board, in a game that Kasparov described as "psychologically brutal" and "mental torture" (ibid.)—and indeed, the same can be said sometimes about real life—there is a time for shameless audacity in order to prevail.

Finally, we come to the Endgame, "the phase in which material is reduced (usually Queens are traded) and the results often settled" (Shahade, 2005, p. 288). All great players memorize the most frequently used Endgames, though the skillful use of intuition comes into play in a big way, often involving spectacular escapes. In a classic Endgame only a few pieces remain on the board, typically a King and a couple of pieces on each side (Shenk, 2006, p. 191). In contrast to the Middlegame when checkmate-oriented moves are most feared, in the Endgame the King may assume a more aggressive role, while the Pawns can be advanced with less of a risk to themselves or threat to their Kings ["The King is a strong piece—use it!" said Reuben Fine (www.chessquotes.com, retrieved 5/3/14)]. In general, the ultimate but not necessarily the immediate goal of the Endgame is to "promote a Pawn" (Hooper & Whyld, 1991, p. 123) and to avoid "Zugzwang" at all costs. Zugzwang ("compulsion to move") is a situation in which the obligation to make a move in one's turn is a serious, often decisive, disadvantage. In other words, every legal move undermines your position. A rather intriguing aspect of chess is that the Endgame of King and rook versus lone King, not an impressive victory, relies on zugzwang (Rachels, 2008, pp. 222–223). As the "Latin lover of chess" and Endgame genius Jose Capablanca noted, "In order to improve your game, you must study the endgame before everything else. For whereas the endings can be studied and mastered by themselves, the middlegame and opening must be studied in relation to the endgame" (www.chessquotes.com, retrieved 5/3/14). As Samuel Beckett noted in his partly chess-inspired "theater of the absurd" masterpiece, *Endgame*, "The end is in the beginning and yet you go on."[25]

It is interesting to note that Beckett was a good friend and chess playmate of Duchamp (Beckett was not a very good player and Duchamp was a master). In fact, *Endgame* was to some extent stimulated by Duchamp's Endgame-focused book on chess (Shenk, 2006, p. 191). One wonders if the bleak Beckett found in the drama of chess insights into the subject matter of his play, one that he wrote in darkly existential and tragicomic terms, namely, those of the master-servant relationship (or the married couple) (www.samuel-beckett.net, retrieved 5/4/14). Beckett viewed the "endgame" of chess as an analogy to "the chess conceit to the endgame of life, in which death is the inevitable." In other words, as in the Endgame, where the result is usually determined prior to the formality of the Endgame occurring, the characters, similar to chess players, reenact "repetitive rituals that are part of their endgame." Calling to mind how a nearly defeated chess player who desperately attempts to survive the final moves even though his destruction is looming, the characters—and we are all characters in this absurdist struggle called life—make everyday routines out of their threatened lives and do whatever it takes to endure yet another day, even though the game, or the game of life, has lost whatever joy it may have once contained (www.sparknotes.com, retrieved 5/4/14).

What does chess wisdom recommend to the player when he is "up front and personal" with the threatening aspects of the Endgame? In other words, what practical wisdom can the grandmaster offer that has extrapolative bearing on the Endgame, metaphorically speaking, when we are face to face with the real-life cyclical and repetitive character of beginnings and endings, the emptiness, alienation and loneliness, and the absurdist aspects (ibid.) of everyday living?

To begin with, it is important to be mindful of the wise words of chess champion Emanuel Lasker who warned, "Do not permit yourself

25 Beckett's play, *Murphy*, also includes a chess theme.

to fall in love with the endgame play to the exclusion of entire games. It is well to have the whole story of how it happened; the complete play, not the denouement only. Do not embrace the rag-time and vaudeville of chess" (www.chessquotes.com, retrieved 5/4/14). What Lasker is saying about Endgame applies also to the art of living, that is, it is a mistake to rigidly focus on the end product or the goal, at the expense of the process. Otherwise you do not learn from and appreciate everything that happens along the way. For as in chess, if you only focus on the Endgame, your chances of ultimately prevailing are greatly diminished because you lack the retrospective consciousness that allows you to properly assess the totality of competitive and psychological circumstances that you are and have been in that inevitably animate the final outcome.

If there is one bit of practical wisdom concerning the Endgame that grandmasters advocate and personify both on and off the wooden board, it is the need to cultivate the capacity for improvisation. Improvisation, dictionary defined as the ability to make or do something drawing from whatever is available, typically because you do not have what you really need, is another way of describing creative reality adaptation. More specifically, improvisation calls for the cultivation of a very different way of thinking than one usually associates with the cerebral grandmaster as well as how most of us go about navigating our everyday lives. Unlike the detached intellectualizing, discursive reasoning and obsessive-like cerebral doings that are rooted in the empiricism and rationalism of the western mindset, improvisation aims to fully engage the immediacy of the human situation in its essential fluidity and changeability. This is the place where "the unconscious delivers the goods," where spontaneous creativity emerges as does the beauty of the unknown (Wardle, 1992, p. 10). Improvisation thus emphasizes the intuitive, "the direct knowing of something without conscious use of reasoning...it is a way of knowing other than intellectual knowing" (ibid., p. ix). Intuition implies a highly-attuned sense of empathy, concentration and spontaneity, imagination, expanded awareness, emotional intelligence, and the ability to be supportive and helpful to others. These and other such qualities of the mind and heart are of course some of the required properties for playing the chess Endgame well (with the exception of being supportive/helpful to one's opponent), as well as living the "good life." As comedic improviser Steve Carell noted, "improv," as it is called in artistic circles, can be conceptualized as similar to chess playing: "I look at improvising as a prolonged game of chess. There's an opening gambit with your Pawn in a complex game I have with one character, and lots of side games with other characters, and another game with myself—and in each game you make all these tiny, tiny moves that get you to the end-game" (http://www.newyorker.com, retrieved 5/4/14). To resolve or to better manage the difficult problems of living that are associated with the Endgame that Beckett has grimly described requires living the valuative attachments most associated with improvisation at its best. The whole person becomes awakened and attentive to the problem of living—mind, body, intelligence and creativity, spontaneity and intuition are utterly responsive to the moment, and to the otherness of life. Moreover, such a way of embracing life without reserve tends to enhance one's capacity to appreciate the sad ironies of life that are funny. When the great Alekhine was asked, "How is that you pick better moves than your opponents?" he responded: "I'm very glad you asked that, because, as it happens, there is a very simple answer. I think up my own moves, and I make my opponent think up his" (www.chessquotes.com, retrieved 4/10/14).

IV. THE APPEAL OF CHESS

Garry Kasparov, perhaps the greatest chess player of all time, aptly described in general terms the appeal and cultural function of chess to players and spectators: "Chess is a mixture of sport, psychological warfare, science, and art" (Shahade, 2005, p. 75). The more psychologically minded Burt Hochberg, the former editor-in-chief of the highly regarded monthly magazine, *Chess Life*, further noted that chess is not only a game, sport, art and science, it is also a "passion, madness, recreation, obsession," in other words, "it is a world" of meaning (Hochberg, 1993, p. xi). Like any world of meaning, chess includes some of the existential tensions that all of us struggle with in our everyday lives such as "freedom, time, utility" and "chance" (Cockburn, 1974, p. 13). As Shenk noted, in chess there is a powerful "dialectic between total freedom and complete restriction, between choice and futility" (2006, p. 90). Saidy, too, views the appeal of chess similarly, "In chess is relived the age-old tension between matter and spirit, control and freedom, domination (mastery of chess) and love (chess as a mistress)"

(Saidy, 1994, p. 308).[26] Moreover, as with other sports, chess includes "images of fear, enactments of pain, anxiety, love, the desire for transcendence," even an enactment of suicidal sacrifice (Cockburn, 1974, pp. 197–198). One just has to consider the proletariat of the wooden board, the seemingly low status Pawn whose effective management is essential to winning a game. Hans Berliner, a champion grandmaster of Correspondence chess and professor of computers noted, "No other piece contributes as much to the success of a position, because of the tyranny of the weak. The Pawn is worth little and can therefore intimidate all pieces of greater value" (www.chessgames.com, retrieved 4/8/14). Also noteworthy is the fact that while on one hand, unlike other pieces, the Pawn's moves cannot be reversed,[27] every Pawn has the potential to be a Queen, the arch symbol of phallic-like power. Perhaps this is the reason that psychoanalyst/grandmaster Reuben Fine quipped, "I'd rather have a Pawn than a finger" (www.chessquotes.com, retrieved 5/4/14). Indeed, the Pawn speaks to the unconscious of the player and spectator, as do all the other pieces and the game as a whole. It is probably for this reason that chess has had such a powerful command over the imaginations, if not the lives, of so many people worldwide. Moreover, as I have suggested throughout this chapter, chess and the chess world provide some helpful insights on how to live the "good life."

While the motivation animating a particular player's and spectator's passion for chess is always an idiosyncratic trajectory, that is, it is driven by a number of interrelated, interdependent and interactive psychological, social and contextual factors, I have argued that perhaps the most important reason for chess's general appeal is that it calls to mind the Oedipal situation, centrally including the murder of the

---

26 The great grandmaster and chess writer Paul Keres noted, "True beauty in chess consists in an elemental struggle between totally different tendencies....It is the multiplicity of the various styles of personalities that gives chess its magic attraction" (Shenk, 2006, p. 86).

27 André Danican Philidor (1726–1795), the first positional thinker, emphasized this point when he further noted that Pawn structure thus has a fundamental strategic importance to the game. "Pawns," Philidor famously said, "are the soul of chess" (Saidy, 1994, p. 10). Former world champion Anatoly Karpov agrees with Philidor: "Pawns not only create the sketch for the whole painting, they are also the soul, the foundation, of any position" (www.chessquotes.com, retrieved, 5/4/14).

father. As Freud wrote, the death of one's father is "the most important event, the most poignant loss, of a man's life" (Freud, 1953, p. xxvi). How much more so when it is through one's own actions, even if it is etherealized violence (Waterman, 1993, p. 18)?[28]

While the claim that chess is a sublimation of the Oedipal drama and family romance and its related thematics such as aggression, homosexuality, masturbation and narcissism is, of course, a debatable one, though one that is in sync with my Freudian outlook, the fact is that it has considerable rhetorical traction when one tries to account for chess's incredibly addictive hold on so many people. Moreover, it is hard to adequately account for the strange and troubling behavior of various famous grandmasters without centrally factoring in these alleged unresolved unconscious Oedipal and other psychodynamics discussed in this chapter. Consider the following few examples: The immortal Paul Morphy, at age 21, during the final game of a blindfold exhibition in Paris against eight of the best players, sat "almost unmovable for ten consecutive hours, without having tasted a morsel of anything, even water, during the whole consecutive period." As I have said earlier, he ultimately lost his mind, probably suffering from melancholic paranoia if you are convinced by Ernest Jones's famous study; Wilhelm Steinitz, the World Champion for twenty-eight years, died believing that "he could move chess pieces by impulses from his brain and defeat God at odds of Pawn and move;" The great Akiba Rubenstein was also paranoid to the point where he thought other players and officials were trying to poison him, even fleeing rooms when others came in. He spent the last thirty years in a psychiatric institution. Alexander Alekhine, a World Champion for seventeen years, was known to throw chess pieces, smash furniture and once drunkenly peed on the floor. In addition to being an alcoholic he was a Nazi collaborator and had five wives, the last of whom he frequently publicly humiliated (Cockburn, 1974, p. 17); and finally as already mentioned, Bobby Fischer was a well-known paranoid and megalomaniacal character while Spassky was probably a depressive one (Fine, 1973, p. 86).[29]

---

28 Etherealized violence is roughly equivalent to adaptive benign or defensive aggression that is typical to all species (Aragno, 2014, p. 260).

29 In his *The Psychology of the Chess Player* Fine includes a discussion of the serious psychopathology in a many champions. Fischer might be characterized as suffering from "malignant narcissism," an "ego-syntonic

No doubt the above examples of psychopathology in some of the greatest chess players do not mean that all chess players or spectators suffer or are prone to suffer from these conditions. However, by looking at the extreme of chess pathology in the greatest players where Oedipal and other related psychodynamics are presumably operative, it is reasonable to assume that these psychological themes resonate to some extent in the typical player and spectator. In other words, what I am claiming is that what, in part, makes chess so powerfully appealing to so many people is that it gives us the opportunity to re-experience the Oedipal situation and familial romance, but with a key difference—with the hope that we will finally undo the trauma of Oedipal defeat and have an Oedipal victory. In child analysis, an Oedipal victory happens when the child feels, or fantasizes, that he has obtained the greater part of love and attention from the parent of the opposite sex. An Oedipal victory can occur within the context of the death of the father (the King) or in other situations, like when an aggressive mother (the Queen) who worships her son shows hatred for her husband's masculinity (Moore & Fine, 1990, p. 135). While the application of these diverse Oedipal and family romance dynamics to chess have been explicated in detail earlier, what makes the chess player and spectator revisit the wooden board over and over again is that the game seductively suggests the possibility of an Oedipal victory, though with a rub. As in real life, an Oedipal victory is psychologically lethal because it leads to intense guilt and the pervasive fear of punishment. In other words, the re-visiting of the Oedipal trauma in the chess devotee reflects the repetition compulsion, that psychological "tendency to repeat patterns of behavior or to re-create situations that may be painful or self-destructive" (Person, Cooper, & Gabbard, 2005, p. 558), but with the hope that this time it will lead to a joyful ending, one of possession of and sexualized intimacy with the mother/Queen. Of course, even in the healthiest of adults, the Oedipal complex is never fully and permanently resolved. Even when a player wins the game the same repressed Oedipal trauma and its derivatives come back to haunt the player in some form later, the so-called return of the repressed, and thus induce another round of obligatory re-enactments meant to put things internally right. The obsessive and compulsive nature of so many chess players in the way they relate to

---

grandiosity combined with cruelty or sadism, and severe paranoid traits" (Kernberg, 1984, p. 276).

the game speaks to this point that the player and spectator are likely driven by these early, unresolved childhood psychodynamics: "My attitude towards the game," said the great Judit Polgar, "especially in my youth could be called obsessive" (Shahade, 2005, p. 88). Albert Einstein, who was a good friend of Lasker, wrote in the foreword of the latter's biography, "The enormous mental resilience, without which no chess player can exist, was so much taken up by chess that he could never free his mind of this game, even when he was occupied by philosophical and humanitarian questions" (midwestchess.com/quotes.htm retrieved 7/28/14). The well-known anti-libidinal, anti-impulsive and anti-emotional (Rycroft, 1995, p. 117) aspects of the obsessional character that is rooted in the anal-sadistic phase of development has been captured by the Armenian grandmaster Levon Aronian, "As a chess player one has to be able to control one's feelings, one has to be as cold as a machine" (www.chessquotes.com, retrieved 5/2/14; www.chessquotes.com, retrieved 5/4/14).[30]

FINAL THOUGHTS

The powerful appeal of chess can be connected to the fact that the game forces the players and spectators to unconsciously feel the pleasurable terminal effects of lethal force, albeit with some ambivalence, symbolized by the war-like nature of the game and, most sharply, when the King is checkmated. This being said, the chess player and spectator also unconsciously intuit something even more starkly significant, though paradoxically reassuring, an insight that is axiomatic for living the "good life": that when all is said and done, as in real life, whether one is a King or a Pawn, lofty or lowly, we all have to contend with the same Endgame that inevitably leads to death. This powerful insight, chess as the great moral and social leveler in which the game, and the game of life, is rigged so that no one gets out alive, has been beautifully immortalized in the ironically comforting Italian saying, "After the game, the King and the Pawn go into the same box" (www.philosiblog.com, retrieved 5/4/14).

30 Speaking of being obsessed with chess, one writer described the negative impact of Duchamp's obsession on his marriage: "Duchamp spent most of one week they lived together studying chess problems, and his bride, in desperate retaliation, got up one night when he was asleep and glued the chess pieces to the board. They were divorced three months later" (Waterman, 1993, pp. 21–22).

CHAPTER 5

TENNIS: A SPORTSMAN'S PASTIME AND A FIGHTER'S GAME

> "When we have matched our rackets to these balls,
> We will in France, by God's grace, play a set
> Shall strike his father's crown into the hazard."
>
> William Shakespeare (*Henry*, Act 1, Scene 2)

"During a match," said the "King of Clay," Rafael Nadal, "you are in a permanent battle to fight back your everyday vulnerabilities, bottle up your human feelings. It is a kind of self-hypnosis, a game you play, with deadly seriousness, to disguise your own weaknesses from yourself, as well as from your rival" (www.hachettebookgroup.com, retrieved 5/12/14).[1] Indeed, tennis, like chess, is a gladiatorial contest between two opponents in which the fight is as much psychological as it is physical. As the highly regarded tennis writer Richard Evans noted, "Tennis is not a gentle game. Psychologically, it is vicious" (www.sportsfeelgoodstories.com, retrieved 5/12/14),[2] reminding us that an ugly mind can inhabit a

1 Formerly ranked number five, Gaston Gaudio made a similar remark, "I think that always myself is my worst opponent. I [sic] always playing against myself first and then to the other one. So I'm playing against two guys during the match...It's like mentally I don't know what is gonna happen in the next ten minutes. Maybe I get depressed in ten minutes. I don't know myself too much...Yeah, I was working with a psychologist, and I still [am]" (oxnardtenniscenter.com, retrieved 5/28/14).

2 Andre Agassi notes about his opponent, "He hates me, and I hate him, and now we're sneering and snarling and trying to wrest this thing from

beautiful body. While on the face of it, tennis may appear to be a "gentleman's game" in which there is a polite etiquette that governs every aspect of a tournament—for example, the spotlessly clean white attire, the funereal-like silence during play, the polite extolling of the opponent's skilled shot, and the end-of-game handshake by the winner to the loser (Whitman, 2010, p. 205)—but to insiders and mavens, it calls to mind war and man's passion for combat and competition. Many of tennis's terms are rooted in warfare vocabulary like "volley," "kill," "cut" "stroke," and "smash" (Whitman, 2004, p. 144), and there is obvious aggressive pleasure in slamming a ball with a racket directed at an opponent. The legendary Billy Jean King superbly made this point when she commented, "Tennis is a perfect combination of violent action taking place in an atmosphere of total tranquility" (www.biographyonline.net, retrieved 5/12/14). Violence and grace can co-exist and become something aesthetically appealing (Gumbrecht, 2006, p. 171). The former French Open winner Yannick Noah viewed the game in a similar manner, stating, "I have always considered tennis as a combat in an arena between two gladiators who have their racquets and their courage as their weapons" (www.tennispsychology.com, retrieved 5/27/14).

This being said, tennis, a game that has its cultural roots in the twelfth century in the peaceful northern French monastic cloisters (Gillmeister, 1998, pp. xi, 34)[3] not only resonates with the millions of ordinary players and spectators because of its militaristic quality, but it also emulates many other challenging aspects of everyday life, including suggesting how one can prevail. As *New York Times* sport's columnist George Vecsey noted, "Tennis is the perfect sporting metaphor for life," that is, for creating and finding meaning in everyday existence (1995, p. 8). In his bestseller, *Open,* the former World Champion Andre Agassi perceptively elaborated:

> It's no accident, I think, that tennis uses the language of life. Advantage, service, fault, break, love, the basic elements of tennis are those of everyday existence, because every match is a life in miniature. Even the structure of tennis, the way the pieces fit inside one another like Russian nesting dolls, mimics the structure of our days. Points become games become sets become tournaments, and it's all

---

each other" (Agassi, 2010, p. 19).

3 Despite its monastic origins, tennis—and golf—have become vehicles for social climbing and forms of social aggression (Gumbrecht, 2006, p. 26).

> so tightly connected that any point can become the turning point. It reminds me of the way seconds become minutes become hours, and any hour can be our finest. Or darkest. It's our choice. (2010, p. 8)

In this chapter I elaborate some of the important themes of tennis as a metaphor for how to live the "good life." Specifically, I want to discuss some of the psychoanalytic formulations about what motivates tennis playing and spectatorship, for without having a sense of what draws a player and spectator to the game, it is impossible to effectively appropriate its practical wisdom. In subsequent sections I discuss the aesthetic appeal of tennis and some of its moral insights that have bearing on the problem of how to live one's everyday life better. For as philosopher David Baggett noted in an interview, "Tennis is something of a microcosm of life," one that teaches "crucial lessons" (www.tennisnow.com, retrieved 5/12/14). It is to this subject that I now turn.

I. PSYCHOANALYTIC NOTES ON TENNIS

If ever there was a sport that required the capacity to emotionally self-regulate, be empathic (in the sense of fathoming what one's opponent is thinking and feeling in order to defeat him), and relationally in sync with the other (especially when playing doubles), tennis is probably it. Moreover, what makes the game so thrilling to play and watch is that like in life, the actualization of these capacities are made more difficult by the complex external realities such as court conditions, the weather (when playing outside), as well as the interaction of perceptual accuracy, time and space (Petrucelli, 2010, p. 583).

With regards to emotional self-regulation, one only has to think of the many abusive and angry outbursts of John McEnroe, Serena Williams, Ilie Nastase and Jimmy Connors at umpires, judges and other players. Most professionals and others likely feel similarly, but wisely have enough self-mastery to avoid the emotional interference (not to mention the imposed penalties for unsportsmanlike behavior) and therefore maintain the all-important concentration that is necessary to play at the highest level. For those who play on the professional circuit, but also for the casual player, there is a lot that is psychologically at stake. As Billy Jean King noted, "A champion is afraid of losing. Everyone else is afraid of winning" (www.biography.com, retrieved 5/12/14). Bjorn Borg felt similarly—"I just hated to lose" (www.endlessquote.com, retrieved 5/12/14)—as did Nadal: "I have no sense of humor about losing" (www.open.salon.com, retrieved 5/12/14). Indeed, with so much feeling and ego invested in a tournament, it is no wonder that tennis players at all levels require exceptionally good self-control to play the game effectively. The question is, what has to be controlled? Beyond mental focus, relaxed concentration and visualization described in sports psychology literature (Gallwey, 1997), what are the mainly unconscious internal states that the great tennis player has to master in order to press on, maybe even win, or if he loses, to not experience it as a massive blow to his self-esteem?

Aggression-Guilt-Punishment

Perhaps what most needs to be mastered in tennis relates to the aggression-guilt-punishment dynamic. As I have already noted, tennis is an extremely aggressive sport, which its courteous etiquette barely masks. The fact that the most lethal tennis stroke is called the "kill shot" supports this observation (Whitman, 1969, p. 205), as does the violent imagery former world champion Pete Sampras expressed: "You are thinking about taking your opponent's heart out and squeezing it until all the blood comes out, even the very last drop, and you have won" (www.independent.co.uk, retrieved 5/12/14).[4] With this much aggression circulating throughout a tennis match, and certainly when the financial and other stakes are as high as they are on the professional circuit, players often unconsciously feel guilty for their murderous wishes, especially if they equate their opponent with an Oedipal father. As in baseball, soccer and chess, boys (and probably girls) are often first taught tennis by their father whom they eventually equal, if not surpass, in achievements. Agassi, for example, noted that the "sweetest

---

4 It is worth noting that the well-known sports journalist Bud Collins stated that tennis can be conceived as "boxing without bloodshed" (Ditouras, 2010, p. 182) while Agassi called it "noncontact pugilism" (2010, p. 214). Psychoanalytically speaking, all sports involve an aggressive discharge, though they are subtly different. For example, while tennis involves slapping, a kind of extremity extension, golf that also involves a slapping motion is more of a phallic extension. American football can be described as mainly phallic-intrusive (Whitman, 1969, p. 199). Agassi seems to have a layman's intuitive sense of the different types of aggression in tennis when he noted, "Tennis is about degrees of aggression. You want to be aggressive enough to control a point, not so aggressive that you sacrifice control and expose yourself to unnecessary risk" (2010, p. 12).

win of my life" was beating his abrasive, if not psychologically abusive "stage parent" father in a tennis game. In that emotionally significant game his father realized he was going to lose and walked off the court before finishing the match. As Agassi proudly noted, "I'll take this win over a wheelbarrow full of silver dollars...because this is the win that made my father finally sneak away from me" (2010, pp. 53, 180). In other instances, guilt is generated by dishonesty on the court, such as in self-servingly manipulating the scoring, feigning injury at the hands of the opponent, or trying to cunningly make one's opponent feel guilty so he falters. As psychoanalyst Theodor Saretsky noted, the crafty tennis player "plays on the other party's guilt. Continuously praise your opponent's shots, and you'll notice how he begins to press. Self-beratement also serves to balance a guilty conscience for being successful and makes your opponent disturbed for upsetting you so. If on occasion you call one of your opponent's 'out' shots 'in,' then later on you can innocently call an 'in' shot 'out' on a crucial play. Practice saying 'Good try,' sincerely; then you can call a lot of close shots 'out' and get away with it" (www.allgreatquotes.com, retrieved 5/20/14).

As Freud taught, for most people whether on or off the tennis court, in their unconscious minds the crime always seeks punishment. In other words, whether we are referring to genuine guilt, that sense of having violated a consciously maintained moral code like "fair play," which purposefully or unintentionally hurts someone, or neurotic guilt, that is, guilt that is not explicable in terms of any violation of one's consciously maintained values and beliefs, such as feeling guilty because winning is equated with an Oedipal victory, the fact is that there is a human tendency to need to be punished as a result of inflicting real or imagined harm on others. As business consultant C. Terry Warner noted, this dynamic can be enacted in a tennis match:

> Except in a very few matches, usually with world-class performers, there is a point in every match (and in some cases it's right at the beginning) when the loser decides he's going to lose. And after that, everything he does will be aimed at providing an explanation of why he will have lost. He may throw himself at the ball (so he will be able to say he's done his best against a superior opponent). He may dispute calls (so he will be able to say he's been robbed). He may swear at himself and throw his racket (so he can say it was apparent all along he wasn't in top form). His energies go not into winning

> but into producing an explanation, an excuse, a justification for losing. (2001, p. 136)

The psychoanalytic "take home" point, then, is this: In a game like tennis where there is so much competitive aggression embedded in every serve and return—"People don't seem to understand that it's a damn war out there," said Jimmy Connors (www.born-today.com, retrieved 5/21/14)—where there is the possibility of various forms of cheating, a player is prone to unconsciously feel guilty, and this may require either an internal or external punishment of some type. As Whitman summarizes, this unconscious equivalence of defeating one's opponent with murder, especially when the opponent is equated with one's Oedipal father (or mother), evokes a troubling expectation of imminent retaliation that is either internally experienced in terms of guilt/punishment, or externally, as a fear of retaliatory punishment by one's dying opponent. As a result of this fantasy, a player may be utterly inhibited about competing because of the magnitude of his murderous wishes toward his opponent, or more likely, this need for punishment is manifested during the match, leading to strangely inconsistent scores or the occurrence of "breaking back" following an achieved service break. A service break, says Whitman, where the "big game" is predominant is practically the same as winning the set (1969, p. 206). Finally, where "nerves and choking" are a major concern as in a "precision-and-timing sport like tennis" (Wallace, 1997, p. 254)—"The fifth set is not about tennis, it's about nerves"—said Boris Becker (www.tennis.com, retrieved 5/21/14), and where we are dealing with a group known for their perfectionism—"I'm a perfectionist. I'm pretty much insatiable. I feel there's so many things I can improve on"—said Serena Williams (http://thebestyoumagazine.co, retrieved 5/21/14),[5] there may be a heightened proclivity to punish themselves during and after the game by relentless critical accusations of having played poorly and missed one's chance to be victorious. In this case, we are dealing with a kind of moral masochism, in which the sadistic super-ego punishes the ego for its losing performance.

5 Agassi also notes, "When I do something perfect, I enjoy a split second of sanity and calm" (2010, p. 29). Andy Murray suggests one of the underlying motives in tennis perfectionism: "In tennis, it is not the opponent you fear, it is the failure itself, knowing how near you were but just out of reach" (www.dailymail.co.uk, retrieved 6/4/14).

In terms of living the "good life," there is a key insight that can be extracted from the above-described dynamics: that mental integrity relies fundamentally on moral integrity, that mental stability can exist only if there is a sense of guiltlessness (Jones, 1974, p. 192). The definition of "fair play," the psychological "capacity and generosity of sympathizing with the pain and the tragedy of the person you beat in a fair fight" applies both on and off the tennis court (Gumbrecht, 2006, p. 72). It is highly unlikely that a tennis player or an ordinary person in real life can display their best abilities without their psychological functioning, capacities and talents being free of unconscious guilt. Unconscious guilt can undermine the psychologically heartiest of persons, for it not only can distract a person from the task at hand, but it is a fertile breeding ground for self-sabotaging punishment.

Symbolism

It may seem like a Freudian stretch to suggest that the erotic has its symbolic expression in such an aggressively competitive game like tennis; however, there is some suggestive evidence that even amidst the gladiatorial contest, there are erotically-tinged aspects that give the game some of its appeal. In fact, as the former Russian winner of two Grand Slams and number one ranked tennis player Marat Safin explicitly noted after winning the Davis Cup, "This victory is too great, I feel so happy that it is hard to explain with words, it is just better than sex" (www.breakingnews.ie, retrieved 5/22/14). Billy Jean King also showed some awareness that sexual derivatives can inform a typical tennis match: "Ladies, here's a hint. If you're up against a girl with big boobs, bring her to the net and make her hit backhand volleys. That's the hardest shot for the well-endowed" (https://newyorknatives.com, retrieved 5/22/14). And finally, Serena Williams referred to the sexualized and exhibitionistic aspect of women's tennis when speaking with the *Cincinnati Inquirer* on her return to the World Tennis Association Tour from injury: "I'll probably be wearing something fun and sexy as usual, but I can't say it will be the 'Catsuit'" (www.oxnard-tenniscenter.com, retrieved 5/28/14).

The most obvious symbolically laden objects in tennis are the ball and racket. While there is no absolute translation of objects and their symbolic meaning, as sometimes a cigar is just a cigar (said Freud), the fact is that it is plausible that in the unconscious mind the ball may symbolize the breast or mother (Whitman, 1969, p. 202). In this context, playing tennis may represent a return to the earliest relationship to the pre-Oedipal mother in which her comings and goings are regarded as beyond the child's power to reliably control. Hitting the ball and having it come back, says Whitman, may enact the sense of mastery of anxiety about separation and abandonment in a manner that calls to mind the child playing with a sewing spindle that Freud mentioned in *Beyond the Pleasure Principle*. A ball can also have other meanings; it can, for example, unconsciously symbolize the testicle or penis or in other instances, semen or food (ibid.). It may in part be due to the unconscious symbolism of the ball that players have been so fussy about the nature of the ball being used. Doubles champion Max "The Beast" Mirnyi noted about the Prince balls used at a San Jose event, "There is something about the size of the balls that is not making me comfortable. They aren't friendly," while Agassi said, "The balls are terribly unpredictable. They skim the net, you make the adjustment and they go 18 feet long. Prince should stick to tennis rackets, that's for sure" (www.oxnardtenniscenter.com, retrieved 5/28/14). "I'll let the racket do the talking," said the irrepressible John McEnroe (www.espn.go.com/espnw/quote/6391571/264/let-racket-do-talking, retrieved 5/23/14).[6] Indeed, a tennis racket can have phallic significance in that it is equated with a protuberance of the body that has aggressive power. "Knock it down his throat" is not an infrequently heard utterance (and even more often, a thought) at a tennis match. Such phallic intrusive wishes in which the gist is to force the ball into taboo territory, the symbolic mother, territory that is protected by a powerful father (or maybe sibling), gives the racket and ball its special meaning as an aggressive phallic equivalent that is enacting an Oedipal fantasy (Whitman, 1969, p. 204). The various parts of a racket such as head, rim, face, neck, butt/butt cap, handle, and strings can also be unconsciously exploited to satisfy erotic fantasies as well as sexual aggressivity. In a rather different and indirect way, former World Champion Andy Roddick suggested that the racket, like a rod or sword, can have phallic meanings when he quipped, "Rod-dick...I had years of psychological issues with that" (www.dailymail.co.uk, retrieved 5/22/14).

---

6 In all racquet sports, the racquet is the "great equalizer" compared to, say, basketball where height matters so much and in American football where strength is so important (Whitman, 1969, p. 200).

There is one other aspect of tennis that has symbolic meaning potential that relates to various forms of sibling rivalry. For example, players are "seeded," a term that emanates from British horticulture in which seeds are dispersed over the ground for planting. Seeded means a player's position in a tournament has been strategically arranged based on his ranking in order not to compete against other ranking players in the early rounds of play. A player who is seeded first is, statistically speaking, expected to be victorious, second is expected to get to the finals, and third and fourth to the semi-finals, et cetera. Moreover, a player who actually gets to the round his seed designated is described as having "justified his seed," a term that has obvious sexual meanings pertaining to phallic potency (Wallace, 1997, p. 218). Thus, with this level of comparison between players built into the very structure of a tournament, it is not surprising that there is a sense of sibling rivalry among players, especially when there is a huge winning prize at stake, the symbolic woman or mother, one that not only includes a beautiful trophy and lots of money, but a narcissistic infusion that often includes young women throwing themselves at their idealized male heroes. Jimmy Connors aptly captured the sibling rivalry among players on the professional circuit: "I was in the locker-room recently with five top-10 players. Not one word was said in twenty minutes. As I walked out, I said, 'It was a pleasure talking with you fellows'" (www.thetennisspace.com, retrieved 5/22/14).

As I have suggested in the chapter on chess, there is something to be intellectually and emotionally gained by psychoanalytically comprehending tennis in terms of metaphor, in particular its unique storylines of sexual symbolism that reflect the classical Freudian outlook. Indeed, the unconscious makes use of symbols in ways that are at the same time manifesting and hiding unconscious thoughts and wishes, such as in dreams and symptom formation where displacement and condensation are operative. When one becomes more mindful of how primary and unconscious processes both express and conceal themselves on and off the tennis court, that is, when one better grasps how one thing is used to represent something other than itself, especially in terms of anxiety-generating unacceptable sexual and aggressive wishes, one becomes more self-aware and capable of developing adequate sublimations, and thus, more effective in one's chosen endeavors.

Relational Dynamics

"An otherwise happily married couple," said the great singles player, Rod Laver, "may turn a mixed doubles game into a scene from Who's Afraid of Virginia Woolf" (www.cockermouthtennis.org/quotes.html, retrieved 5/23/14). In light of the aggressive, sexual and competitive nature of tennis it is not surprising that when each team consists of one female and one male player, all hell can break out. That is, mixed doubles can be a venue for all types of neurotic relational dynamics to show themselves. For example, mixed doubles tend to reduce unconscious guilt by sharing the guilty feeling associated with winning. In losing, it allows for the relief of shame by having someone to blame and/or commiserate with. Mixed doubles also puts into sharp focus competitive comparisons between men and men and women and women in a more blunt and public way that makes losing feel like more of an upset to one's masculine or feminine self-esteem. Other dynamics related to exhibitionistic and narcissistic wishes also get stimulated which can make winning feel very important and losing a terrible blow to one's ego.

Also worth mentioning is the fact that within the context of a gladiatorial contest, doubles is an example of the best of the human capacity for working together to achieve a common aim. For example, choosing a partner that compliments one's style of play to co-produce a sense of creative synergy and winning "togetherness" is important. At its best, there is a lived experience of being with one's partner, that is, there is an intimately experienced common rhythm of intention and power toward a common goal (Arnold, 1985, p. 7). The psychological gist of doubles is that the other's needs are regarded as equal to, and in some instances, more important than one's own. In this sense the goal is to make the player remember that he is not alone on the court, especially when he messes up, gets into a slump or has a crisis of confidence. Longstanding doubles players have an empathically nuanced understanding of each other and most often know exactly what the other psychologically needs to function at his best throughout a tournament. A player intuitively responds to the emotional needs and body language of their partner in a manner that is almost balletic in character. Like in any psychologically compelling reciprocal and interdependent relationship, if a partner is distressed, obsessing over a bad stroke, or choking, a player would quite likely try to make him feel better and get him back "on track." As John McEnroe noted when speaking with The Tennis Channel on his 1992 Davis Cup doubles win with Pete Sampras, "Pete and I played doubles, and we were down two sets to love, and I try to rally Pete to get him going so something good could happen. And it did, and we turned it around and ended up winning in five sets. Pete, he may not admit this, but he hugged me and he told me he loved me" (oxnardtenniscenter.com, retrieved 5/28/14). Thus, the values and sensibility that are required to play doubles well, such as individual commitment and group effort, remind us that in important relational matters the needs of the self and other are inextricably bound and knotted together, and that what ultimately counts in life is less the fate of the individual "I" than that of the collective "we."

II. THE BEAUTY OF TENNIS

No doubt baseball, soccer, chess, and cycling aficionados would disagree with David Foster Wallace's assertion, "I submit that tennis is the most beautiful sport there is, and also the most demanding," but it is noteworthy that Wallace would so unabashedly make the debatable claim. For Wallace, it is tennis that has "a level of abstraction and formality (i.e. 'play')" that he believes is required for "a sport to possess true metaphysical beauty" (1997, p. 235). Rather than enter the amorphous and confusing scholarly world that attempts to delineate so-called metaphysical beauty, I want to describe what some aficionados have claimed makes tennis beautiful to play and watch that has bearing on living the "good life."

Wallace noted that what constitutes tennis's athletic artistry is that it requires amazing "body control, hand-eye coordination, quickness, flat-out speed, endurance, and the strange mix of caution and abandon we call courage" (1997, p. 235). As Agassi noted, "A strong body listens. It obeys. A weak body commands. If your body is weak it tells you what to do. If your body is strong it'll actually listen to you when you tell it to do something. If you build it right you can overcome some of the obstacles of age and recovery" (www.oxnardtenniscenter.com, retrieved 5/28/14). Former champion Eugene Scott commented on the unique nature of speed in tennis, "Speed in tennis is a strange mixture of intuition, guesswork, footwork and hair-trigger reflexes. Many of the players famed for quickness on court would finish dead last in a field of schoolgirls in a race over any distance more than ten yards" (www.sportsfeelgoodstories.com, retrieved 6/1/14). Tennis, says Wallace, also requires a high level of intelligence; for example, a single shot in one exchange with a skilled opponent in one point of a match requires the integration of an extraordinary mixture of interdependent, interrelated and interacting mechanical elements. Given that a net at the center is only three feet high and the two opponents are rather unrealistically in fixed positions, the effectiveness "of one single shot is determined by its angle, depth, pace, and spin." Moreover,

> each of these determinants is itself determined by still other variables—for example, a shot's depth is determined by the height at which the ball passes over the net combined with some integrated function of pace and spin, with the ball's height over the net itself determined by the player's body position, grip on the racquet, degree of backswing, angle of racquet face, and the 3-D coordinates through which the racquet face moves during that interval in which the ball is actually on the strings. The tree of variables and determinants branches out, on and on, and then on even farther when the opponent's own positions and predilections and the ballistic features of the ball he's sent you to hit are factored in. (Wallace, 1997, pp. 235–236)

In a second essay, Wallace further delineates tennis beauty, which is unlike diving or figure skating where the goal of the sport is to be beautiful. In tennis, the kind of beauty can be called "kinetic beauty," one that has little to do with sexual or societal norms, but rather with the human being's reconciliation with the reality that he is a corporeal being. "The kinetic sense" refers to the player's "ability to control the body and its artificial extensions through complex and very quick systems of tasks" (Wallace, 2010, p. 15). Wallace has the incomparable Roger Federer in mind when he is describing this perfect amalgamation of art[7] and science that brings about the personification of "kinetic beauty:

> Federer's forehand is a great liquid whip, his backhand a one-hander that can drive flat, load with topspin, or slice—the slice with such snap that the ball turns shapes in the air and skids on the grass to maybe ankle height. His serve has world-class pace and a degree of placement and variety no one else comes close to; the service motion is lithe and uneccentric, distinctive (on TV) only in a certain

7 The question of whether tennis, or for that matter any sport, is an art form (e.g., a performing art) is an ongoing debate in the philosophy of sport literature. See, for example, Best (1985).

> eel-like all-body snap at the moment of impact. His anticipation and court sense are otherworldly, and his footwork is the best in the game... (ibid., p. 11)

Not only is Federer a great power-baseline player (a defensive style),[8] but he displays high intelligence, anticipatory skills, situational awareness on the court, a well-honed capacity to psychologically mislead and outfox his opponents; he combines speeds and spins, he shows great tactical forethought as he misdirects and camouflages his intentions, and he has excellent peripheral vision and a wide range of kinesthetic abilities instead of the usual rote pace (ibid., p. 20).

Thus, what makes tennis so aesthetically beautiful is not only its utter physicality amidst the unbelievably fast speed of the balls and player reactions, but the mode of deep thought (Wallace, 1997, p. 236) and feeling that is required to accomplish this integration of so many complex, moving and unpredictable variables, all implemented in a spontaneously improvised, seemingly natural and graceful manner. Tennis players at their best both manifest and evoke in spectators an acute mindfulness of how wonderful it is to have a body that touches and perceives, that can elegantly glide through space and interact with physical matter, what Wallace calls "sensuous epiphanies" (2010, p. 21). For those players and spectators who are properly attuned to the bodily senses, these sense perceptions can become points of entry and intimate connection to something felt to be divine-like.[9] These

8 A baseline player plays from the back of the court, near the baseline, with an eye to exchange groundstrokes rather than to come close to the net. A volleyer attempts to come close to the net and hit volleys, exerting intense pressure on his opponent. All-court players reside somewhere in between these two styles and obviously to some extent all players mix up these styles, as the court surface and the opponent influences the style of play. As Pete Sampras noted in 2006 on the lost art of the serve and volley, "The art...is pretty much extinct. You have some guys that do a little bit of it, but across the board, everyone stays back and just trades groundies. I miss the contrast. I miss one guy coming in and the other guy defending. I think that's the best tennis. But that's just a sign of the times. It's just the kind of direction it was at Wimbledon the last couple years. The part of the court that's worn out is the baseline, not the net. So, you know, if I'd be playing today, I'd be licking my chops on grass" (www.oxnardtenniscenter.com, retrieved 5/28/14).

9 Wallace refers to the "sacred grass of Wimbledon" and "the cathedral of Center Court," suggesting that tennis at its best can inspire so-called

"immortality experiences," as I have called them elsewhere (Marcus, 2015) are an antidote to the sham, drudgery and broken dreams that most of us struggle with in our everyday lives, for they provide a sense of "experiential transcendence," that intense feeling when "time and death disappear." Such experiences of being enamored with existence centrally involve "losing oneself," and can occur in a number of enthralling contexts including during a tennis tournament (Lifton, 1976, pp. 33–34).

Thus, if one wants to experience the beauty involved in tennis one must first be able "to perceive aesthetic qualities keenly, subtly, precisely, sophisticatedly, sensitively," and this requires practical knowledge about tennis or any other potentially aesthetically pleasing experience of technical beauty (Arnold, 1985, p. 3). Beauty can best be experienced when one has cultivated the way of seeing, including the knowledge base that is pertinent to, and in sync with, the phenomenon at hand. In most instances, beauty, especially the more subtle types as in tennis and other sports, requires that a person be emotionally open and responsive to what is before him and have a highly developed sports intellect and imagination. Second, in tennis and other similar activities, what one has to focus on in particular is the grace of the movement, the individual player's "fluency of presence" where both memory and possibility reside (O'Donohue, 2004b, pp. 119, 121). To the engaged observer, the body movement of a tennis player suggests his concealed internal world as his body language contains his unique signature, and intuiting this body/soul connection adds to the beauty of the game. Third, watching a great tennis tournament reminds us that if the body is the mirror of the soul, including suggesting the player's personality and character, if it is indeed a potentially "sacred threshold" as some have claimed, it calls out to be respected, attended to and comprehended in terms of its spiritual potential (O'Donohue, 2004a, p. 47). For instance, greater attunement to the body can loosen up the most rigid notions and soften the most hardened viewpoint, just as "it can warm and heal the atrophied feelings that are the barriers exiling us from ourselves and separating us from each other" (ibid., p. 59). Indeed, Wallace has suggested that tennis greats and for that matter, all top professional athletes are in many ways our society's "holy men." For "they give themselves over to a pursuit, endure great privation and pain to actualize themselves at it, and enjoy a relationship

religious feelings in players and spectators (2010, pp. 8, 9).

to perfection that we admire and reward...and love to watch even though we have no inclination to walk that road ourselves." In short, "they do it 'for' us, sacrifice themselves for our (we imagine) redemption" (Wallace, 1997, p. 237).

Also worth noting is that tennis can especially exemplify what has been called the "good contest" that involves struggle and "good strife" in which competitors relate to each other as partners in a common undertaking (Arnold, 1985, p. 6), sharing a journey together that potentiates excellence on the court (Baggett, 2010b, p. 48). Intrinsic to the "good contest" is the original meaning of the word competition, "to question and strive together." The "good contest" is not characterized by the values and beliefs associated with a gladiatorial combat, including the wish to humiliate and destroy one's adversary, but rather, it exemplifies "full-blooded challenge and effort in an atmosphere of uncompromising but friendly rivalry." Each player is thankful to the other for comporting himself as an honorable and worthy adversary. In other words, in a "good contest" each player is transformed by his competitive experience, he learns something new about himself, he feels deepened and expanded, and is more fulfilled than when he entered the contest (Arnold, 1985, p. 6).

III. TENNIS AND MORAL UNDERSTANDING

I have suggested that what the great Trinidadian Marxist intellectual C.L.R. James said in his masterpiece, *Beyond a Boundary*, about cricket to a large extent also applies to tennis. It combines "dramatic spectacle, the relation between event and design, and visually beautiful aspects" to such an extreme degree that it assumes the status of an art (Huston, 2010, p. 201). Moreover, like all great art, there are moral aspects to it that are suggestive of what valuative attachments and beliefs are most helpful in one's efforts to live the "good life." As Billy Jean King aptly noted, "Tennis taught me so many lessons in life. One of the things it taught me is that every ball that comes to me, I have to make a decision. I have to accept responsibility for the consequences every time I hit a ball" (www.quotery.com/billie-jean-king, retrieved 5/24/14). Indeed, tennis demands a sense of radical individual accountability. It is an "up front and personal" and lonely contest between two opponents battling to defeat the other. "It's one-on-one out there, man," said former champion Pete Sampras, "There ain't no hiding. I can't pass the ball" (www.topendsports.com, retrieved 5/25/14). The informal terms "clutching," prevailing in a critical situation during a game, and "choking," an act in which a player collapses when he is expected to win no matter what the other player does, aptly depicts the individual responsibility that the one-on-one nature of tennis particularly personifies. There is a larger point at work here, namely, that in many contexts the self both finds and creates its meaning through its assertion of individual freedom and power. Moreover, a robust sense of personal agency and autonomy is required to effectively assume responsibility for how one responds to life's challenges, including prevailing in competitive situations.

Tennis can also teach us something about the capacity to be alone. As Agassi noted, only boxers can comprehend the loneliness of a tennis player, and yet, he says that boxers at least have their encouraging corner men and managers with whom they confer. He further says,

> Even a boxer's opponent provides a kind of companionship, someone he can grapple with and grunt at. In tennis you stand face-to-face with the enemy, trade blows with him, but never touch him or talk to him, or anyone else. The rules forbid a tennis player from even talking to his coach while on the court. People sometimes mention the track-and-field runner as a comparably lonely figure, but I have to laugh. At least the runner can feel and smell his opponents. They're inches away. In tennis you're on an island. Of all the games men and women play, tennis is the closest to solitary confinement.... (2010, pp. 8–9)

Agassi says that to cope with his loneliness he turns deeply inward. He talks to himself, and this self-talk which begins "in the afternoon shower" is geared to building his self-confidence and optimism. What Agassi is in fact describing is his robust capacity to be alone, even though he is playing against an opponent amidst a crowd of spectators. The capacity to be alone, Donald Winnicott famously noted, is connected to the ability to dream,[10] that is, to fantasize that which unconsciously calls to mind a nurturing and stable parental caregiver's presence, a psychological parent who evokes a powerful upsurge of hopefulness. As Martina Hingis said, "I was always at peace [on the court] because of the way my mom treated me" (www.justquotes.com,

---

10 Former Wimbledon champion Marion Bartoli noted about her career, "It was like, yeah, dare to dream. I kept dreaming. I kept my head up. I kept working hard, and it just happened" (www.tennispanorama.com › Features, retrieved 6/1/14).

retrieved 6/1/14). Agassi further describes this inspired and inspiring parental presence:

> This is when I begin to say things to myself, crazy things, over and over, until I believe them. For instance, that a quasi-cripple can compete at the U.S. Open. That a thirty-six-year-old-man can beat an opponent just entering his prime. I've won 869 matches in my career, fifth on the all-time list, and many were won during the afternoon shower. With the water flowing in my ears—a sound not unlike twenty thousand fans—I recall particular wins. Not wins the fans would remember, but wins that still wake me at night. (ibid., p. 9)

Agassi is depicting the fact that the capacity to be alone is possible because in a certain sense one is not actually psychologically alone, but rather there is a parental presence that is equated with the best of a parent as comforter, protector and hope giver. As Agassi's comments suggest, the capacity to be alone allowed him to relinquish any self-undermining agenda and assume a more playful relatedness to himself and, ultimately, to his opponent and the tournament as a whole.

While tennis is an individualistic sport, it also puts into sharp focus that at its best personal agency and autonomy should be linked to ethical responsibility. Indeed, without one's opponent there would be no tennis match and no opportunity to strive for and display excellence. In a sense, a player is only as good as his opponent, emphasizing their co-dependency and interdependence of fate. One only has to think of some of the most uplifting moments in a tennis tournament to sense the presence of the ethical, players jumping over the net after a hard fought match and shaking hands and staying friends, or a player correcting a line call that favors his opponent (Baggett, 2010a, p. 3). After helping the United States advance into the Davis Cup semifinals, Andy Roddick noted, "I don't care if I win another match for the rest of the year, if we can hold up that (Davis) Cup, I really don't care. That's probably the one time of the year where you can say that and be that selfless and mean it" (www.oxnardtenniscenter.com, retrieved 5/28/14).

These expressions of sportsmanship (and teamwork), and the grace, dignity and style of a Rod Laver or Arthur Ashe, suggest that a sport or any competitive activity can be played less for narcissistic, exhibitionistic or aggressive gratification, and more for the pleasure it gives for its own sake, while affirming an attitude of fairness, courtesy, mutual respect, and a sense of camaraderie with one's competitors. As sports philosopher Randolph Feezell noted, sportsmanship involves viewing one's "opponent as both competitor and friend, competing and cooperating at the same time" (Valentini, 2010, p. 137). The terms "good loser" "sore loser" and "good winner" all point to the importance of the ethical in tennis (and all sports), and this observation has critical bearing on how one ideally comports oneself in everyday life. The fact is that in the game of life, a sense of teamwork, cooperation, collaboration and group effort play a huge role in bringing out the best in oneself and others. As the former World Number One player Jim Courier noted, "Sportsmanship for me is when a guy walks off the court and you really can't tell whether he won or lost, when he carries himself with pride either way" (www.tennisquote.com/post, retrieved 5/28/14).

Thus, if one wants to equate a tennis game at its best with the game of life, then an attitude of sportsmanship rather than gamesmanship is the ethical ideal, meaning to avoid trying to win a game by doing things that are not technically breaking the rules but are meant to destroy the concentration and confidence of the other player.[11] While in tennis and life there are occasions where prevailing involves using various ploys and tactics to gain a psychological advantage, in the long term such a way of being in one's personal life can be guilt-inducing and can corrupt the individual's integrity. Winning in tennis and prevailing in life is only sweet when it is honorable, a self-assertion of excellence that is always respectful to the other, a virtuous victory.

Tennis also puts into sharp focus the role of luck in everyday existence. As Woody Allen depicted in his engaging film *Match Point,* dictionary defined as the situation in a tennis game when the player who is winning will win the match if they get the next point, it can be a matter of pure luck on which side of the net the ball falls. That is, as in life, tennis often involves chance and fate. "That's what tennis is all about. Anything can happen," said the highly ranked Spanish star David Ferrer, "Until the end of the match, you can't really say it's done" (www.tennisquote.com/page/6, retrieved 5/25/14). While luck appears to have its inexplicable and arbitrary role in tennis and life, there also seems to be at least some loose correlation with the amount

11 McEnroe and Connors temper tantrums were probably meant to generate external distractions so that opponents would lose their concentration and serving cadence (Perry, 2005, p. 122).

of effort and practice one has put in prior to the so-called lucky moment. As the popular saying goes, luck is the residue of hard work and design.[12] "Find something that you're really interested in doing in your life," said Chris Evert, "Pursue it, set goals, and commit yourself to excellence. Do the best you can" (www.searchquotes.com, retrieved 5/28/14). The point is that while there is undeniably an aspect to tennis and life that is out of our control, a kind of arbitrary determinism, for chance to favor a person seems to require an incredible dedication of time and personal resources to excelling at the chosen activity.

IV. CONCLUSION: IN PRAISE OF TENNIS

"It's difficult for most people to imagine the creative process in tennis," said former singles and doubles Grand Slam winner Virginia Wade, "Seemingly it's just an athletic matter of hitting the ball consistently well within the boundaries of the court. That analysis is just as specious as thinking that the difficulty in portraying King Lear on stage is learning all the lines" (www.sportsfeelgoodstories.com, retrieved 5/28/14). As I have tried to show, while the creative aspects of tennis may be less obvious to the casual onlooker compared to other sports, once one becomes more attuned to the "nuts and bolts" and nuances of the game, its ability to powerfully captivate emerges. As philosopher and recreational player David Baggett noted,

> The sport still mesmerizes me. I love the strategy, the angles, the power, the challenge of it all. The thousand variables, the need for mental resilience, the rugged individualism of it, the back and forth and side to side, the spins and slices and serves—everything about the games enthralls me as a player. The sheer beauty, and the occasions it affords for excellence, at times have seemed to me nothing less than sublime... (2010a, p. 1)

Indeed, there is a breathtaking "focused intensity" that the great tennis player gets "lost" in for hours, a kind of disengaged obliviousness to the spectators and ordinary life that we love watching (Gumbrecht, 2006, pp. 51, 52). By focused attention I mean the player is in his own world, ultra concentrating on one thing: hitting and returning the ball in a manner that vanquishes his opponent. As Arthur Ashe noted,

---

12 One is reminded of the South African golf great Gary Player's quip, "The more I practice, the luckier I get" (www.quoteinvestigator.com, retrieved 6/3/14).

"The ideal attitude is to be physically loose and mentally tight," that is, the opposite of paralysis by analysis is composure, calm and resilience (www.cmgww.com, retrieved 6/1/14; Gumbrecht, 2006, p. 165).

While in this "zone"[13] the player's physical and emotional capacities are functioning close to their maximum, and in some instances his performance morphs into something even more glorious, that is, into one of those magical moments when we experience a kind of athletic perfection that is utterly beautiful to watch. In these moments there is a sense that the player's body has gone somewhere it has never ventured before, as if he has crossed an absolute threshold of human performance. These spontaneously improvised moments of displayed greatness are nothing short of sublime and thus have a "freeze-frame" impact on our psyche, a kind of encapsulated psychological presence that becomes one of our significant sports memories to which we joyfully, if not gratefully, return (Gumbrecht, 2006, pp. 73, 79, 184, 86, 231).

Thus, once one learns how to intelligently play and/or appreciate the game like an experienced player, it is hard not to agree with Baggett's glowing characterization. Moreover, tennis, like all sports, can educate a player and spectator to the importance of affect regulation of a wide range of challenging self-states, especially those related to sublimating aggression and narcissism. Tennis also teaches the importance of maintaining autonomy and integrity amidst competitive and other challenging situations, as well as an ethical outlook, one that is

---

13 Being in the "zone," defined as residing in a state of consciousness where actual skills perfectly correlate with the perceived performance demands, is similar to Mihaly Csikszentmihalyi's famous concept of "flow," a state of total engagement in an activity for its own sake without any conscious ego involvement. At these peak moments when a player is in the "zone": "He's out of his mind"; "He's playing over his head"; "He's unconscious"; "He doesn't know what he is doing" (Gallwey, 1997, p. 7). In other words, tennis players perform at their best when they are not self-occupied and self-reflective. Rather, when in the "zone" and "flow" there is a deeply pleasurable loss of self-consciousness; time awareness and reality is positively distorted, players are effortlessly, if not automatically, capable of generating context-dependent, setting-specific responses that are perfectly attuned to the requirements of the task. As Agassi noted, "Freed from the thoughts of winning, I instantly play better. I stop thinking, start feeling. My shots become a half-second quicker, my decisions become the product of instinct rather than logic" (2010, p. 135).

other-related, other-regarding and other-serving even amidst striving for individual excellence and victory. Calling to mind its English upper-crust origins, tennis at its best affirms the timeless principle that honorable defeat is preferred to an inglorious victory, meaning that losing can also have drama, dignity and grace (Whitman, 1969, p. 208; Gumbrecht, 2006, pp. 82, 74). As Arthur Ashe aptly advised, "You've got to get to the stage in life where going for it is more important than winning or losing" (www.cmgww.com, retrieved 6/1/14).

CHAPTER 6

GOLF: A GAME OF CIVILITY

Golf should be essentially a game of good fellowship; it should, and generally does, constitute a bond of union between any strangers who casually meet.

H. S. C. Everard, 1890 (Apfelbaum, 2007, p. 223)

"Sport is a wonderful metaphor for life," said actor/director Robert Redford, and "[o]f all the sports that I played, skiing, baseball, fishing, there is no greater example than golf, because you're playing against yourself and nature" (www.quotestree.com, retrieved 6/1/14). Indeed, even more than tennis, golf has been described as a "rugged individualist" sport (Laumakis, 2010, p. 146). As the former World Number One tennis player Caroline Wozniacki noted, "Golf can be tougher than tennis when things go wrong, because you can't explain things by saying that your opponent played better than you. It's a cruel sport in that way" (www.endlessbacon.com, retrieved 6/9/14). Like tennis, golf has been described as "the loneliest sport." Former American professional golfer Hale Irwin noted, "You're completely alone with every conceivable opportunity to defeat yourself. Golf brings out your assets and liabilities as a person. The longer you play, the more certain you are that a man's performance is the outward manifestation of who, in his heart, he really thinks he is" (www.golflifelessons.com, retrieved 6/6/14).[1] That golf is played outside on a rolling 9- or 18-hole area of terrain, with greens, fairways,

1 Of interest is what the incomparable Jack Nicklaus noted: "Golf is my love and golf is my life, but candidly tennis seems to me in many ways a better game than golf. It's less expensive, takes less time, provides more exercise, demands as high a level of skill in a different way, is intensively competitive, can be played 'mixed' and has fewer social or financial barriers" (www.golfdigest.com, retrieved 6/9/14).

and hazardous roughs that are designed to aggressively challenge a player's skills speaks to its "man against nature" character. In golf you are not so much playing against an opponent, quipped the legendary amateur player Bobby Jones, "you are playing old man par" (www.golflifelessons.com, retrieved 6/10/14).[2] Also worth mentioning is that golf courses, similar to gardens, are designed creations using nature as the raw materials and thus, they have an aesthetically pleasing, if not tranquilizing effect on players and spectators, including allowing one to forget how miserable this world can be. "No other game," said American professional golfer Tom Watson, "combines the wonder of nature with the discipline of sport in such carefully planned ways. A great golf course both frees and challenges a golfer's mind" (www.golfdigest.com, retrieved 6/11/14).

In this chapter I discuss some of the unique psychological features of golf using the same organizational categories as previous chapters, namely, the unconscious meanings of golf, and what makes the game beautiful and morally instructive, always with an eye to mining insights into how playing and watching golf can enhance our capacity to the live the "good life."

I. THE UNCONSCIOUS MEANINGS OF GOLF

Castration Anxiety

It is no Freudian overreach to suggest that golf is a sport that has obvious sexual symbolism, certainly for men who have always been the majority of players. Simply think of the evocative imagery of a long club hitting a small ball into a hole in the middle of a lush green patch of grass. Indeed, golf has been psychoanalytically characterized as a sport of phallic extension where there is a club/penis analogy such that the sexual act is re-enacted in every swing. As Irish professional golfer Rory McIlroy noted, "You know I need that *cockiness,* the self-belief, arrogance, swagger, whatever you want to call it, I need that on the golf course to bring the best out of myself" (italics added; www.edition.cnn.com, retrieved 6/16/14). Professional player Mac O'Grady wondered, "Will my masculinity be threatened if I hit the ball well and still shoot 72?" (Apfelbaum, 2007, p. 120). Professional

2 Par is defined as the number of strokes an expert golfer is expected to need to complete an individual hole, or all the holes on a golf course.

golfer Jan Stephenson was even more explicit when she noted, "Golfers make better lovers because they have such great touch. In golf you have to be good in all areas. You have to be powerful, be strong have stamina and be able to control yourself. All those things are important in making love" (ibid., p. 33). Golf has also been described using erotically tinged language by non-professional players as "a mistress as fickle as she is bewitching" (James, 1957, p. 5), a "capricious goddess" (P. G. Wodehouse), a "tempestuous, lousy lover" (Dinah Shore). H. N. Wethered noted that "undulation is the soul of golf" and by Billy Orville said, "Golf is a lot like sex. Even when you cheat you still have to get it up and in. And that gets tougher and tougher to do every year" (ibid., pp. 28, 32, 25, 35).

If this simple formulation of there being a club/penis analogy is plausible, it partly accounts for why millions of players and spectators enjoy the game, for golf provides sublimated gratification of sexual wishes and needs.[3] However, one of the most striking aspects of golf that serious players often describe is that it can never really be mastered; it is a game that is impossible to perfect. Indeed, "Golf," said ESPN sports talk anchorman Mike Greenberg, "is a game of endless failure and frustration" (www.golfdigest.com, retrieved 6/10/14). "Gentle" Ben Crenshaw, as he is nicknamed, the winner of two Masters Tournaments, explains, "Golf is the hardest game in the world. There is no way you can ever get it. Just when you think you do, the game jumps up and puts you in your place" (www.izquotes.com, retrieved 6/10/14). Jack Nicklaus described golf similarly when he quipped, "Professional golf is the only sport where, if you win 20% of the time, you're the best" (www.west-point.org, retrieved 6/10/14). Given these observations that emphasize the extremely challenging if not exasperating nature of golf, it would appear that players and spectators intuitively recognize that they enact their never-ending unconscious sexual and aggressive conflicts and their ongoing psychological elaboration in playing the sport (Adatto, 1964, p. 828).

In light of this alleged club/penis analogy it is not surprising that castration anxiety has been mentioned as the main psychodynamic conflict in golf. Indeed, one golfer who was treated in psychoanalysis

---

3 To give the reader a sense of golf's popularity, there are about 30 million golfers in the United States, which includes approximately 17% aged five to seventeen and 19% aged eighteen to twenty-nine (Beller & Stoll, 2010, p. 66).

developed a certain mistake in his swing, namely the bending of his left elbow, which suggests castration anxiety (ibid., p. 836). Castration anxiety is typically connected to forbidden Oedipal desires that evoke a fear of, if not a need for, punishment in the form of losing one's penis or its symbolic equivalent. In the case of golfers, this need for punishment often manifests itself in a player undermining his self-confidence and self-efficacy. As the American actor/singer and recreational golfer Howard Keel noted, "The only way to enjoy golf is to be a masochist. Go out and beat yourself to death" (www.pilgrimsrestgolfclub.co.za, retrieved 6/11/14). Jack Nicklaus made a similar observation, "Golfers have a tendency to be very masochistic. They like to punish themselves for some reason. A lot of them like tough courses" (www.quotestorage.com, retrieved 6/11/14). Not only do golf players put their psychological ego through frequent hammering, they also unconsciously put their bodies through similar ordeals. While to the casual observer golf has the appearance of being a gentle sport compared to American football or basketball, the fact is that it is incredibly physically demanding. Players are prone to all types of injuries related to the wear and tear of their rigorous training and competitions, and in this sense the body ego also gets hammered.[4] As Australian professional golfer Greg Norman commented, "My doctor asked me how many golf balls I had hit in my career. I'm lying there in bed calculating somewhere between four and five million golf balls I had hit to do that on my body" (www.compleatgolfer.co.za, retrieved 6/11/14). One wonders why anyone would want to put themselves through all of this mind and body punishment, unless, of course, it was needed to reduce unconscious guilt and the like for forbidden wishes. In short, golf can be used to re-play various psychosexual and other conflicts associated with one's child development, especially, but not only, Oedipal and phallic exhibitionistic ones.

Due to the phallic and other erotically-tinged meanings of golf there is some evidence that female players derive unconscious gratification through playing golf. For example, one of the greatest professional

4 As Lee Trevino noted, "I've been hit by lightning, had back operations, torn ligaments in my thumb and a million other things. But I'm still playing, because I have the best physical therapist in the world. She's 60 years old, is about 6-foot-5 and just beats the hell out of me. Her thumbs are like hammers...Longevity comes with a price" (www.worldgolfchampionships.com, retrieved 6/12/14).

female golfers, Australian Karen Webb noted, "Golf is my boyfriend right now," while female athlete/actress and golf devotee Gabrielle Reece said, "I don't have a life, I really don't. I'm as close to a nun as you can be without the little hat. I'm a golf nun" (www.izquotes.com/quote/194617, retrieved 6/12/14; www.ottawagolf.com/files/lineoftheday.txt, retrieved 6/12/14). As with any sport, golf is usable for re-enacting a wide range of unconscious conflicts whose personal meaning and significance is only discernible in terms of a particular person's idiosyncratic psychological trajectory. In one reported analytically-treated case, a woman analysand equated the ball not with a phallic or genital symbol, but rather, with her mother's body. Playing golf was a way of searching for her mother's body, which reflected her wish to be nurtured, to find her mother's breast, as well as the fear that her anger destroyed it, and thus she would forever be without the possibility of being loved (Adatto, 1964, p. 832).

Motor Mastery and Regressive Wishes

It was one of the greatest ball strikers in history, Ben Hogan, who noted that swinging properly in golf, which includes one's grip, posture, alignment, rhythm and balance, is counter-intuitive: "Reverse every natural instinct and do the opposite of what you are inclined to do, and you will probably come very close to having a perfect golf swing" (www.golf.about.com, retrieved 6/11/14). As Adatto noted, to hit correctly and well the golfer must permit the club to become an extension of his left arm, even though the right arm along with the rest of the body provides the power needed to implement the shot at a distance. The fact that the left arm becomes trained in a new way creates considerable difficulty to the beginner, who has typically used the dominant right arm to participate in similar activities (e.g., baseball batting). The fact that golfers wish they had learned these motor skills in childhood so that they feel "natural," that is, they acquire the longed for automatic muscle memory, points to the regressive wishes associated with game. In fact, players must have a strong desire to experience the free flow of childhood motor mastery, a kind of muscle eroticism, in order to tolerate this initial frustrating phase of learning the mechanics of how to swing and the laws of ball flight.

Moreover, how the golfer approaches this challenge of learning correct swinging often reveals a lot about his general outlook and character (Adatto, 1964, p. 829). As Australian professional golfer Stuart

Appleby noted, "I always say golf's a really good exposer of a player's personality" (www.ottawagolf.com, retrieved 6/11/14). As mentioned above, "golf is not a game of perfect," and at its highest levels it tends to draw people who are hugely competitive and obsessive about their mode of play but also have a fatalistic attitude, meaning the capacity to accept whatever happens and make the best of it, even if it is begrudgingly so (Rotella, 1995, p. 113, 122). Bobby Jones, for example, epitomizes this view and suggests its application both on and off the golf green: "Golf is the closest game to the game we call life. You get bad breaks from good shots; you get some good breaks from bad shots, but you have to play the ball where it is" (www.golflifelessons.com, retrieved 6/6/14). Jack Nicklaus has aptly made this point in a way that puts into sharp focus the ambivalence associated with this inner attitude:

> Self-control demands self-honesty above all else. Learn to fight emotionalism with realism. Accept first and foremost the cold fact that every shot you hit, good or bad, is the product of only one person: YOU. Accept, secondly, that you rarely if ever will play or score quite as well as you think you can and should. I never have. (www.golfdigest.com, retrieved 6/12/14)

Nicklaus is touching upon the duality of the professional player's internal attitude: on the one hand, golf appeals to perfectionists in its exactitudes of measurements and attention to the mechanical details of swinging, ball flight and the like; on the other, it requires a stark realism, as one almost always fails at achieving the ideal shot. Compare the precision of golf to baseball. As former All-Star first baseman and recreational golfer Ken Harrison noted, "In baseball you hit your home run over the right-field fence, the left-field fence, the center-field fence. Nobody cares. In golf everything has got to be right over second base" (www.izquotes.com, retrieved 6/13/14). In a certain sense it is this double structure to golf that makes the game so pleasurable. As the winner of five major woman's championships, Yani Tseng noted, "In golf, it's almost impossible to be perfect on each shot; that's the fun and challenge of golf" (www.espn.go.com, retrieved 6/13/14).

As with many other activities, perfectionism can be a great motivator to achieve excellence in golf; however, unless it is modulated by reasonable self-reflection that moves against the "all or nothing" outlook it can be intimately tyrannical. Indeed, perfectionism can lead to many problems in life. For example, it makes the experience of mistakes, failures and other setbacks feel devastating to one's self-esteem and self-concept, usually in the form of sadistic attacks on the self that lead to depression, anxiety and other self-undermining states; it cultivates an obsessive need for approval and affirmation from others while at the same time making the perfectionist overly sensitive to criticism; and finally, perfectionists tend to set unrealistic goals that are doomed to failure, thus creating cycles of self-loathing. While the great golfers are in quest of excellence, they are not usually perfectionists in the self-destructive manner described above. They understand that what is essential to excellence is an ultra-realistic acceptance that in most instances, imperfection rules the day. It is precisely this downsizing of one's ego and narcissism—call it humility—that golf teaches after nearly every swing. Indeed, golf is much more about how good you are at accepting, responding, and scoring with your misses, than it is a game of perfect shots (Rotella, 1995). As Ben Hogan noted, "I never played a round when I didn't learn something new about the game" (www.golflifelessons.com, retrieved 6/6/14), while Jack Nicklaus said, "Don't be too proud to take a lesson. I'm not" (www.forbes.com, retrieved 6/12/14).

Aggression

Golf, like any sport, also has its aggressive side. Lee Trevino, for example, noted, "Show me a golfer who doesn't have a mean streak, and I'll show you a weak competitor" (www.worldgolfchampionships.com, retrieved 6/12/14). Fuzzy Zoeller, who has won ten PGA Tour events quipped, "Every golfer has a little monster in him. It's just that type of sport" (Apfelbaum, 2007, p. 80). The character of aggressive expression in golf has some interesting aspects. Oberndorf provides an anecdote from an analysand he treated that shows how this unmastered aggression is re-enacted in golf:

> When the patient's compulsion to work gradually weakened and he began to play golf he once remarked that golf is really a solitary game for there is no comeback from the ball such as one would receive if one approached any living thing with equal aggression. Golf reminded him of earlier days when he spent much time playing solitaire at cards and would alternate the game with frequent masturbation. In golf the primitive impulses to violence reappeared and he said that he actually felt temporarily "crazier" on the golf

> course than he had been during some phases of his serious mental illness. To him the only pleasure derived from golf consisted in the moment when he struck the ball and all of his viciousness, bitter aggression and latent sadism found release. (1951, p. 83)

In order to prevent the expression of raw aggression in golf there are elaborate requirements of etiquette and sportsmanship and contempt for gamesmanship (at least on the professional level). However, what is most interesting is what the typical player is doing inside his own head to channel his aggressive wishes into effective, if not winning, play. Nicklaus opines on this point:

> Power is overemphasized in modern golf to a point where it's become totally out of proportion to the basic nature and enjoyment of the game. Golf is a game of precision, not strength...Where's the fun, where's the challenge in just beating at the ball? Any idiot can do that and if he's strong enough he'll score well. That's not what golf's about. It's a thinking man's game. (www.golfdigest.com, retrieved 6/12/14)

While in the minds of some players and spectators there may be a certain amount of machismo in, say, the long drive—that is, hitting the ball in a manner that suggests strength, power and virility—compared to the short game that may suggest femininity and delicacy (Rotella, 1995, p. 86), what is most important according to Nicklaus is that golf is "a thinking man's game." The World Golf Hall of Fame professional player Chi Chi Rodriguez made the same point from a slightly different perspective: "Golf is a thinking man's game. You can have all the shots in the bag, but if you don't know what to do with them, you've got troubles" (www.golf-mavin.com, retrieved 6/12/14).[5] Indeed,

5 As David McNaron pointed out, in many ways golf straddles conceptual distinctions, such as between a sport and a game, including as a contemplative sport/game. Yet, for the most part the best golf is played unconsciously. "Don't think; play!" There is both a calculative and a meditative/intuitive aspect to golf. Consider, for instance, the way a competent golfer approaches each shot. First comes the rational, calculative part as the player evaluates the upcoming shot. "How far, exactly, is one's ball from the green and hole, or the place one wishes to lay up? What kind of lie does one have? Is there wind, and if so, how strong and from what direction is it blowing? Is there trouble? What kind of shot would be best?" When all this is determined (quickly, one would hope), then the golfer steps back behind the ball and visualizes the shot he wants to hit, visualizes it all the way to the hole. He will take one or two practice swings. Then he steps up to the ball, moves his

golf players have finely-developed thinking skills that creatively draw from, but are not distorted or confused by, aggressive proclivities. In this context, thinking is not so much erotically tinged as in aspects of chess, but is focused more like a heat-seeking missile. Nicklaus notes,

> Beyond good hand-eye coordination, perhaps my greatest inherent gift in regard to golf is the ability to compartmentalize my mind, to switch it at will totally from one activity or concern to another, then, for the required duration of the new focus, blank everything else out 100 percent. (ibid.)

Indeed, golf technique requires that before one swings one must lock the mind and eyes into the smallest possible target, think consistently and have a sound pre-shot routine, learn to quiet the restless "monkey mind," remain in the here and now, and concentrate tightly on the upcoming shot. In other words, as Rotella put it, the player must passionately believe that "[t]he correlation between thinking well and making successful shots is not 100 percent," while "the correlation between thinking badly and unsuccessful shots is much higher" (1995, p. 220). To accomplish this kind of mindset requires the capacity to fend off id-driven primary process thinking, in particular modulating angry and competitive feelings that can interfere with focusing under pressure. Golfers compared to other athletes have a lot of time to think on the green, which can lead to self-defeating thoughts. As former football quarterback and recreational golf player John Elway noted, "The patience that goes with the game, the little things that go along with the game, you have so much more time to think in golf than you do in football—you have to keep your thoughts positive. I'm not sure I've got that mastered" (www.quotestorage.com, retrieved 6/14/14). Thus, what a skillful golfer can do is use the aggressive side of his personality in the quest for excellence, or as analysts would describe it, for the sake

---

feet around to address position and executes the swing. Moreover, the best golf is played quickly. The calculative part is sometimes reduced to merely seeing. As McNaron says, "I see the line of a putt immediately. I don't have to do much by way of lining up the putt. I quickly step up to the ball and knock it in the cup, sometimes from a distance. Thinking and calculation belong more to practicing than to playing golf. One does, of course, have to think about what one should do on each hole and shot; when, for example, to hit at the flag and when to hit a more conservative shot. Many shots are played for misses, good misses. But the mind should be as quiet as possible through all of this" (personal communication, 7/21/14).

of mastery and adaptation. Actor Lucas Black, who has been rated as one of Hollywood's 100 best golf players, aptly describes this internal dialogue in layman's terms: "If you're thinking clearly and are content about where your life is—to where you can just think about the present, think about the now—that's what you need to do to hit good golf shots. I know there are a lot of distractions, but when you're thinking clearly, you're more free. You've got to have that freedom on the golf course" (www.huffingtonpost.com, retrieved 6/13/14). Indeed, it is precisely this psychological challenge, golf conceived as a rigorous mind game, that constitutes much of its pleasure. It is "the mental aspect of golf," says former professional golfer Johnny Miller, that "makes golf such a great sport" (www.tampabay.com, retrieved 6/13/14).

As with any competitive sport, one of the most salient aspects of the "mental aspect" of golf is the way the player deals with his fear. "Of all the hazards, fear is the worst," said one of the top players for forty years, Sam Snead (www.forbes.com, retrieved 6/12/14).[6] There is probably no feeling state in golf that is more undermining of self-confidence and self-efficacy than fear. Comparing tennis to golf, tennis champion Ivan Lendl suggests one reason this may be so: "In tennis, you can have a bad half-hour, but you can't in golf. You can lose the first set in tennis and still win. In golf, if you make three (double bogeys) in a half hour, you are done" (www.heraldtribune.com, retrieved 6/13/14).[7] The smooth swinging professional golfer Lloyd Mangrum further elaborates this unique feature of golf when he said, "Golf is the only sport I know of where a player pays for every mistake. A man can muff a serve in tennis, miss a strike in baseball, or throw an incomplete pass in football and still have another chance to square himself. In golf, every swing counts against you" (www.golflifelessons.com, retrieved 6/6/14). In sum, in golf if you seriously mess up early on in the game, the chances of winning are very unlikely and thus, the rational fear of not performing well is extremely high in most players. In this sense playing golf is similar to the performing arts like acting. There is a feeling of aloneness and vulnerability that has both rational and irrational

6 As with other sports, part of the appeal of golf is that there is simultaneous fear and pleasure being experienced. It is this terrifyingly sublime feeling that occurs when terror and pleasure are an integrated experience (Fudge & Ulatowski, 2010, p. 25).

7 A bogey is defined as a score of one stroke over par at a hole. A double bogey refers to the completion of a hole in two strokes over par.

components to it that must be reckoned with. This is especially apparent when the rational fear of falling behind or losing morphs into anxiety, or irrational fear, in which falling behind or losing a game is animated by longstanding neurotic issues related to self-esteem and self-concept that are lodged in one's childhood. Again, similar to actors at their best, at the highest level golfers have cultivated a degree of impartiality when they are playing, call it engaged detachment, such that they more reasonably manage their fear of failure and modulate their anxiety. As Snead noted, "To be consistently effective, you must put a certain distance between yourself and what happens to you on the golf course. This is not indifference, it's detachment" (www.golfdigest.com, retrieved 6/14/14).

Perhaps the main aspect of this detachment is trust, that is, trust in his swing. As Rotella notes, most fear-prone players think about the mechanics of the swing, such as how they cock their wrists, keep their head still, or how they begin the downswing, and thus they lose their rhythm and grace which almost always leads to an inconsistent and unreliable shot, regardless of whether they are driving or putting. Thus, what is needed is a trained swing that is trusted. Trusting is not natural or simple for the majority of golfers, and they may experience it only from time to time, such as when they use a favorite club that helps them swing more determinedly or fluidly or when they are on a hot streak. However, the best golfers trust their swing with every club and score, even when they are facing especially difficult circumstances (Rotella, 1995, pp. 40–43). It is for this reason that golf, a sport where exactitude and precision is crucial at every swing, requires a mind that is resilient and accepting. Chi Chi Rodriguez beautifully noted this point with regards to the art of putting: "I've heard people say putting is 50 percent technique and 50 percent mental. I really believe it is 50 percent technique and 90 percent positive thinking, see, but that adds up to 140 percent, which is why nobody is 100 percent sure how to putt" (www.just-one-liners.com, retrieved 6/12/14).

"Golf is me," said Tiger Woods, and my guess is that many less-illustrious players and spectators have a similar conscious if not unconscious belief about themselves (www.quotestorage.com, retrieved 6/13/14). This suggests that golf must resonate on the deepest levels of self-identity such that there exist parallels between what is psychologically needed to play the game of golf and the game of life well. While I have described some aspects of the cast of mind that makes for a great golfer and has bearing on living the "good life," like mastering unconscious sexual and aggressive conflicts and developing cognitive and emotional resiliency, the fact is that these qualities of mind and heart are likely common to the achievement of excellence in any sport, though with different emphases and nuances. As Australian professional golfer Bruce Crampton aptly put it, "Golf is a compromise between what your ego wants you to do, what experience tells you to do, and what your nerves let you do" (www.coloradoavidgolfer.com, retrieved 6/13/14). This being said, what perhaps makes golf a unique sport is that in certain ways it emulates the life cycle, or at least our psychological experience of those series of changes that we all go through and ultimately return to the starting state to begin again. This is the rather hope-infused notion that there is an endless repetition and cyclicality to life, one that implies that regardless of how bad things get the sun always rises. Indeed, the professional golfer and NBC commentator Peter Jacobson has made this precise point that directly speaks to the art of living the "good life": "One of the most fascinating things about golf is how it reflects the cycle of life. No matter what you shoot—the next day you have to go back to the first tee and begin all over again and make yourself into something" (www.forbes.com, retrieved 6/12/14). Part of golf's appeal is this possibility of self-renewal.

II. THE BEAUTY OF GOLF

"What other people may find in poetry or art museums," said the legendary Arnold Palmer, "I find in the flight of a good drive" (www.yourgolftravel.com, retrieved 6/12/14). The drive from the tee is one of those highly pleasurable moments in golf, not only because it is such a complicated and difficult thing to do well,[8] but also because it is potentially beautiful to experience and observe. Repeated research shows that the simple joy of hitting the golf ball well ranks highest among players. In one survey of "avid golfers" taken a decade ago, 29% of respondents selected "ball striking" as their top reason for enjoying the

8 The elusive, if not impossible to actualize, ideal swing has been described as follows: "The fixed head position, the slightly inside-the-line backswing that stops parallel to the ground at the top and in line with the target, the inside-out path of the clubhead during the acceleration, the path swing, the smooth follow-through dissipating all unused kinetic energy, all in perfect tempo" (Holt & Holt, 2010, p. 211).

game. The second most selected reason was the companionship, "the people you play with," at 19%. Interestingly, no other response drew more than 9% of the vote; posting a good score came in at 8% (www.realclearsports.com, retrieved 6/13/14). When a golfer has mastered the mechanics of the swing, and the ball is solidly hit on the "sweet spot" of the clubface (the right speed and contact angle), there is a lovely sound that rings in the ears of the players and spectators. Add to this the long flight of a nicely hit ball as it gracefully flies across the fairway, and we have something beautiful to experience and watch (Lunsford, 2010, p. 228). Fudge and Ulatowski perfectly describe this moment:

> One of the greatest joys is to hit a drive that seems to hang in the air for an eternity, framed by trees on both sides, a lush green fairway below, and a clear blue sky above, only to drop down gently near its target. When accompanied by a sense of quiet wonder...when the beauty of the scene is all-pervasive, the experience is of the splendid sublime...what ultimately makes the shot sublime is its fundamental simplicity and the evocation of the eternal. (2010, p. 26)

Golf provides many points of entry to engaging beauty, such as Palmer's perfectly hit long drive, the equipment, the gorgeous courses, and the moral beauty that players show. Gini, for example, comments on his father's love of his collected wood clubs:

> He waxed every one of them regularly every year, and he had a few of his favorite clubs professionally sanded, stained, and varnished. Later in my life, I vividly remember the first time he used a titanium "wood." After hitting half a bucket of balls, he sat next to me with tears in his eyes. "God," he said, "I wish I had this club thirty years ago when I could have done something with it. I could have improved my game by four or five strokes. This just isn't fair!" (2010, p. 13)

All of us can relate to Gini's melancholic father who felt that life, at least at times, isn't fair, that it is fundamentally characterized by lost opportunities and missed moments. However, what is most important is the way his father related to his clubs, with love and affection, reminding us that we are meaning-giving beings who are capable of giving profoundly personal significance even to inanimate objects. Moreover, this meaning-giving capacity is the basis for our self-identity, in part because it generates memories. The fact that sports memorabilia is sought after speaks to this point. Not only do such collections allow us to escape from the harshness of everyday life into a comfortable, magical world, not only do they have a sentimental value, but they allow us to renew our tangible connections to sports that we love (www.sportscardforum.com, retrieved 6/13/14). In a somewhat different though related way, this human capacity to poignantly project meaning into a sports object was beautifully depicted in the adventure film *Cast Away*. "Wilson" was the soccer ball that Chuck (Tom Hanks) talked to after his plane crashed and he was marooned on an uninhabited island, forced to survive only with the remnants of the crash. "Wilson" became Chuck's best friend, and when Chuck left the island on a self-made raft in pursuit of rescue and "Wilson" fell from the raft after a terrible storm and was lost, it left a despairing Chuck besieged with loneliness. In anguish Chuck cries out to "Wilson" as the soccer ball drifts away, "Wilson, I am sorry. I am so sorry Wilson..." In a certain sense, Gini's father's relationship to his "woods" and Chuck's to his beloved "Wilson" teaches us something about living the "good life," namely, that to the extent that one can creatively envision and enliven the inanimate world, one is able to beautifully deepen and intensify one's attachment to, and appreciation of, the ordinary physical world that we often take for granted.

Given that golf courses are created by architects and other design professionals it is not surprising that they have a pronounced aesthetic appeal. While the playing fields used in baseball, soccer and football have a certain subtle beauty, they all are built using exacting measurements of required length and width and have fairly unattractive grandstands. In contrast, golf courses do not have such rigid and well-delineated dimensions and features (Fudge & Ulatowski, 2010, pp. 16–17). Golf courses have been viewed by some sports scholars as artworks, similar to how gardens have been conceptualized (ibid.; Marcus, 2015). Part of the appeal of golf courses is that, like a garden, they are aesthetically integrated into the surrounding environment as opposed to being separated from it as are other sports fields. Also, again similar to a garden, a golf course is designed with its aesthetic appeal being firstly in mind, while these considerations are secondary or, more likely, tertiary when designing a baseball or soccer field. Finally, the golf course as garden can be viewed as a manifestation of Eros, a "luminous and numinous presence that ha[s] depth, possibility and beauty." The golf course, in other words, caresses human presence and thus evokes a soulful "erotic charge" that calls to mind a mystical, divine or eternal presence (O'Donohue, 2004a, pp. 131, 101, 76, 100). "Golf is the most fun you can have without taking your clothes off," quipped Chi Chi Rodriguez (www.usgolftv.com, retrieved 6/14/14). The late British historian of leisure and sport John Lowerson emphasized that "[p]laying golf should be an aesthetic as well as a sporting experience." Moreover, while golf was originally a sport played on wild seaside terrain in Scotland,

> Around the turn of the century there was a clear move toward this [intentional design], and the grander golf clubs began to develop courses...It could be seen in course layout, especially in the development of bunkers and the intertwining of fairways, rough and trees to combine an adequate golfing challenged with pleasant views. In this sense the very private world of the "exclusive" golf clubs matched that of the similarly alienated formalized parks of the grander country houses. (ibid., p. 22)

While golf course architecture has become a sub-specialty that involves varying aesthetic ideals and practices, what is important for my discussion is that both the player and spectator have the opportunity to appreciate the beauty embedded in the physical context in which golf is played, and I don't mean appreciation of the golf course as a passing interest, but as a crucial part of the totality of circumstances that make golf the aesthetically pleasing sport it is to the serious player and spectator. Golf courses have been described as "some of the most beautiful places on earth" by golf aficionados, even as resembling a heavenly "paradise": "Sweeping vistas of closely manicured fairways, colorful flowers and foliage, scattered groupings of trees, ponds with aquatic vegetation, beautifully designed bridges crossing over streams, and on some courses like Pebble Beach, magnificent ocean views" (Lunsford, 2010, p. 228).[9] No wonder Ben Crenshaw said, "This is the best. This is just perfect, so serene, so peaceful. There's nothing like [golf]" (Apfelbaum, 2007, p. 665).

---

9 Pebble Beach Golf Links is a golf course located in Pebble Beach, California. It is the only public golf course to have hosted many U.S. Opens. The final hole at the course is one of the great finishing ones in golf: "It curves left all the way, following the line of the cliffs. The tee shot is played across the corner of the cliffs, how much of the dogleg is cut depends on the player's bravery" (Campbell, 2001, p. 133). A "dogleg" hole is one that bends, changing direction at some point along its length, called the "corner."

Moreover, what is unique to this appreciation is that the golf course is not simply aesthetically beautiful the way a garden is, but as I have said, it generates fear in players and it is a player's opponent, thus reflecting the two sides of nature, productive and destructive. "Forget your opponents," said Sam Snead, "always play par," meaning that it is the golf course and course management that most matters if one wants to prevail (www.stevensadowskijr.com, retrieved 6/13/14). This appreciation of the golf course as an opponent to fear is balanced by the player's experience of the course as a generative ally. The winner of six PGA tournaments, Lou Graham put it like this: "If you try to fight the course, it will beat you" (www.facebook.com/GolfballsDotCom, retrieved 6/13/14), while Jack Nicklaus, who designs courses, noted, "I've wanted to design golf courses ever since I was a kid. I suppose it comes from the way I've played the game. To find the proper way to play any hole, I've always begun by asking myself what the architect has tried to do with it" (www.golfdigest.com, retrieved 6/13/14).

III. THE MORAL BEAUTY OF GOLF

One of the distinguishing features of golf is that players are required to call their own penalties and scoring is kept by fellow players instead of officials. This puts into sharp focus the moral issues of honesty and trust. On the professional level, compared to most other sports, gamesmanship, the use of unconventional but not strictly illegal tactics to gain an advantage, is considered a gross violation of the etiquette of the game (though this is less so with recreational golfers), and good sportsmanship and a heightened sense of civility is the expected behavioral norm. One has only to compare golf with tennis, which also has pronounced etiquette expectations; for example, consider the angry outbursts of John McEnroe, Serena Williams, Ilie Nastase and Jimmy Connors. They would never happen, let alone be tolerated, by golf players, spectators or officials.

There have been some notable golf examples of the integrity and civility that professional golf demands, perhaps speaking to its "gentlemanly" origins: During the 1925 U.S. Open, Bobby Jones unintentionally moved the ball by brushing the surrounding grass with his iron. Though there were no spectators, rules officials, or other players who saw the ball move, and even though it did not give Jones advantage in his following shot, he called a penalty on himself, which ultimately cost him the tournament. When praised for his remarkable integrity, Jones famously replied, "You might as well praise me for not breaking into banks" (Fudge & Ulatowski, 2010, p. 24). During the 1996 Canon Greater Hartford Open, Greg Norman disqualified himself from the tournament when he realized that he had used an illegal ball (Beller & Stoll, 2010, p. 80). Meg Mallon, who four times won the LPGA major tour, assessed herself a 1-shot penalty when she dropped her golf ball on her coin. She said, "You can't live with yourself if you don't call it. I just couldn't play feeling that way" (ibid., p. 69). Many more examples can be cited that illustrate how integrity, responsibility to the other, and civility distinguish golf from most other sports. Consider football, basketball, lacrosse, soccer and hockey, where typically players are educated and socialized into believing that gamesmanship is, for the most part, acceptable behavior. As Beller and Stoll noted, in these team sports how one plays the game is not nearly as important as triumphing. That is, "the ultimate goal is to gain an advantage, no matter who is or is not watching, to ensure victory." It is not surprising that research indicates that on measures of moral reasoning (how they view moral issues), in general, golfers score higher than all other individual and team sports (ibid., pp. 73, 74, 79). As the English humorist P. G. Wodehouse aptly put it, "Golf...is the infallible test. The man who can go into a patch of rough alone, with the knowledge that only God is watching him, and play his ball where it lies, is the man who will serve you faithfully and well" (www.golftoday.co.uk, retrieved 6/13/14).

Golf is also noteworthy because there is so much time for chatting during play, and as a result, it tends to foster strong friendships that, like any good friendship, includes trust. Because of the relative lack of physical prowess that is needed to play golf, one can play the game well into old age. Indeed, companionship is without a doubt one of the major draws in golf, especially at the non-professional level. Professional golfers probably also have stronger friendship circles among players compared to other sports. After all, a golf game includes a lot of walking and talking and it takes many hours to play 18 holes. Such extensive opportunity for contact with one's fellow players is an important part of the experience for most players. Where baseball players converse with their teammates, in golf they also speak with their opponents (Wible, 2010, p. 241). Quite plausibly it is the friendship factor that is built into the golf experience that accounts for its emphasis on individual honesty and civility, reminding us that when it comes to moral action it is a "good" community of likeminded people that can be a great facilitator of individual moral behavior. As McNaron concludes, golf provides the conventions that promote integrity and civility, "the game presents an image of a good community, one that harmonizes the desire to excel with civility." In other words, "golf elicits the aspiration to become a better person," and it is precisely this motivation that is a fertile breeding ground for developing the necessary qualities of mind and heart that allow one to live the "good life" (McNaron, 2010, p. 61).

Through its handicap system, golf is one of the few sports that allow golfers of all skill levels to compete on an evenhanded basis, emphasizing that equality and fairness are among its "core" values (Wible, 2010, p. 242). "Handicap" is a numerical representation of a competitor's playing ability. The lower a golfer's handicap, the better he is. For example, a 2 handicapper is better than a 10 handicapper, who is better than a 20 handicapper. In fact, handicaps are intended to represent a golfer's potential rather than only being an average of a golfer's playing scores. A player who averages 20-over-par is not likely to have a handicap of 20; rather, his handicap will most likely be more than a few strokes lower than 20 due to the way handicaps are calculated. The point is that golf highly values equality and fairness and the handicap indexes are used so that golfers of varying playing abilities can compete fairly against one another. Just imagine that in principle a Jack Nicklaus or Tiger Woods can enjoy competing against, and possibly be defeated by, a recreational player with a 15 handicapper when the scores are adjusted by the handicap system. Sports like tennis and baseball do not provide such an officially structured opportunity and players do not usually enjoy playing against opponents who are obviously inferior (www.golf.about.com, retrieved 6/16/14; Wible, 2010, p. 242).

Finally, there is a certain kind of moral beauty in the way professional golfers inventively approach their craft, reminding us that excellence on and off the golf course requires self-creation and self-mastery. While on the surface professional golfers play to make a living, they also consciously and/or unconsciously use their clubs in a similar way that artists use paintbrushes. Indeed, professional golfer Tom Watson made this very point, "Golf to me is not a business; it's an art form, like a Picasso or a Steinbeck novel" (Apfelbaum, 2007, p. 662). In other words, to paraphrase John Stuart Martin, author of *The Curious*

History of the Golf Ball: Mankind's Most Fascinating Sphere, at each swing of the club, the ball is transformed into a vital extension, an image of one's innermost self. Thus, at its best, in the act of playing, golfers are inventing themselves, affirming their personal identity and fashioning themselves into a "work of art."

This capacity for self-creation and recognized excellence requires a high degree of self-mastery of a wide range of challenging emotions. A sprinkling of quotations from professional golfers suggests what constitutes this self-mastery on the way to excellence. Billy Casper said, "Golf puts a man's character on the anvil and his richest qualities—patience, poise, restraint—to flame" (ibid., p. 109). John P. Marquand noted, "Confidence is what you need in golf" (ibid., p. 121). Said Alex Morrison, "The excellence of anyone's game depends on self-control" (ibid., p. 122). Byron Nelson offered, "Every great player has learned the two Cs: how to concentrate and how to maintain composure" (ibid., p. 127). Finally, Jack Nicklaus stated, "Golf should make you think, and use your eyes, your intelligence, and your imagination. Variety and precision are more important than power and length" (ibid., p. 131). Many more quotations from golf legends can be cited, but the point is clear—as in life, golf excellence requires a cast of mind that includes psychological qualities such as confidence, or even a self-assurance that comes perilously close to cockiness; short term memory loss, that is, not getting too down after a bad shot or lingering in the negative emotion, but moving on to the next shot with a singular focus; a creative mind's eye to get oneself out of tough situations; and a competitive fire that wants to honorably win (www.bleacherreport.com, retrieved 6/17/14).

IV. FINAL THOUGHTS

The great American author and humorist Mark Twain must have had a very bad day when he famously said, "Golf is a walk ruined." In fact, it has been claimed that golf integrates two preferred American pastimes: going on contemplative long walks and hitting things with sticks. In contrast to Twain's critical comment, the American sportscaster and recreational golfer Bob Ryan evocatively described golf's effect on the soul: Golf is "a passion, an obsession, a romance, a nice acquaintanceship with trees and water" (www.golftoday.co.uk, retrieved 6/16/14). Arnold Palmer further elaborated the appeal of the game: "Golf is deceptively simple and endlessly complicated; it satisfies the soul and frustrates the intellect. It is at the same time rewarding and maddening—and it is without a doubt the greatest game mankind has ever invented" (www.golfmagic.com, retrieved 6/17/14). As I have demonstrated, golf is not only a very enjoyable (though extremely frustrating) game for the reasons that Ryan and Palmer point out, but also for the competition, exercise and aesthetics the golf course offers. Perhaps even more importantly, golf provides insights into what really matters in life, such as personal integrity, civility, camaraderie, and being part of a decent and supportive community. Golf played at its best provides a vehicle for actualizing those qualities of mind and heart that are optimal to living a flourishing life. It is for this reason that P. G. Wodehouse correctly observed, "To find a man's true character, play golf with him" (www.brandongaille.com, retrieved 6/16/14).

CHAPTER 7

CYCLING: THE FREEDOM-LOVING SPORT

> "The bicycle, the bicycle surely, should always be the vehicle of novelists and poets."
>
> Christopher Morley (www.worldliteraturetoday.org, retrieved 6/30/14)

Former Beatle John Lennon reported a deep and abiding longing that he had as a child:

> I wanted to own my own bicycle. When I got the bike I must have been the happiest boy in Liverpool, maybe the world. I lived for that bike. Most kids left their bike in the backyard at night. Not me. I insisted on taking mine indoors and the first night I even kept it in my bed. (www.bikefortcollins.org, retrieved 6/30/14)

Indeed, just about every adult remembers getting their first bike, and even better, that moment when they first propelled themselves without any assistance from training wheels or a supportive parent or caregiver. This was the pure pleasure of experiencing individual liberation, freedom and self-direction, "even pride of ownership" (Herlihy, 2004, p. 1). The well-known author of *The Man in the Gray Flannel Suit*, Sloan Wilson, described this moment from the side of the parent, indicating how psychologically important this is to the parent who wants to help his child potentiate himself: "The hardest part of raising a child is teaching them to ride bicycles. A shaky child on a bicycle for the first time needs both support and freedom. The realization that this is what the child will always need can hit hard" (www.socialenterprise.org.uk, retrieved 6/30/14). One only has to think of that wonderful coming of age comedy/drama film, *Breaking Away*, to grasp the powerful symbolic meaning of a bicycle for psychological development. Dave is a working-class lad growing up near the upper crust side in the college town of Bloomington, Indiana. He just graduated high school and is clueless about what to do with his life. He gets it into his mind to vie for the affection of a college girl who is dating one of the college boys while at the same time he becomes utterly obsessed with competitive bicycle racing. Dave dreams about becoming a champion Italian bicycle racer; he fantasizes about the fame, respect and wealth that it will bring him, including winning the heart of the college girl. In his attempt to make himself feel like the "real thing," Dave drives his straight-laced, conventional father bonkers with opera records, Neapolitan cuisine and ersatz Italian. Throughout the film, it is the bike that signifies Dave's wishes to separate from his parents and home world, and to individuate as he realizes greater autonomy, masculine effectiveness and the capacity to lean into the future with life-affirming anticipation. Thus, in adolescence, the bicycle can be used as a literal and figurative vehicle for sublimating the upsurge of unwieldy sexual and aggressive drives, that is, it can be part of a defense mechanism that allows him to express these unacceptable impulses by transforming them into a more socially acceptable form. A bicycle can also function as an important psychological grounding experience in the service of identity consolidation.

In this chapter I focus on what makes recreational and competitive cycling so appealing worldwide.[1] In particular, I will suggest how it can serve as a rich source for joyful self-discovery and life-affirmation. As cycling devotees have correctly claimed, while cycling provides greater physical fitness, inexpensive transportation and is environmentally friendly (Mapes, 2009, p. 8), perhaps more than any other sport, it is conducive to a more contemplative way of being, and therefore, it has some important insights to teach us about fashioning the "good life." As the author of *Sherlock Holmes*, Sir Arthur Conan Doyle, aptly recommended, "When the spirits are low, when the day appears dark, when work becomes monotonous, when hope hardly seems

1 It has been estimated that worldwide there are about a billion bicycles in use today and approximately thirty-six million Americans cycle at least once a year. American men travel on bicycles more than twice as much as women and the ratio of male to female club cyclists and racers has been estimated to be about 10 to 1. Cycling worldwide is about a six billion dollar industry (Mapes, 2009, p. 20; Womack & Suyemoto, 2010, p. 91).

worth having, just mount a bicycle and go out for a spin down the road, without thought on anything but the ride you are taking" (www.thebikebeat.com, retrieved 6/30/14). Indeed, ever since the invention of the modern bicycle in Victorian Europe in the late nineteenth century (Herlihy, 2004, p. 6), recreational cycling has always had its calm, thoughtful and for that matter delightful side to it, and this has been part of its popular appeal regardless of one's background. The late U.S. President John F. Kennedy famously noted, "Nothing compares to the simple pleasure of a bike ride" (www.m.bikeradar.com, retrieved 7/5/14).

In addition to the contemplative aspect of recreational cycling, competitive racing is a template for how to effectively manage the mind and emotions, especially in extremely challenging if not painful circumstances both on and off the racecourse. Competitive cyclists at their best are masters of using their images and thoughts to increase their emotional control and enhance their performance (Miller & Hill, 1999, p. 2). As American novelist Donald Antrim commented, "But to say that the race is the metaphor for the life is to miss the point. The race is everything. It obliterates whatever isn't racing. Life is the metaphor for the race" (www.bicyclekingdom.com, retrieved 7/3/14). As I will suggest later, the great race cyclists (and to a lesser extent other types of cyclists) have the uncanny capacity to imaginatively create a unique and compelling internal reality that temporarily brackets everyday concerns and allows cyclists to reside in a different dimension of the spirit, one that evokes a sense of personal transformation, if not spiritual transcendence (Miller & Hill, 1999, p. 237). In this sense, like other sports, cycling can be aptly conceptualized as a metaphor of life in that it provides a powerful example of how one can use the faculty of the imagination, one's imagery, thoughts and self-talk, to generate the positive experiences and outcomes that one wants (ibid., p. 118). More generally, what makes competitive cycling so metaphorically rich with practical wisdom about the art of living the "good life" is that it puts into sharp focus three intertwined aspects of the human condition that we all struggle with in one way or the other: "man versus nature, man versus man, and man versus himself" (Tinley, 2010, p. 79). Similar to golf, but in a much more pronounced way, outdoor competitive cycling such as the Tour de France displays the human capacity for glorious self-affirmation against nature, man and oneself, all in the service of athletic excellence. The qualities of mind, heart and spirit that these great endurance athletes exemplify is a way of being that can be instructive and uplifting to the average person who faces similar challenges and the harshness of everyday life.

Finally, a word about the wacky and wonderful "culture" of cyclists, that is, the differences among the wide ranges of riders, especially in terms of what draws them to the sport. Jill Homer (2007, pp. 40–42), a devoted cyclist and Alaskan newspaper editor, has perceptively and amusingly compared cyclist to dogs in trying to understand what makes them tick. In terms of better contextualizing the main focus of this chapter, bicycle riding in its many forms is a metaphor for the art of living the "good life," it is illuminating to hear how a cyclist "insider" who loves to ride conceptualizes her community of bike riders.

First, Homer says, there are the "commuters," the Labrador retrievers. "Throw them a good bicycle, and they'll keep coming back" (ibid., p. 40). For example, they enjoy a good game of "catch," that is, racing to catch green lights. These riders are very sociable, they tend to be domesticated and are just fine with being "leashed" to the exact same roads day in and day out.

Next are the "recreational riders" who call to mind toy poodles because they are mostly out there for exhibitionistic reasons. These riders have the best bicycles in the neighborhood, and they are only used a couple of times a year for show. Such riders "coast gingerly along smooth pavement, chrome sparkling in the sunlight, all the while smiling dreamily" (ibid.) to capture the attention and admiration of the casual onlooker.

The "extreme mountain bikers" are the exact opposite of the recreational riders as they are like huskies "pulling their powerful bodies over terrain that evolution never intended them to cross" (ibid.). The bicycles of these riders show all of their wear and tear of a fully lived life, covered in mud and blemished by deep scars. Such riders "live on the cusp between tame and wild," and they are completely prepared for the toughest riding conditions. Interestingly, while these riders work effectively in groups they are known for their autonomous personalities, and are never completely satisfied when they descend from the summit of the mountain.

The "recreational mountain bikers" are analogous to golden retrievers. Similar to their husky brothers, they adore going on long journeys on the mountain, jumping about in the mud, and calling upon their maximum energy and effort whenever they ride. The difference between them and the "extreme mountain bikers" is that they can also be just as satisfied "to curl up on the couch when the weather gets bad" (ibid., p. 41).

The "club riders" are the Shetland sheepdogs and they are most often the happiest riders in large groups. They frequently are "nipping at the heels of the other riders to keep a good drafting speed as they move in formation along the road" (ibid.). Club riders do not suffer riders who fall behind the group very well; in fact, says Homer, "they cringe at the sight of stragglers" (ibid.).

In contrast to club riders, "road racers" are like greyhounds as they break out of the pack when it ultimately matters. Similar to greyhounds, "they move in graceful unity until the time comes to rush forward in a stunning burst of speed" (ibid.). According to Homer, their sleek, Lycra-clad bodies were designed for speed, and only speed. As a "breed," they can be rather delicate, and they are prone to freezing in the cold of winter, thus, they are "unable to carry the weight of life's necessities on their ultra-light bikes" (ibid.).

Finally, the "cycle tourists" call to mind the lovable Saint Bernards. These are "big, bulky, slow, but built to last" dogs, "built to withstand the rain and snow and ice and wind that gets in the way during the long haul" (ibid., p. 42). Like Saint Bernards, the "tourist" rider is capable of carrying big loads on their bicycles, efficiently pulling them when required, moving at a steady and secure speed until they arrive at their final destination, and this is whether the final destination is four or four thousand miles away.

Homer's observations are interestingly amplified by cycling writer Hank Barlow's comments about what draws riders to "off-road" cycling. In his view, mastery of this form of biking reflects the "personalities" of the riders:

> Analyzers study every element. Finessers search for the line of least resistance. Muscle barons assume sheer power will overcome all obstacles. Then there are the free lancers. They hop on any bike and go. They're superb riders and their learning process is purely visceral...They're masters of instant—choreography—doing whatever's necessary to keep going. (Strickland, 2001, p. 37)

Another sub-group of cyclists are the "sprinters," and not surprisingly since sprinting is the most explosive and volatile aspect of cycling, it too reflects the personalities of the riders. As Davis Phinney, a former

Olympiad and professional road racer noted, "I like the danger and the speed. It brings out the primal feeling. It's like pushing the adrenalin button" (ibid., p. 88).

As Homer and Barlow's analyses of the many different types of bikers suggest, biking is a rich and varied sport in terms of motivation and practice. For the most part, what is common to all of these types of riders is the search for adventure and perhaps even more, for meaningful human connection among a group of people who may be prone to feeling somewhat alone in the world. Daniel Behrman, in his *The Man Who Loved Bicycles*, put this point just right when he also used a dog analogy:

> The world lies right beyond the handlebars of any bicycle that I happen to be on anywhere from New York Bay to the Vallee de Chevreuse. Anywhere is high adventure, the walls come down, the cyclist is a loner, it is the only way for him to meet other loners. And it works. One seldom exchanges anything but curses or names of insurance companies with another driver, the car inhibits human contacts. The bicycle generates them; bikes talk to each other like dogs, they wag their wheels and tinkle their bells, the riders let their mounts mingle. (www.kba.tripod.com, retrieved 7/11/14)

I. PSYCHOANALYTIC MUSINGS ON BICYCLES

Aron Raab, a professor of religious studies, describes the meaning of receiving his first bicycle as a little boy:

> I was still a toddler when my parents gave me a shiny red tricycle and six years old when a beautiful "Flying Camel" green bicycle, adorned with a silver decal bearing its namesake, appeared by my side. Since then I have felt a deep love toward bicycles and appreciation of their generosity, ferrying me without complaint or squeak to play, school, work, friends, and my beloved. This gratitude was shared also by Albert Einstein who reportedly discovered the theory of relativity while on a bicycle...(www.worldliteraturetoday.org, retrieved 6/30/14)[2]

There are at least three aspects of Raab's reflection that are psychologically noteworthy. First, that the tricycle and bicycle was given to

---

2 Einstein said, "I thought of that [the theory of relativity] while riding my bicycle" (www.library.arlingtonva.us › Articles › Collection Arlington County, retrieved 7/4/14).

him by his parents, acts that Raab experienced as nurturing, supportive and encouraging of his autonomy and integration; second, the toddler's "little boy" tricycle was given up for a "big boy" bicycle, the "Flying Camel" with its "cool" decal that was perfectly in sync with, and reinforcing of, Raab's developmentally typical and life-affirming phallic stirrings; third, Raab felt grateful to his trusty bicycle (and indirectly, to his parents) for its vital help in actualizing himself in work and love. No doubt these childhood-emanating sentiments animate many competitors. As Ivan Basso, the Italian professional racer noted, "I'm still that eight-year-old kid who rode up the Stelvio [a mountain pass in northern Italy]. I'm still that kid in my legs, in my head and in my heart" (www.cycling-passion.com, retrieved 7/1/14). "Johnny G" (Goldberg), as he is known, the entrepreneurial South African immigrant and cyclist/body builder, famous for his inventions of the Spinner stationary bike and Krankcycle, described his first bike in a way that powerfully points to its multiple self-actualizing meanings for his adult psychological development:

> I was four years old when I got my first bike and fell in love with cycling. A bike was more than a workout tool. It was a place to sink my sorrows, to dream. It was a place to break through boundaries, to get myself out of this box or cage. It was a place for me to liberate myself, to find peace and harmony. To take that trip on the coat tails of God. To find the sense of freedom that lots of people find using the bike. (Wallack & Katovsky, 2005, p. 64)

Bicycle riding is thus most often intimately tied to one's loving parents or caregivers who provided the first bicycle and who taught one to ride. As with so many sports in western culture, it is probably the father who is more often the parent who first introduces a child to the magical world of bicycle riding, and if the pastime has traction beyond its recreational value, also cultivates a child's interest in competitive racing. It is in part because of a bicycle's connection to one's childhood and parents or caregivers that they have great symbolic potential for the average person. It is therefore not surprising that bicycles and bike riding are often turning up in the weird and wonderful realm of phantasmagoric symbols, namely, the "royal road to the unconscious," as Freud famously called dreams.

This symbolic richness of bicycles is especially the case when we are mindful of the main function of a bicycle in real life—to get you somewhere. This can be taken literally, like using a bicycle to get to the local grocery shop, or metaphorically, as when children regard their bicycle as a "silent steed" (e.g., as in the film *ET*) that is galloping in pursuit of an enemy. Moreover, for many people it is learning how to ride a bicycle that represents their first experience with the development of an important body skill, and this sense of bodily mastery becomes the basis for increased self-empowerment and freedom. In this context, the bicycle becomes a fantasized integral part of the rider's body, that is, of his legs, feet and arms, as do the cluster of enhancing thoughts and feelings that are generated as the bicycle becomes merged with the person's body ego and overall self-experience. One rider described the bike as a kind of supportive and protective exoskeleton, "a device that efficiently magnifies my power and makes me stronger even when I'm not tethered to it" (Mapes, 2009, p. 16). Moreover, to be a cycling champion one has to have a perfect match of man with machine. Greg LeMond, the first American to ever win the Tour de France, was described by an Olympic team consultant as "a study in perfect riding posture and bike fit. He did not fight the bicycle" (Miller & Hill, 1999, p. 79). Another cyclist and freelance writer compared "bonding" to her bike as "similar to a love affair" (Joyce, 2007, p. 30)[3] while the prolific English writer H. G. Wells also noted that "[t]o ride a bicycle properly is very like a love affair; chiefly it is a matter of faith" (Strickland, 2001, p. 174). The bicycle, in other words, is transformed into a potentiating extension of the rider that evokes an upsurge of kinesthetic vitality and aliveness and this, too, helps to make the bicycle and bike riding a repository of symbolic potential and insight (Larsen, 2010, p. 27; Austin, 2010, p. 179).

Consider some of the many symbolic meanings that bicycles can have in dreams (www.dreamhawk.com, retrieved 7/16/14), though its most plausible symbolic meaning depends on the idiosyncratic trajectory of the dreamer—that is, no bicycle in a dream has a fixed meaning, as its ultimate meaning is the one that the analysand and analyst co-produce as they probe its "deep structure" and personal significance to the analysand. A bicycle race may suggest that one views life

3 In 1895 Ann Strong suggested a different take on the love of a bicycle in the *Minneapolis Tribune*: "The bicycle is just as good company as most husbands and, when it gets old and shabby, a woman can dispose of it and get a new one without shocking the entire community" (www.pedalqueens.com, retrieved 7/18/14).

in terms of a competition in which the dreamer likely feels he is somehow not performing as well as he wants to and is falling behind. Such anxiety about achievement may reflect self-esteem deficits, like a lack of self-confidence connected to phallic wishes, especially compared to others. That biking is centrally about maintaining balance means that when a person dreams of falling off a bicycle, it points to him feeling personal weakness or a lack of self-assurance in the face of some imminent challenge. When a person is riding a flying bicycle in a dream this may express a wish to succeed amazingly in something that one cares about, especially if one feels anxiety, like self-doubt, about successfully meeting the challenge. In this instance the flying bicycle may represent a wish to be omnipotent and therefore triumphant. Riding a bicycle downhill often depicts a dreamer's views about risk taking, whether he has the courage and confidence to face something that is difficult, or it may reflect a fear of losing a foothold in a situation, losing control, as in "going downhill." It can also suggest that one believes that progress and success feel easy. Riding uphill may point to feeling that any progress amidst a task will be slow and arduous. Pushing a bicycle in a dream may indicate that one feels that the help they have received was not worth the effort. A stolen bicycle in a dream in which the dreamer is the thief can signify that he feels he cannot manage without the assistance from the outside. Likewise, if one's bicycle is stolen it suggests that one feels inadequate to the challenge ahead or that he fears losing his ability to prevail, a derivative of castration anxiety. Dreaming about a bicycle as a desired object may suggest a wish for help as one travels along one's existential odyssey. As Henry Miller wrote in *My Bike and Other Friends*, in wakeful moments, "I took to calling my bike my friend. I carried on silent conversations with it. And of course I paid it the best attention" (Strickland, 2001, p. 15).

Finally, quite often a bicycle is a classic phallic symbol. "I guess I just have bigger ovaries," said the former downhill biker superstar Missy Giove (www.strava.com, retrieved 7/4/14). John Howard, a former Olympic cyclist, once called his bicycle "My 'Iron Mistress'" (Wallack & Katovsky, 2005, p. 44). The phallic meaning of cycling was aptly though inadvertently described by the "racing fanatic," as he describes himself, professional philosopher Steen Nepper Larsen:

> The primitive bike technology fosters an *ecstatic-present-attentive* being. One might say that I become bigger than my own flesh (and I'm big enough at 6ft. 7in.!), when I fasten my metal and rubber to

> my skin and extend my outer extremities. The racing bicycle is the extension of the body and the ultimate skin of thought and awareness. (2010, p. 30)

Though not referring explicitly to dreams, the literary writer Flann O'Brien, author of *The Third Policeman*, described his love relationship with his bicycle that may suggest why bicycles turn up so frequently in dreams as erotically-tinged objects:

> How can I convey the perfection of my comfort on the bicycle, the completeness of my union with her, the sweet responses she gave me at every particle of her frame. I felt that I have known her for many years and that she had known me and that we understood each other utterly. (Strickland, 2001, p. 20)

There are many other ways that bicycles are represented in dreams, but my point is that since the bicycle is so deeply associated with childhood experiences and concerns it generates and satisfies unconscious sexual and aggressive wishes, including those strange, bizarre and frequently changing subjectively meaningful imaginings. As H. G. Wells said in his comic novel *Wheels of Chance*, "After your first day of cycling, one dream is inevitable. A memory of motion lingers in the muscles of your legs, and round and round they seem to go. You ride through Dreamland on wonderful dream bicycles that change and grow" (www.online-literature.com, retrieved 7/1/14).

The Meaning of Movement for the Cyclist

While the unconscious meaning of a bicycle is highly individualized and varied, I want to focus on two aspects of bike riding that seem most illuminating in terms of gaining insights into the art of living the "good life." Bicycle riding, especially in racing, is about the real and symbolic theme of movement and it is concerned about the passage of time, two aspects of existence that we are all to some extent mindful of in our everyday lives. Just think of the word "cycle" as in "life cycle," and how it applies to the sport to grasp this likely unconscious link. Thus, the enlivening sense of movement and the poignant passage of time are powerful affect-saturated concerns connected to bicycle riding and racing (Chomet & Stein, 2006, pp. 1129, 1130, 1128). As Mario Cipollini, the former Tour de France champion known for his amazing sprinting ability said, "The bicycle has a soul. If you succeed to love it, it will give you emotions that you will never forget" (www.cycling-passion.com, retrieved 7/1/14).

In his 1887 self-published classic *Ten Thousand Miles on a Bicycle*, Karl Kron wrote, "All creatures who have ever walked have wished that they might fly, with highwheelers [a bicycle with a large front wheel and a much smaller rear wheel] a flesh and blood man can hitch wings to his feet" (www.archive.org, retrieved 7/1/14). In a way that is different from other activities that give one the sense of flying, biking is an easily accessible way to feel what it must be like to be a bird in flight. Bike riding is thus a way of creating a heightened kineticism, one that is expansive, self-directed, and enormously pleasurable. As I have suggested, the wish to fly represents a longing for radical freedom, especially escape from the worries and troubles associated with the ground, and in this sense it can be said to express a transcendent longing.

While cycling recreationally or competitively may embody the childhood wish to fly, it is probably derivative of a developmentally earlier and more profound state of mind, what in Taoist thought, particularly in the work of philosopher/mystic Chuang Tzu, has been called the "floating life." The "floating life" is manifested in the wish to ride like the wind, to drift like a cloud, to flow like water, or to wander in the great forest without any thought of return. As cycling writer Scott Martin noted, "Picture its bare-bones beauty. The delicate balance of power and elegance you use to make it fly" (Strickland, 2001, p. 52).[4] This floating metaphor calls to mind Winnicott's work that relates play to the creative process. It may even embody the longing for the "oceanic" feeling that Freud thought depicted the regressive ego-feeling associated with infant at the breast and Roman Roland, who first used the term in a letter to Freud, to describe the mystical cosmic sentiment that he believed was the basis of religion (Rycroft, 1995, p. 118). Strickland, a cycling journalist, supports this "oceanic formulation": "It is not until we find the bicycle that we rediscover flight, the unstrained weightlessness we knew in the womb, the easy, lofting movements and sweeping curves possible with a subtle tilt of our bodies. The bicycle ride is something we remember from before we had memory..." (Strickland, 2001, p. 172).

4 Political scientist Louis J. Halle, Jr. noted that in particularly "long downslopes, this is to know the freedom of the wind" (Strickland, 2001, p. 73).

For Chuang Tzu, the floating person is playful in that he has the capacity to shift and roam, he refuses to be pigeonholed by any given stereotype, he is not aligned with any fixed system, and is not overly serious about anything. This is the psychological context for the floating person's ability to cope, survive and flourish (Marcus, 1988, p. 87). Thus, the "floating life," this fantasized return to the best of childhood existence, is unconsciously re-enacted every time an adult gets on his bicycle. It allows a person to empty himself of all extraneous and cumbersome thoughts and feelings and reside in a state of detachment from everyday life to engage in flexible, spontaneous adaptation to the external world. "Unimpededness," says philosopher/cyclist Larsen, "is our primary state" (2010, p. 28). Moreover, as in childhood, not being attached to anything and being able to move freely tends to create a deeply pleasurable mental calmness and joy to be alive. Thus, creating the "good life" requires the capacity to be free-floating and free-wheeling, including manifesting a high degree of buoyancy in recovering speedily from disappointment and failure. It is this quality of mind, heart and spirit that, in part, constitutes the cheerfulness and optimism of the person who artfully lives his everyday existence.

To add to the uplifting nature of cycling conceived as a return to the "floating life" is the fact that the sport is often done outside amidst "Mother Nature." Consider the ultimate race, the Tour de France—a yearly, multiple-stage, three-week competition that is mainly held in France (though it briefly includes other countries), during which the competitors are thoroughly enmeshed in and engaged with "Mother Nature," which both severely challenges and nurtures competitors in their quest for athletic excellence. Indeed, as Chuang Tzu notes, it is the beauty, bounty and regenerative power of "Mother Nature" that is conducive to creating the "floating life," for it requires fusing with the Tao (the absolute and unique underlying source of the universe that determines everything) through action modeled on "Mother Nature." It is precisely the free, flowing and unrestrained movement of the cyclist as he improvises and accommodates the arduous course that is in sync with the Tao, and thus ironically it tends to produce an upsurge of inner calm amidst a fiercely competitive race that is both physically and mentally painful. This duality of structure of the cyclist's experience of the Tour de France, and for that matter of achieving the "floating life," was aptly depicted by two former competitors and now retired professional racers. Danish rider Per Pedersen depicts the ongoing conscious struggle with the extreme harshness of "Mother Nature": "First week you feel good, the second week you lose strength. Third week, fucked" (www.bicyclekingdom.com, retrieved 7/3/14). The Dutch cyclist Theo de Rooij noted what lies beyond the harsh surface experience of the Tour de France, beyond the physical and mental pain, namely an unconscious glimpsing of the transcendent aspect of the race and the "floating life": "Sure, it's the most beautiful race in the world!" (www.cyclingtips.com.au, retrieved 7/4/14). As in ordinary life, on the racecourse the well-known observation that agony precedes ecstasy often seems to be true. Moreover, it reminds us that there is an irreversibility to lived time; there are no "dress rehearsals" or "do overs" in life, and so one better be willing and able to completely throw oneself into the experience one is amidst, which means embracing life without reserve.

The Meaning of Time for the Cyclist

Cycling on the professional competitive level is utterly concerned about the passage of time. "It was eleven [seconds] more than necessary," said cyclist Jacques Anquetil, a five-time winner of Tour de France, after winning a race by twelve seconds (www.allgreatquotes.com, retrieved 7/5/14). For the racer, time can be experienced as tyrannical taskmaster, but it can also be something gently instructive. Certainly this is the case for the recreational rider. For example, in a long-distance ride, one has to conceive of time with a different cast of mind than with most everyday activities, with a gracious acceptance of the rhythm and tempo associated with the long haul. Hales, a philosopher and devoted long-distance cyclist, describes this outlook within the context of an 80-mile ride in a rainstorm:

> I remember feeling like a mechanism, tucked in, my legs rhythmic pistons, water sluicing over me like machine oil, hammering out the miles. There was a sort of perverse pride I felt, riding all day in the cold rain and getting coated in road grit. It was only through obedience to the implicit orders of cycling that I could learn its virtues. To ride is to reduce life to simplicity, with no other demands but to keep pedaling. "Why should we live with such hurry and waste of life?" Thoreau writes in *Walden*. Simplify, simplify. (Hales, 2010, p. 164)

What Hales is admirably depicting is the wonderful symbiosis between the bike and the body mentioned earlier, such that machine and human are an integrated whole. Even more importantly, he is evoking the joy of the body ego, that part of the ego that Freud said was derived from bodily sensations and which constitutes the elemental ground of one's sense of self. As Hales's narrative suggests, this requires the capacity to not only delay gratification in terms of the endpoint of his ride, but to cultivate the ability to appreciate and enjoy the unfolding physical/mental experience as it is occurring in real time. This is what simplifying life means, being able to be present in one's here and now experience without distraction, without getting "off track" by thoughts and feelings lodged in a retrospective or prospective consciousness. It also means beginning something and finishing it, as in many ways life is an ongoing series of problems to be solved: "With cycling, I had to learn the devotion, almost the meditation, of the long thunder of the deed" (ibid.). Thus, there is something important to learn about the relationship between doing and becoming, particularly in long-distance cycling (Larsen, 2010, p. 33). Action done with the fullness of one's whole being, without looking for shortcuts or cheating, is the basis for becoming something otherwise, something more, even something better. "The great thing about cycling," said manufacturer of bicycles and their components Mike Sinyard, is that "what you put in, you get directly back. That is so different than other things in life, which are very confusing—there's not a direct correlation. But this is a direct deal" (Wallack & Katovsky, 2005, p. 156). In other words, part of the beauty of cycling is that it is occurring in a realm of immediate information delivery and continuous information feedback (Strickland, 2001, p. 29). Larsen further elaborates this outlook on the riding experience when he notes, for example, that the here and now becomes something different than a point on the time line; rather, the rider becomes utterly enmeshed in a protracted moment: "Time falls off its hinges and achieves fullness. To bike is to see the homogenous, low quality clock time vanish" (even though a bike may have a computer and heart monitor feeding the rider information) (Larsen, 2010, p. 31). The author of *The Call of the Wild*, American writer Jack London beautifully summed up the appeal of recreational bike riding from the point of its surface pleasures in real time:

> Ever bike? Now that's something that makes life worth living!...Oh, to just grip your handlebars and lay down to it, and go ripping and tearing through streets and road, over railroad tracks and bridges, threading crowds, avoiding collisions, at twenty miles or more an hour, and wondering all the time when you're going to smash up. Well, now, that's something! And then go home again after three hours of it...and then to think that tomorrow I can do it all over again! (Penn, 2010, p. 9)

Following Freud, what biking as London describes it seems to instantiate is that our sense of time emerges as a potentiating force as a consequence of experiencing a delay between the desire to do something, like riding, and the gratification of doing so. That is, we experience the motivating power of time between the primary processes that tend to deny time and the adaptive inclinations of secondary processes (Rycroft, 1995, p. 184). London's lively quote reminds us that time need not be a tyrannical force in everyday life that tells us that we are getting closer to death with every passing minute. Rather, like in childhood, time can also be experienced as an eternal repository of pleasurable and attainable possibilities, provided that one is willing and able to tap into its unconscious primary process aspects that often embody a transcendent vision (e.g., through fantasy). John Howard, the great Olympic cyclist, captured this point rather well while also pulling together many aspects of our discussion thus far, including touching on the next topic, the aesthetically pleasing aspects of cycling:

> I found myself practicing a very profound, personal form of worship when I turned those pedals. On a bike, passively covering ground for two or three hours, I would experience a wonderful sense of self-discovery, of being a part of a universe that was much more powerful than myself. I say passive for a reason. I can remember covering 20 or 30 miles and having no recollection of being anything but in a complete form of perfect bliss. (Wallack & Katovsky, 2005, p. 44)

For Howard, and perhaps for other riders too, this moment of "perfect bliss" implies a radical reconfiguration, if not spiritualization of time, as if it has been stretched out for all eternity. Indeed, bike riding can evoke that wonderful feeling of completion and sureness that is most often associated with all journeys between awakening and surrender, reminding us that the experience of the beautiful is a kind of homecoming with eternal echoes (O'Donohue, 2004b, p. 2). "Cycle tracks will abound in Utopia" said H. G. Wells (www.bikehub.co.uk, retrieved 7/13/14).

II. THE AESTHETICALLY PLEASING ASPECTS OF CYCLING

One cycling devotee, a "non racer" as he proudly calls himself, and a professor of kinesiology, described some of the characteristics of the "beautiful ride":

> The smoothness and effortlessness of the experience; the organic feels of the ride fitting together from beginning to end; the dissolution between the challenges of the route and the efficiency of my efforts in the saddle; the satisfaction I feel when my resulting performance seems to be far greater in measure than my perceived effort...the fluidity of my ride. (Hopsicker, 2010, p. 25)

Hopsicker is putting his finger on how bike riding can allow us to intensely experience a wide range of our sensory-filled physical world, what has been called "the sensuous life," those movements and feeling states, the distances and varying speeds, and the sights and soundscapes that are alive and well if only one focuses on them. For those with the appropriate attunement, bike riding is thus a rich venue for experiencing more deeply and widely "our aesthetic, sensory-rich existence—an existence filled with fragrances, feels, forms, colors, sounds, rhythms, tensions, climaxes, and resolutions" (ibid., p. 17). Charlie Cunningham, the founder of Wilderness Trail Bikes, further elaborates on Hopsicker: "You're moving through a wonderful natural environment and working on balance, timing, depth perception, judgment...It forms a kind of ballet" (Strickland, 2001, p. 31). Such receptivity to the "spiritual voluptuousness" of the world can be equated with a kind of "sensuous beatitude," one that points to an "infinite opening" and transcendent vision (Eigen, 1986, pp. 304, 349).

Not only does bike riding barrage the senses in a mostly pleasurable way but the way one rides a bike, especially the incredible skillfulness of the master riders, has been described as something of a physical art form. "Think of bicycles," said well-known bicycle designer Grant Peterson, "as rideable art that can just about save the world" (www.thebicycleworks.org, retrieved 7/12/14). Peterson may be overstating the world-saving nature of bike riding, but his claim that bike riding can be reasonably conceived as a "rideable art" strikes me as worth reflecting on, for it may, in part, account for what makes biking satisfying to so many people. Chester Kyle, an engineering professor, has provided one of the most thoughtful ways of understanding what makes bike riding an artful activity:

> The interaction of the body, mind, muscles, terrain, gravity, air and bicycle are so complex that they defy exact mathematical solutions. The feel and handling of a bike borders on art. Like the violin, it's been largely designed by tough, inspiration and experimentation. (www.cycling-passion.com, retrieved 7/1/14)

Henri Desgrange, the founder of the Tour de France in 1903, further explains Kyle's insight by reference to the amazing "climbing" of the late French professional road racer and *Tour* champion, Henri Pelissier: "Henri Pelissier's climbing ranks as art. He climbs using the full range of his abilities, from the force of his legs to the acumen of his mind and surety of his judgment. Pelissier knows how to play his instrument" (Strickland, 2001, p. 61).

Thus, there is a consensus among serious cyclists that cycling has its beautiful side to it, especially in the way the great racer generally comports himself. David Millar, Scottish winner of four stages of the Tour de France, emphasized this point when he noted that bike riding is "based so much on form, on aesthetics, on class—the way you carry yourself on the bike, the sort of technique you have" (www.project4cycling.com, retrieved 7/14/14).

Perhaps it was the improvised words of the professional racer Lee Rodgers who best captured what makes bike riding so beautiful. After a hard stage in Tour de Langkawi, a multiple-stage race held in Malaysia, Rodgers stood by two colleagues on a terrace overlooking a golf course observing the golfers playing. One of the colleagues turned to Rodgers and said, "Man, we chose the wrong sport." After that interchange, Rodgers spontaneously wrote the following words in his diary blog, words that deserve being quoted in their entirety, for they aptly summarize what is aesthetically pleasing about endurance cycling:

> Yeah. And right then I agreed with him. But we did choose the most beautiful [sport]. The most epic. The daftest. The most furious, the most poetic, romantic, brutal, life-affirming and soul-destroying sport of all, the sport that drives its flawed geniuses to destruction and its devotees to distraction. It's the simple love affair of man

> with machine, human-powered machine, and it's the one toy from childhood we get to keep, that grown men and women still get to play with, all over the world, no matter how old, no matter what culture, race, creed or ideology. It's the thing that gave you the freedom to leave your neighborhood and to explore the world around and when we race, it's the same barnstorming thrill you had when you sped down your block, racing home from school against Pete Barnes to see who could get to the edge of the cul-de-sac first. It's that same rush, that same freedom, the same Breath of Sheer and Unadulterated Life. The sport of kings. Beat that. (www.velonews.competitor.com, retrieved 7/11/14)

What does all of this beautiful "bike talk" have to do with the average person's efforts to live the "good life"? First, it emphasizes the importance of being attuned to our marvelous physicality, and in particular to enjoy the play of the body in motion. Mark Remy, for example, wrote in *Bicycling Magazine* about the sheer pleasure of the body/bike in motion and its instructive import for everyday living:

> The best routes are the ones you haven't ridden. You could pedal the same loops year after year. Many people do, literally or figuratively. But to grow, you need new rides. Risks. Turn down lanes you've long seen but never traveled. Get lost once or twice, then double back to where you started and try again. Live like this and you come to see unknown territory not as threatening, but as intriguing. (www.kba.tripod.com, retrieved 7/11/14)

My point is that most of us have become estranged from the body, a rich and powerful creative resource, and therefore we cannot craft in a decisive manner the body-mind-heart synergy that makes for intense living. Bike riding emphasizes a usable truth—to discover the creative possibilities of the body, our repressed psychophysicality one might call it, one must be able to enjoy the play of the body in motion. In adolescence, for instance, the phase of development that is characterized by frequent experimentation in personal identity, the enjoyment of bike riding as an activity morphs into a moment of self-exploration. Such questions as "how long can I go; how fast can I take the bend; what is my top speed," resonate on a deeper psychological level of self-esteem and self-concept. The point is that the adolescent is playing with his body's capacities as a way of fashioning a credible and acceptable identity, and to some extent, this process that is in its extreme in adolescence should take place throughout the adult life cycle.

As Ilundáin-Agurruza and McNamee further noted, by exploring the limits of one's physical and psychological make-up, "we push the plasticity of our character and identity too" (2010, p. 256).

Lastly, bike riding puts into sharp focus a profound existential truth that the way the feet relate to the ground really matters. Skillful cycling requires pedaling in a rigorously and artfully controlled cadence to keep the bike moving efficiently, safely and satisfyingly on the ground amidst the random challenges of the trail. Cycling coach Mike Walden called pedaling the "essence of our sport" (Strickland, 2001, p. 100). This strong, foot-generated movement of the bicycle, with rubber tires that grip the ground, emphasizes a psychological point that has applicability beyond the racecourse, namely, the vital importance of a person making contact with the ground, a powerful metaphor for being stable or existentially "grounded." Grounded, for example, means being balanced (and bicycle riding is literally all about balance) and sensible, and making good decisions as one faces life's challenges. In fact, bike riders often view themselves as if they are psychologically part of the ground, as intimately linked to "Mother Nature" in a similar way to how they view their bicycle as their exoskeleton. As professional road- and cross-country racer Bob Roll noted, "Mountain biking should be a Buddhist relationship between you and the environment you're in, where you're the environment and the environment is you..." (ibid., pp. 184–185). In both instances, these literal and figurative attachments to the ground and bicycle reflect the human capacity to have, and to benefit from, a life-affirming relationship with the physical world that we are inextricably a part of as much as that for which we are responsible.

III. THE MORAL ASPECTS OF CYCLING

David Millar described the moral struggle, the pain and suffering that endurance racing encompasses: "It seemed romantic but also tragic—people would be winning but then lose it all, or crash but fight on, break bones but get back on their bikes and try to finish. Just getting to the end was seen as an achievement in itself" (www.izquotes.com, retrieved 7/13/14).

Unlike pain and suffering[5] that feels like "God is throwing rocks at you," adversity that is experienced as if it were an expression of cosmic sadism, endurance racers and others choose to put themselves through their ordeal; in fact, they relish it. While one might explain this in terms of the usual psychoanalytic suspects such as masochistic inclinations and the like, there also seems to be other, more wholesome, even life-affirming motives animating the activity. The winner of three Tour de France races, Greg LeMond, noted, "I have always struggled to achieve excellence. One thing that cycling has taught me is that if you can achieve something without a struggle it's not going to be satisfying" (www.winwisdom.com, retrieved 7/13/14). Of course, LeMond is affirming conventional psychological wisdom that there is a correlation between the effort one puts into surmounting a challenge and the resultant satisfaction that is felt when one has prevailed.

I have already commented on the various motivations for why people are attracted to different types of cycling. While all competitive sports require the capacity to endure demanding training and competitions, in cycling the problem of self-overcoming, that is, "purposeful self-determination or creation" (McCary, 2010, p. 19), especially emotional self-control in the face of physical pain and suffering, is particularly salient. As Felice Gimondi, a former Italian pro racer and world champion noted, "Basic physical strength is necessary. The body's legs and muscles have to be there. But you stay on bikes for hours and hours so you need to have a little imagination. You need to be intelligent and calm. You need to be in control. You need mental control" (Miller & Hill, 1999, p. 29). Indeed, in the world of sports psychology, cycling is perhaps the best example of where athletes have to learn how to transform pain and suffering into power, "Feel it, See it. Believe it. Do it" (ibid., pp. 75, 4). While it is beyond the scope of this chapter to review in detail the many techniques that sports psychologists have developed to help cyclists excel in their demanding sport, like creative visualization, power imagery, positive self talk and a "winner's" attitude (ibid., p. 2), I do want to offer one often underappreciated observation about the problem of pain and suffering management in the service of

5 While pain and suffering are not necessarily psychologically the same, in the cycling literature the terms are often used interchangeably, so I have adopted this custom. Philosophers also have made a distinction between these two categories of human experience.

cycling excellence, for it has bearing on the inevitably trying aspects of human existence that must be surmounted in living the "good life."

Scott Martin, an ex-Marine and one of the top para-cycling athletes in the country, has vividly put into sharp focus the painful aspects of cycling and what it takes to press on:

> To be a cyclist is to be a student of pain....at cycling's core lies pain, hard and bitter as the pit inside a juicy peach. It doesn't matter if you're sprinting for an Olympic medal, a town sign, a trailhead, or the rest stop with the homemade brownies. If you never confront pain, you're missing the essence of the sport. Without pain, there's no adversity. Without adversity, no challenge. Without challenge, no improvement. No improvement, no sense of accomplishment and no deep-down joy. Might as well be playing Tiddly-Winks. (www.bicyclekingdom.com, retrieved 7/3/14)

Elsewhere Martin detailed the nature of the pain associated with his cycling: "Pain is a big fat creature riding on your back. The farther you pedal, the heavier he feels. The harder you push, the tighter he squeezes your chest. The steeper the climb, the deeper he digs his jagged, sharp claws into your muscles" (www.indoorcyclingassociation.com, retrieved 7/15/14). LeMond has made similar observations: "I know the pain of cycling can be terrible: in your legs, your chest, everywhere. You go into oxygen debt and fall apart. Not many people outside cycling understand that" (Miller & Hill, 1999, p. 44). John Stamstad, a legendary mountain bike endurance racer, offered an intriguing counter-intuitive take on the problem of cycling pain when he said, "I used to do a lot of mental callousing. It took me a long time to feel that pain is good" (Strickland, 2001, p. 203). That is, rather than "fight" the pain by denying, deflecting or ignoring it, Stamstad was receptive and responsive to it and thereby converted it into a motivating ally. Teho de Rooiy, a professional road racer, seems to have had a similar view, crude as he may have expressed it: "Paris-Roubaix [a one-day road race in France] is a pile of shit. You're up to your neck in mud and you're riding in mud and you don't have time to piss. It's a pile of shit. It's the most wonderful race in the world" (Strickland, 2001, p. 220).

What is striking about Martin, LeMond, Stamstad and de Rooy's comments is their incredible willpower and determination, notions that are often underemphasized in psychoanalytic circles. As Nietzsche noted in *Beyond Good and Evil*, "in real life it is only a question of *strong* and *weak* wills" (McCary, 2010, p. 15). While willpower has its unconscious roots and meanings, the fact is that consciously experiencing oneself as having a high degree of willpower, as being a causal agent that can effectively intervene in one's circumstances, is a necessary component of mental toughness, self-determination and well-being. Otto Rank, one of Freud's earliest devotees, who wrote about the importance of the role of choice, will, creativity, responsibility and humanistic ethics in psychotherapy encouraged his patients to exert willpower in order to develop autonomy and independence. Many of Rank's ideas have been appropriated by post-Freudian thinkers, though there is a need for further psychoanalytic research into the psychology of willpower. The point is, to view oneself as largely self- and inner-directed versus other- and outer-directed, as being capable of living one's life by personal decision rather than feel that the external world, the social context, is the final arbiter of one's feelings, thoughts and actions, is vital amidst pain and suffering. As Nietzsche notes, "One must test oneself to see whether one is destined for independence and command...one should not avoid such tests" (ibid., p. 17). I am thinking of a patient of mine with a life-threatening illness who came to the realization that if she wanted out of her ordeal, she had the courage and ability to kill herself. This self-awareness actually motivated her to keep fighting her disease. Without an "inner center of gravity," one is pretty much doomed to feel like a piece of driftwood being tossed to and fro by the ocean's waves. As Mahatma Gandhi noted, "Strength does not come from physical capacity. It comes from an indomitable will" (Gandhi, 2000, p. 40).

It is worth noting that the problem of enduring suffering has been identified as *the* central factor in terms of what makes a champion rider. LeMond, for example, noted, "The key is being able to endure psychologically. When you're not riding well, you think, why suffer? Why push yourself for four or five hours? The mountains are the pinnacle of suffering" (Lewis, 1999, p. 5). Pain, when conceived as a core component of suffering, can utterly undermine a racer's willpower and determination as it leads to truncated and inhibiting defensive thoughts, and if it goes on long enough without being countered by positive self-talk, it leads to demoralization and giving up. The late Australian coach and manager Charles Rays noted this very point:

> Do not give up when you find you have to suffer greatly to get results. Never forget that winners are the ones who can suffer the best. It's the no-hopers who cannot suffer. The inability to suffer

> is almost always the real reason riders do not succeed in our sport. The person who can suffer the best has the best chances of getting to the top. (Miller & Hill, 1999, p. 45)

In the cycling world, suffering is often linked to fear that makes matters much worse. Suffering and fear feed off each other and are dialectically related. When it comes to endurance riding, what racers frequently speak about is their fear of losing control of their riding, of "breaking down, of failure, of embarrassment, and of crashing and getting injured" (ibid., p. 63). Fear and suffering are often entwined; suffering can involve the actualization of one's greatest fears which makes the suffering feel even worse and hugely diminishes performance. The problem with fear is that it causes organismic seizing up and reduces breathing effectiveness (to battle this, one should twin positive thoughts with rhythmic breathing), a vital component for the successful racer, and it cuts deeply into one's power, resilience and self-confidence, causing mental anguish which impacts on one's ability to effectively ride. In other words, fear potentiates mental suffering and mental suffering potentiates fear, and together they not only drastically undermine performance but can take a competitor completely down. No man dies but by his own hand, as the saying goes.

The legendary Graeme Obree, "The Flying Scotsman," who in 1993 and 1994 twice broke the world hour record, however, explained succinctly how he managed his fear in addition to the usual sports psychology and technology: "My biggest fear is not crashing on a bike… It's sitting in a chair at 90 and saying, 'I wish I had done more'" (www.cycling-passion.com, retrieved 7/14/14). What Obree is saying in his quiet simplicity speaks to the heart of the matter when it comes to managing pain and suffering both on and off the race course. That is, without the capacity for metabolizing distressing emotions one is doomed. As I will suggest shortly, the antidote to fear and other distressing emotions is love, but not only love of riding, climbing, speed, training, competition, challenge, other riders, or even loving oneself, as the sports psychologist recommend (Miller & Hill, 1999, p. 137). It also involves enmeshing oneself with the fullness of one's whole being in a transcendent, deeply humanizing moral vision, one that integrates one's deepest drives and valuative attachments. As cycling writer Mike Ferrentio noted, "For every moment of hassle and pain, there is one of revelation and joy" (Strickland, 2001, p. 140). The disgraced cyclist,

Lance Armstrong, astutely elaborates Ferrentio's point in his memoir *It's Not About the Bike: My Journey Back to Life*: "I'm into pain…because its self-revelatory….There is a point in every race when a rider encounters his real opponent and understands that it's himself….Will I discover my innermost weakness, or will I seek out my innermost strength….You might say that pain is my chosen way of exploring the human heart" (Armstrong, 2001, pp. 269–270).

By emotionally metabolizing a situation characterized by pain and suffering it is necessary to "process" the evoked feelings in a manner that makes them more "manageable," at least relative to who one is. This internal work includes putting the troubling or painful feelings into an organized, intelligible and ultimately emotionally modulated cognitive perspective. In psychoanalytic parlance, this requires considerable "ego strength," the application of "reason and common sense" to the totality of circumstances one is in (Rycroft, 1995, p. 43). While the subject of coping with pain and suffering is an enormously complex one, I here want to focus on only one essential point, which is perhaps the most important aspect of effectively emotionally metabolizing the troubling feelings; that is, the invocation of a meaning-giving, affect-integrating, action-guiding valuative attachment that links the pain and suffering to a "higher" order of meaning of ultimate concern. As Nietzsche said, "He who has a why to live can bear almost any how" (Kleiser, 2005, p. 6). It is this ability that great racers have in which they view the challenge of effectively managing their mind and emotions, self-overcoming as I have called it, as an overarching valuative attachment that provides them with the guts and grit, the mental toughness to carry on and even prevail. Indeed, Alexi Grewal, an Olympic gold medalist, put this point just right: "The real race is not on the hot, paved roads, the torturous off-road course or the smooth-surfaced velodrome. It is in the electrochemical pathways of your mind" (Miller & Hill, 1999, p. 5). In this instance, it is the belief that one can, indeed one must, attain a sense of personal control, self-efficacy, willpower and determination, problem-solving performance, and creativity and courage, which becomes the rider's overarching valuative attachment. In addition, when this self-overcoming cluster of beliefs and feelings that one can prevail is combined with a larger transcendent vision, a rider feels there is nothing that can stop him. Nicknamed the "Cannibal" because of his insatiable drive for success, the greatest cyclist in history, Belgian Eddy Merckx, affirms this very point: "At the beginning stages, it is definitely the total physical development that is important. Later on, you develop more mental concentration, mental preparation to maintain the physical capacity. Next, you develop the spiritual" (ibid., p. 231). Exactly what constitutes the "spiritual" is not clear in the case of Merckx, though he was a believing Catholic; however, throughout this chapter I have insinuated that many riders have adopted some kind of religious or secular spiritual or spiritual-like transcendent outlook that animates their riding commitment and practice. Missy Giove, the former downhill champion, for example, noted, "I think when you're on the edge of life like a downhill racer is, you have to be spiritual. For me it would be odd not to think about death and spirituality" (Strickland, 2001, p. 74).

Indeed, the endurance cycling sports literature on the "zone" tends to support the notion that cyclists are able to surmount the tremendous pain and suffering of the Tour de France, Giro d'Italia and the Vuelta a España, the three-week long races that make up the Grand Tours, by entering into a different realm of the being that cyclists have described as a "spiritual experience, a transcendent state, going beyond the self, a mystical experience" (Lewis, 1999, p. 2). This involves a total absorption in the ride and residing in what has been called "kairos" time, being utterly engrossed in the here and now and losing a sense of the passage of time even though many hours of racing may have occurred in real time. As Lewis further points out, cyclists also have a quality of "hypnotic susceptibility" which permits them to dissociate from the pain and suffering that they must endure during the race. It is this dissociative process, integrated with the complete focus and absorption in "transcendental awareness" that possibly best explains the racer's extraordinary ability to perform under the most extreme circumstances (ibid., p. 5).

What I have called a "higher" order meaning of ultimate concern, in the case of cycling, self-overcoming that includes a transcendent vision, is a heartfelt valuative attachment that helps a person metabolize his troubling, if not painful feelings amidst pain and suffering, by making them interpretable or as Geertz says, "sufferable." During World War II, in the extreme situation of the Nazi concentration camps, for example, "believers," like devout Jews, Christians, Jehovah Witnesses and steadfast Marxists, had a symbolically mediated relation between themselves and the extreme situation they were in that gave a specific life-affirming meaning to their environment in the camps, one that was "symbolic of transcendent" truth. In the case of devout Jews, this was a set of religious symbols which provided "a cosmic guarantee not only for their ability to comprehend the world, but also, comprehending it, to give a precision to their feeling, a definition to their emotions" that enabled them to better endure their ordeal and maintain a modicum of autonomy, integration and humanity. Intense, relentless, brute pain could be endured "by placing it in a meaningful context, providing a mode of action through which it can be expressed, being expressed understood, and being understood, endured" (Geertz, 1973, pp. 98, 100, 104, 105). As Erving Goffman wrote, "Strong religious and political convictions have served to insulate the true believer against the assaults of the 'total situation'" (1961, p. 66).[6]

While endurance cycling and the trials and tribulations of everyday life cannot be reasonably compared to the suffering of concentration camp inmates, what was psychologically true in the extreme circumstances of the camps has some applicability to the challenges of everyday life. That is, emotionally metabolizing pain and suffering is perhaps best accomplished when one is able to give meaning to one's experience by developing an ethical response to it, one that is for the other, whether this is a real or imagined other. To the extent that one can perceive pain and suffering as an ethical problem that requires an other-directed, other-regarding, other-serving response, one is more likely to be able to best metabolize the challenging emotions associated with the dire personal ordeals mentioned above. While the concentration camp ordeal represents perhaps the most extreme stressful context, the fact that some inmates were able to draw on their self-transcending values and beliefs to maintain their autonomy, integration and humanity points to what the average person needs to develop in terms of effectively coping with other less extreme, but still daunting, everyday personal pains and sufferings. In other words, to cope with the above-mentioned, everyday distressing situations requires that individuals have the capacity to imagine a moral order beyond themselves, one that provides the psychological, moral and communal context for putting moral duty and responsibility for the other above self-interest. Indeed, while cycling is centrally about individual self-overcoming, most often the great racers conceive of their striving for athletic excellence in a manner that goes beyond themselves in

6 For an in-depth study of psychological survival in the Nazi concentration camps, especially as it relates to the "believers," see Marcus, 1988.

some form. Certainly this is the case when one considers the team aspects of the sport. As the 2013 Tour de France winner Chris Froome noted, "In sport you always think the strongest guy should be going for it and getting the best results. The thing is, cycling also has a very important team aspect, which I don't think that a lot of people fully grasp" (www.cyclingnews.com, retrieved 7/13/14). Whether we are referring to an elite group of cream of the crop riders or a small collection of good friends who ride together when they are able, cyclists understand that they very much need each other to actualize their potential: "Sprinters need lead men, climbers need their teammates to help them gain ground in the mountains or at least to get to the bottom in the right place in the pack" (Austin, 2010, p. 181). Sean Yates, the great former British professional road racer, put this point just right:

> I never go into a race saying, "I want to win this." The thing that motivates me is riding for someone, either leading out a sprinter or helping a climber or defending a jersey. And when I'm in that situation, in any of those situations, then I perform much better because I'm motivated. (Strickland, 2001, p. 148)

Womack and Suyemoto have also noted that while cycling is in some of its features "an individual activity and sport, its practice and flourishing require significant community participation and reliance on others" (2010, p. 84). For example, they describe that "from race planning to training to bike maintenance and commuter advocacy, application of care ethical principles" are operative (ibid.). In contrast to men, female racers report a portrayal of identity and goals that are more relational in nature: "growth and developments as riders over time (both locally within the race and in the long term), education (lessons learned from others are important), and connections with others, both their opponents and their teammates" (ibid., p. 88). As I said earlier, for the competitive cyclist sometimes this other is conceived of as riding for, or at least with, God, the Green Environment or Family, or another deeply held transcendent conviction. As Chepe Rodriguez, the winner of the 1996 Tour de France quipped, "I dedicate this victory to God, my mother, my family and those who pay me" (Strickland, 2001, p. 257).

While I am not trying to claim that competitive cycling is fundamentally "for the other" (though there is the team dimension) rather than "for oneself," I am suggesting that even in this highly individualist and solitary sport we can see that the capacity to be other-directed, other-regarding and other-serving—even if this mainly means to a valuative attachment of self-overcoming, of creating oneself according to one's own ideal (McCary, 2010, p. 20), that is linked to a transcendent vision—is an important aspect of athletic excellence, and by extension, adult flourishing in everyday life. As Paul de Vivie, the illustrious publisher of *Le Cycliste* and the father of French bicycle touring noted, "Never ride just to prove yourself" (www.sirbikesalot.com, retrieved 7/21/14).

IV. FINAL REFLECTIONS: BIKE RIDING IN OLD AGE

At the highest level of competition, endurance racing depicts the human inclination to push oneself beyond what is usually regarded as reasonably doable. It illustrates how humans want to be radically self-reliant by drawing on their own internal physical, psychological and spiritual resources to survive, to flourish, and especially to triumph over the nearly impossible challenge. That is, the endurance cyclist affirms how vital it is to maintain one's autonomy, integration and human dignity, to use one's personal freedom to self-overcome, to self-fashion the ideal person one wants to be, whether the consummate athlete, or in everyday life, the consummate person. Moreover, while there are financial and other external rewards associated with professional endurance racing like the Grand Tours, the fact is that spectators are awed by the way these seemingly superhuman athletes strive for cycling excellence, if not victory, especially in their willingness to endure extreme pain and suffering for what boils down to a fleeting moment of glory for oneself and one's team (Elcombe & Tracey, 2010, p. 246). Self-affirmation, the recognition and assertion of the existence and value of one's individual self, feeling "I can because I must," and delivering, so to speak, seems to be a need, or at least a heartfelt desire that many people have to sustain a modicum of self-respect. Indeed, I have suggested some of the praiseworthy values and beliefs and other personal qualities that constitute the way of being of these extraordinary endurance racers that the average person struggling to live the "good life" can appropriate as they face challenges in their everyday lives. As Strickland noted, while "not everyone can be a great rider, anyone can have a great ride" (2001, p. 198).

I want to conclude this chapter by returning to where I began my discussion, namely, the simple meaning of the ordinary bicycle and recreational bike riding in childhood. Indeed, the bicycle has been described by journalist/cyclist Bill Strickland as "an unparalleled merger of a toy, a utilitarian vehicle, and sporting equipment," a human-powered machine that "approaches perfection in each use" (ibid., p. 16). However, rather than focus again on actual childhood experience, I want to comment on what at its best can be another form of childhood, namely, old age (Ilundáin-Agurruza & McNamee, 2010, p. 264). Seniors who ride bikes often relate to the machine with a sense of living one's childhood dreams, of "spinning spokes and spinning daydreams" (Bellofatto, 2007, p. 48) as they re-invent themselves, fashioning a "new life" as it were, by rediscovering the best of their old one. Playing off Robert Frost's poetic masterpiece, for the senior, bike riding can be a way of symbolically re-finding the beckoning road that was not taken, one that one imagines would have been the more satisfying, the one that is frequently associated with the most enlivening aspects of one's formative years. As one of the inventors of the mountain bike, 64-year-old Gary Fischer noted, "If you don't mountain bike, try it. Those new physical experiences will keep you a kid at heart" (Wallack & Katovsky, 2005, p. 34). John Howard, a former Olympic cyclist who is now 67, put this point rather well:

> After a life of competition, I no longer compete. It's beautiful, I go out and experience the bicycle the way it should be...[as] a life tool...I have reached a point where I know that there is no immortality. What is important for me is to prolong, elongate the process of life and to experience it on a positive, blissful level. Play with it. (ibid., p. 48)

Professional mountain biker Marla Streb provided a similar reflection:

> The most important thing that mountain biking taught me is that if I can climb a mountain, I can do anything. Mountain biking taught me that I am strong, tough, and brave. That I am never too old. That I like to get dirty and play like a child. (ibid., p. 262)

The American historian Henry Adams, who learned to ride at age 50 after his wife died, noted that biking was "a means of new life. Nothing else offered itself" (Strickland, 2001, p. 175).

In addition to taking pleasure in being outdoors in nature, moving at a speed that works against feelings of boredom or depression—"A bicycle ride is a flight from sadness," said James E. Starrs (www.bicyclekingdom.com, retrieved 7/3/14)—and engaging in exercise that stresses your body rigorously enough to release those wonderful pleasure-inducing endorphins (Mapes, 2009, p. 24), in a deep psychophysical, if not primal way, bike riding calls to mind the exhilaration associated with the best of childhood: to be able to do as one pleases, to be unconstrained by social ties or responsibilities, in short, "to be footloose and fancy free." Thus, one would have to be rather daft to not heartily agree with H. G. Wells's conclusion, "Every time I see an adult on a bicycle, I no longer despair for the future of the human race" (www.worldwidebikeride.com, retrieved 7/14/14)!

CHAPTER 8

CONCLUSION

In Arthur Ashe's inspired and inspiring 1993 memoir, *Days of Grace,* finished a few weeks before he died of HIV that was contracted from a blood transfusion he received during heart bypass surgery, the tennis great spoke to his beloved adopted daughter, Camera, who at the time was 6 years old. In the last chapter entitled "My Dear Camera," Ashe gave his daughter a directive for the future:

> Whatever else you learn in school, I would like you to master at least two "life sports," those you can play long after you are out of school. Sports are wonderful; they can bring you comfort and pleasure for the rest of your life. Sports can teach you so much about yourself, your emotions and character, how to be resolute in moments of crisis and how to fight back from the brink of defeat. In this respect, the lessons of sports cannot be duplicated easily; you quickly discover your limits but you can also build self-confidence and a positive sense of yourself. Never think of yourself as being above sports. (Ashe & Rampersad, 1993, pp. 38–39)

Ashe is eloquently and poignantly conveying the heart of what I have been imparting in this book, that whether one is passionately playing or watching sports (though as I have mentioned, though performing and spectating have psychological similarities they are not the same), the average person can learn a lot of practical wisdom that is applicable to living the "good life." With illustrative sports as the vehicle—soccer, baseball, chess, tennis, golf and cycling—I suggest some of the ways that playing and watching these games can contribute to crafting a flourishing life, one that embraces, with the fullness of one's whole being, beauty, truth and goodness. In all of these sports, each in their different way, humans are engaged in play, or "action…carried out for the sheer pleasure of acting, the exertion of powers for the sheer pleasure of exerting them" (Graeber, 2014, p. 40). Sports provide an organized setting for the free exercise of a human's most complicated powers and capacities that are experienced as a deeply satisfying end in and of itself (ibid., p. 41).

Like play in childhood, this play experience can have a transformative effect that can both be and feel self-transcendent. Social critics have described sport as something of a replacement religion in modern western society. For example, Beneke and Remillard point out that while religious affiliation and church attendance in the United States is hugely decreasing (and this is likely true in Europe and elsewhere), tens of millions of people are creating "powerful cohesive communities" around their beloved sports teams. As churches close down, money is poured into new sports stadiums. More than 60% of Americans regard themselves as devoted fans, which is double the percentage from a half of century ago. In a sense, the "modern sports stadiums function like great cathedrals once did" in their capacity to evoke strong feelings of community and transcendence (Beneke & Remillard, 2014). On an individual level, sports allow a player and, via identification, the observer to be a "religio athlete," to engage the deeper realms of personhood and moral value, including the worthwhile valuative attachments of fair competition and striving for excellence that have origins in Greece (Parke, 2012). As John Wooden, Legendary UCLA Basketball Coach famously said, "Sports do not build character. They reveal it" (www.voices.yahoo.com, retrieved 6/19/14).

In this conclusion I briefly return to the main premise of this book, that what makes sports so compelling, beyond the entertainment of observing the remarkable physical and mental abilities of athletes as they compete, is the fact that each sport taken as a totality of circumstances is a "parable of life" that wonderfully portrays the challenges and problems in living that ordinary people face as they attempt to create the "good life." Indeed, while there is tremendous "family resemblance" among all sports, that is, common psychological aspects of playing and watching that are operative in serious engagement with any sport, each sport has its own "storylines" that constitute "moral fables." The titles of my chapters—soccer, the beautiful game; baseball, the immortal game; chess, the royal game; tennis, a sportsman's pastime and a fighter's game; golf, a game of civility, and cycling, a "freedom-loving" sport—all point to the importance of sport as a conveyor of positive moral values and instructive and uplifting metaphors that can animate how to live the "good life." Moreover, as I have tried to suggest in my psychoanalytically-informed renderings, each sport allows an individual to sublimate a wide range of sexual and aggressive wishes in a life-affirming manner that is consciously and unconsciously deeply pleasurable for participants and spectators. Sports can make the here and now more complex and revitalize the past "with a glorifying and sometimes sobering aura," this being part of its fascinating transfiguring aesthetic power (Gumbrecht, 2006, pp. 15, 16). It is precisely this creative experience of playing and watching sports that can be a fertile breeding ground for the birth of the transcendent.

Playing and watching sports, at least at its best, can provide a person with that all-important sense of plentitude and cohesion, that guiding sense that things fit together into an integrated whole, that works against the emptiness of meaning that one has to fight in everyday life. This is part of the sacred function of sport, "to help live, to help bring things to life" (Marcel, 2005, p. 79). Most importantly, in order to experience this transformative, transcendent spiritual power of sports, one has to be able to let oneself move into what has been called the "fairy space" that sports tends to evoke in the skilful athlete and spectator; that is, to let oneself enter into the mysteriously magical internal space in which the infinite is evoked (ibid., p. 128). The key personal quality that needs to be operative to enter "fairy space" is the capacity to profoundly feel, that is, to allow oneself to deeply participate in the sports experience in a way that is analogous to falling in love. This erotically tinged capacity to enter into this "fairy space," to engage and reside in the love experience, what the great Christian Socratic philosopher Gabriel Marcel called "the limitless fecundity of the spirit" (ibid, p. 118), with mind, body and soul, requires a complex form of responsiveness. When one fully enters into this "fairy space," one is privileged to be transformed by a new and radiant presence, a presence that endures beyond the summoning moment of a great goal or home run, and can be affectively recalled in a similar manner as with an absent beloved. In short, what sports can do is open "a secret door in time and [reach] in to the eternal," it can be a unique kind of presence that awakens us to an eternal depth which is utterly life affirming and deeply pleasurable (O'Donohue, 2004a, p. 62). Thus, for many athletes and spectators, this experience of playing and watching sports is nothing short of a "saving light" (ibid., p. 53). Such a "grace moment," as one might call it, suggests the quasi-magical, transformative power of sports to transmit ideas, direct the will, and reinforce faith in life (and in some instances, God), whether this is described in religious or secular language. Indeed, as I have quoted throughout this book, athletes and spectators have described sports in decidedly redemptive language, suggesting what passionate sports participation and spectatorship can be at its best. Sports can bring us back to ourselves, especially to that lovely phase of childhood called toddlerhood, when we were thoroughly engaged in life. As Margaret Mahler (1975, p. 70) noted, the toddler with his growing motor and cognitive skills enjoys a "love affair with the world." To return to the "fairy space" metaphor, sports are like "fairy dust," that magical powder that makes strange and unlikely things happen, which in the hands of Peter Pan gives the power of flight to whoever is sprinkled with it. It is precisely this flight of the soul, that deeply felt sense of sparkling charm, magic and the marvelous that sports provides us. As the late physician and bestselling sports author George A. Sheehan beautifully noted,

> Sport is where an entire life can be compressed into a few hours, where the emotions of a lifetime can be felt on an acre or two of ground, where a person can suffer and die and rise again on six miles of trails through a New York City park. Sport is a theater where sinner can turn saint and a common man become an uncommon hero, where the past and the future can fuse with the present. Sport is singularly able to give us peak experiences where we feel completely one with the world and transcend all conflicts as we finally become our own potential. (2013, p. 189)

Indeed, whether player or spectator, in a certain sense one can't help but feel an upsurge of pure gratitude for having easy access to such wonderfully joyful experiences.

BIBLIOGRAPHY

Adatto, C. (1964). On Play and the Psychopathology of Golf. *Journal of the American Psychoanalytic Association, 12*, 826–841.

Adler, S. (2000). *The Art of Acting* (H. Kissel (Ed.)). New York: Applause.

Agassi, A. (2010). *Open: An Autobiography*. New York: Vintage Books.

Andrews, A. (2012). *Baseball, Boys, and Bad Words*. Nashville, TN: Thomas Nelson.

Apfelbaum, J. (Ed.) (2007). *The Gigantic Book of Golf Quotations*. New York: Skyhorse.

Aragno, A. (2014). The Roots of Evil: A Psychoanalytic Inquiry. *Psychoanalytic Review, 101*:2, 249–288.

Armstrong, L. with Jenkins, S. (2001). *It's Not About the Bike: My Journey Back to Life*. New York: Berkley Books.

Arnold, P. J. (1985). Aesthetic Aspects of Being in Sport: The Performer's Perspective in Contrast to That of the Spectator. *Journal of the Philosophy of Sport, xii*, 1–7.

Ashe, A. & Rampersad, A. (1993). *Days of Grace: A Memoir*. New York: Ballantine.

Austin, M. W. (2010). From Shoes to Saddle. In: J. Ilundáin-Agurruza & M. W. Austin (Eds.), *Cycling: Philosophy for Everyone: A Philosophical Tour De Force* (pp. 173–182). Malden, MA: Wiley-Blackwell.

Baggett, D. (2010a). Introduction: The Love of Wisdom. In: D. Baggett (Ed.), *Tennis and Philosophy: What the Racket Is All About* (pp. 1–5). Lexington, KY: The University Press of Kentucky.

Baggett, D. (2010b). Why Roger Federer is the Best or is it McEnroe. In: D. Baggett (Ed.), *Tennis and Philosophy: What the Racket Is All About* (pp. 26–53). Lexington, KY: The University Press of Kentucky.

Beckham, D. (2008). *People Magazine*, 3/20/08, http://www.people.com/people/article/0,,20185337,00.html.

Beller, J. M., & Stoll, S. K. (2010). How Golf Builds and Shapes Moral Character. In: A. Wible (Ed.), *God and Philosophy: Lessons from the Links* (pp. 65–84). Lexington, KY: University Press of Kentucky.

Bellofatto, G. (2007). Joy Ride: Life is a Bike. In: J. Joyce (Ed.), *The Bicycle Book: Wit, Wisdom & Wanderings* (pp. 49–52). Hardwick, MA: Satya House Publications.

Benedetti, J. (1998). *Stanislavski and the Actor*. New York: Routledge.

Beneke, C. & Remilliard, A. (2014, February 14). America's National Religion. *The Week*, p. 12.

Berlin, I. (2009). *The Hedgehog and the Fox: An Essay on Tolstoy's View of History*. London: Phoenix.

Best, D. (1985). Sport is Not Art. *Journal of Philosophy of Sport, XII*, 25–40.

Borghini, A. & Baldini, A. (2010). When a Soccer Club Becomes a Mirror. In: T. Richards (Ed.), *Soccer and Philosophy: Beautiful Thoughts on the Beautiful Game* (pp. 302–316). Chicago: Open Court.

Bouton, J. (1984). *Ball Four Plus Ball Five*. Aurora, ON: Madison Books.

Brooke, S. L. (2006). *Creative Art Therapies Manual: A Guide to History, Theoretical Approaches, and Assessment, and Work with Special Populations of Art, Play, Dance, Music, Drama, and Poetry Therapies*. Springfield, IL: Charles C. Thomas.

Burman, H. (2012). *Season of Ghosts: The '86 Mets and the Red Sox*. Jeffferson, NC: Mcfarland & Company.

Campbell, M. (2001). *The New Encyclopedia of Golf*. New York: Dorling Kindersley Book.

Camus, A. (1960). *Resistance, Rebellion, and Death: Essays* (J. O'Brien (Trans.)). New York: Vintage International.

Cant, G. (n.d.). Why They Play: The Psychology of Chess. www.chess.com : Forums : Off Topic, retrieved 4/19/14.

Charlton, J. (2002). *The Military Quotations Boos: More Than 1,200 of the Best Quotations about War, Leadership, Courage, Victory and Defeat*. New York: Thomas Dune Books.

Chomet, S. & Stein, A. (2006). Tricycles, Bicycles, Life Cycles: Psychoanalytic Perspectives on Childhood Loss and Transgenerative Parenting in Les Triplettes de Bellevile (2003). *International Journal of Psycho-Analysis, 87*, 1126–1134.

Cockburn, A. (1974). *Idle Passion: Chess and the Dance of Death*. New York: Village Voice/Simon and Schuster.

Cohen, M. (1974). *Baseball the Beautiful*. New York: Links Books.

Colman, A. M. (2009). *Oxford Dictionary of Psychology*. Oxford, UK: Oxford University Press.

Coriat, I. C. (1941). The Unconscious Motives of Interest in Chess. *The Psychoanalytic Review, 28*, 30–36.

Crowe, J. (2010). The Loneliness of the Referee. In: T. Richards (Ed.), *Soccer and Philosophy: Beautiful Thoughts on the Beautiful Game* (pp. 347–356). Chicago: Open Court.

Delius, C. (2008). The Sunday I Became World Champion. In: J. Turnbull, T. Saterlee & A. Raab (Eds.), *The Global Game: Writers on Soccer* (pp. 251–254). Lincoln, NE: University of Nebraska Press.

Dickson, P. (Ed.) (2008). *Baseball's Greatest Quotations*. New York: HarperCollins.

Ditouras, H. (2010). The "Kournikova Phenomenon." In: D. Baggett (Ed.), *Tennis and Philosophy: What the Racket Is All About* (pp. 182–199). Lexington, KY: The University Press of Kentucky.

Dubath, P. (2008). Zidane and Me. In: J. Turnbull, T. Saterlee & A. Raab (Eds.), *The Global Game: Writers on Soccer* (pp. 245–250). Lincoln, NE: University of Nebraska Press.

Dura-Vila, V. (2010). Why Playing Beautifully Is Morally Better. In: T. Richards (Ed.), *Soccer and Philosophy: Beautiful Thoughts on the Beautiful Game* (pp. 141–148). Chicago: Open Court.

Eigen, M. (1986). *The Psychotic Core*. Northvale, NJ: Jason Aronson.

Elcome, T. (2010). Is Ronaldo a Modern Picasso? In: T. Richards (Ed.), *Soccer and Philosophy: Beautiful Thoughts on the Beautiful Game* (pp. 161–171). Chicago: Open Court.

Elcombe, T. & Tracey, J. (2010). Stretched Elastics, the Tour De France, and a Meaningful Life. In: J. Ilundáin-Agurruza & M. W. Austin (Eds.), *Cycling: Philosophy for Everyone: A Philosophical Tour De Force* (pp. 241–252). Malden, MA: Wiley-Blackwell.

Eylon, Y. & Horowitz, A. (2010). What's Luck Got to Do with It? In: T. Richards (Ed.), *Soccer and Philosophy: Beautiful Thoughts on the Beautiful Game* (pp. 107–120). Chicago: Open Court.

Ferris, K. (2001). *Manchester United in Europe: Tragedy, Destiny, History*. London: Mainstream Press.

Fine, R. (1952). *The Middlegame in Chess*. New York: McKay. (Reprinted by Random House, 2003)

Fine, R. (1965). *The Psychology of the Chess Player*. New York: Dover.

Fine, R. (1973). *Bobby Fischer's Conquest of the World's Chess Championship: The Psychology and Tactics of the Title Match*. Bronx, NY: Ishi Press International.

Fleming, J. & Strong, S. M. (1943). Observations on the Use of Chess in the Therapy of an Adolescent Boy. *Psychoanalytic Review, 30*, 399–416.

Foucault, M. (1987). On the Genealogy of Ethics: An Overview of Work in Progress. In: H. L. Dreyfus & P. Rabinow (Eds.), *Michel Foucault: Beyond Structuralism and Hermeneutics* (pp. 227–252). Chicago, IL: University of Chicago Press.

Foucault, M. (1989). The Ethics of the Concern for Self as a Practice of Freedom. (S. Lotringer (Ed.)). *Foucault Live, Collected Interviews, 1961–1984*. New York: Semiotexte.

Freud, S. (1915). Thoughts for the Times on War and Death. In: J. Strachey (Ed. & Trans.), *The Standard Edition of the Complete Psychological Works of Sigmund Freud*. London: Hogarth Press, Vol. 14, pp. 273–300.

Freud, S. (1919). The "Uncanny." *The Standard Edition of the Complete Psychological Works of Sigmund Freud*, Vol. XVII.

Freud, S. (1927–1931). Civilization and its Discontents. In: J. Strachey (Ed. & Trans.), *The Standard Edition of the Complete Psychological Works of Sigmund Freud*. London: Hogarth Press, Vol. XXI.

Freud, S. (1949). Three Essays on Sexuality. In: J. Strachey (Ed. & Trans.), *The Standard Edition of the Complete Psychological Works of Sigmund Freud*. London: Hogarth Press, Vol. VII.

Freud, S. (1953). The Interpretation of Dreams. In: J. Strachey (Ed. & Trans.), *The Standard Edition of the Complete Psychological Works of Sigmund Freud*. London: Hogarth Press, Vols. IV & V.

Freud, S. (1958). On Beginning the Treatment (Further Recommendations on the Technique of Psycho-Analysis I). In: J. Strachey (Ed. & Trans.), *The Standard Edition of the Complete Psychological Works of Sigmund Freud*. London: Hogarth Press, Vol. 12, pp. 121–144.

Fudge, R. & Ulatowski, J. (2010). On the Beauty and Sublimity of God. In: A. Wible (Ed.), *God and Philosophy: Lessons from the Links* (pp. 15–32). Lexington, KY: University Press of Kentucky.

Galeano, E. (2009). *Soccer in Sun and Shadow* (M. Fried (Trans.)). New York: Nation Books.

Gallwey, W. T. (1997). *The Inner Game of Tennis* (Rev. Ed.). New York: Random House.

Gandhi, M. (2000). *The Words of Gandhi: Second Edition* (R. Attenborough (Ed.)). New York: New Market Press.

Geertz, C. (1973). Religion as a Cultural System. In *The Interpretation of Cultures* (pp. 87–125). New York: Basic Books.

Giamatti, A. B. (1998a). *A Great and Glorious Game: Baseball Writings of A. Bartlett Giamatti* (K. S. Robson (Ed.)). Chapel Hill, NC: Algonquin Books of Chapel Hill.

Giamatti, A. B. (1998b). *Take Time for Paradise: Americans and their Games*. New York: Summit Books.

Gill, D. (Ed.) (2005). *Doolally: Mad For Leeds*. West Yorkshire, UK: PDG Books.

Gillmeister, H. (1998). *Tennis: A Cultural History*. New York: New York University Press.

Gini, A. (2010). The Importance of Play. In: A. Wible (Ed.), *God and Philosophy: Lessons from the Links* (pp. 9–14). Lexington, KY: University Press of Kentucky.

Goffman, E. (1961). *Asylums*. New York: Anchor Books.

Goldblatt, D. (2006). *The Ball Is Round: A Global History of Soccer*. New York: Riverhead Books.

Goodwin, D. K. (2013). Foreword. In: J. Sexton, with T. Oliphant & P. J. Schwartz, *Baseball as a Road to God: Seeing Beyond the Game* (pp. 1–3). New York: Penguin.

Gould, S. J. (2003). *Triumph and Tragedy in Mudville: A Lifelong Passion for Baseball.* New York: W.W. Norton.

Graeber, D. (2014, March 14). Do Atoms Play? *The Week*, pp. 40–41.

Grimwood, T. & Miller, P. K. (2010). The Boy Done Good: Football's Clichés. In: T. Richards (Ed.), *Soccer and Philosophy: Beautiful Thoughts on the Beautiful Game* (pp. 379–388). Chicago: Open Court.

Gumbrecht, H. U. (2006). *In Praise of Athletic Beauty*. Cambridge, MA: Harvard University Press.

Hadot, P. (1997). *Philosophy as a Way of Life*. Oxford, UK: Blackwell.

Hagman, G. (2005). *Aesthetic Experience: Beauty, Creativity, and the Search for the Ideal.* Amsterdam: Rodopi.

Hales, S. D. (2010). Cycling and Philosophical Lessons Learned the Hard Way. In: J. Ilundáin-Agurruza & M. W. Austin (Eds.), *Cycling: Philosophy for Everyone: A Philosophical Tour De Force* (pp. 162–172). Malden, MA: Wiley-Blackwell.

Hamilton, M. J. (2004). There's No Lying in Baseball (Wink, Wink). In: E. Bronson (Ed.), *Baseball and Philosophy* (pp. 126–138). Chicago: Open Court.

Herlihy, D. V. (2004). *Bicycle*. New Haven, CT: Yale University Press.

Hochberg, B. (Ed.) (1993). *The 64-Square Looking Glass: The Great Game of Chess in World Literature*. New York: Times Books.

Holmes, R. (1999). *The Hutchinson Atlas of Battle Plans: Before and After*. Chicago: Helicon.

Holt, J., & Holt, L. E. (2010). The "Ideal" Swing, the "Ideal" Body. In: A. Wible (Ed.), *God and Philosophy: Lessons from the Links* (pp. 209–220). Lexington, KY: University Press of Kentucky.

Homer, J. (2007). Of Dogs and Cyclists: The Difference Between Riders. In: J. Joyce (Ed.), *The Bicycle Book: Wit, Wisdom & Wanderings* (pp. 39–42). Hardwick, MA: Satya House Publications.

Hooper, D. & Whyld, K. (1991). *The Oxford Companion to Chess, New Edition*. Oxford, UK: Oxford University Press.

Hopsicker, P. M. (2010). Learning to Ride a Bike. In: J. Ilundáin-Agurruza & M. W. Austin (Eds.), *Cycling: Philosophy for Everyone: A Philosophical Tour De Force* (pp. 16–26). Malden, MA: Wiley-Blackwell.

Hornby, N. (1992). *Fever Pitch*. New York: Riverhead Books.

Hoyningen-Huene, P. (2010). Why is Football So Fascinating? In: T. Richards (Ed.), *Soccer and Philosophy: Beautiful Thoughts on the Beautiful Game* (pp. 7–22). Chicago: Open Court.

http://betweenthelines.in/2014/01/book-2review-soccer-sun-shadow-eduardo-galeano-translated-mark-fried/

Huston, M. R. (2010). Losing Beautifully. In: D. Baggett (Ed.), *Tennis and Philosophy: What the Racket Is All About* (pp. 200–219). Lexington, KY: The University Press of Kentucky.

Hutchinson, A. C. (2000). *It's All in the Game: A Nonfoundationalist Account of Law and Adjudication: The Game*. Durham, NC: Duke University Press.

Ilundáin-Agurruza, J. & McNamee, M. (2010). Life Cycles and the Stages of a Cycling Life. In: J. Ilundáin-Agurruza & M. W. Austin (Eds.), *Cycling: Philosophy for Everyone: A Philosophical Tour De Force* (pp. 253–265). Malden, MA: Wiley-Blackwell.

Ilundáin-Agurruza, J. M. & Torres, C. R. (2010). Embellishing the Ugly Side of the Beautiful Game. In: T. Richards (Ed.), *Soccer and Philosophy: Beautiful Thoughts on the Beautiful Game* (pp. 185–196). Chicago: Open Court.

Imre, R. (2010). Hungary's Revolutionary Golden Team. In: T. Richards (Ed.), *Soccer and Philosophy: Beautiful Thoughts on the Beautiful Game* (pp. 290–301). Chicago: Open Court.

James, S. L. (1957). Foreword. In: B. Hogan, *Five Lessons: The Modern Fundamentals of Golf* (pp. 5–7). New York: Simon and Schuster.

Johnson, A. G. (1995). *The Blackwell Dictionary of Sociology: A User's Guide to Sociological Language*. Oxford, UK: Blackwell Publishers.

Jones, E. (1974). The Problem of Paul Morphy: A Contribution to the Psychology of Chess. In *Psycho-Myth, Psycho-History: Essays in Applied Psychoanalysis* (pp. 165–196). New York: Hillstone.

Jones, J. M. (n.d.). Nearly Half of Americans are Baseball Fans: Football is the Top Sport. www.gallup.com/poll/22240/nearly-half-americans-baseball-fans.aspx, retrieved 10/28/13.

Kent, M. A. (2010). Aristotle's Favorite Sport. In: T. Richards (Ed.), *Soccer and Philosophy: Beautiful Thoughts on the Beautiful Game* (pp. 47–62). Chicago: Open Court.

Kernberg, O. (1984). *Severe Personality Disorders: Psychotherapeutic Strategies*. New Haven: Yale University Press.

Kilpatrick, D. (2010). Nietzsche's Arsenal. In: T. Richards (Ed.), *Soccer and Philosophy: Beautiful Thoughts on the Beautiful Game* (pp. 37–46). Chicago: Open Court.

Kleiser, G. (2005). *Dictionary of Proverbs*. New Delhi: S. B. Nangia.

Kraus, J. (2004). There's No Place Like Home! In: E. Bronson (Ed.), *Baseball and Philosophy* (pp. 7–19). Chicago: Open Court.

Krauthammer, C. (1993). The Romance of Chess. In: B. Hochberg (Ed.), *The 64-Square Looking Glass: The Great Game of Chess in World Literature* (pp. 5–12). New York: Times Books.

Lambert, A. (2010). The Evolution of the Football Fan and the Way of Virtue. In: T. Richards (Ed.), *Soccer and Philosophy: Beautiful Thoughts on the Beautiful Game* (pp. 215–230). Chicago: Open Court.

Larsen, S. N. (2010). Becoming a Cyclist. In: J. Ilundáin-Agurruza & M. W. Austin (Eds.), *Cycling: Philosophy for Everyone: A Philosophical Tour De Force* (pp. 27–38). Malden, MA: Wiley-Blackwell.

Lasker, E. (1960). *Lasker's Manual of Chess.* Garden City, NY: Dover.

Laumakis, S. J. (2010). Finding the (Fair) Way with Confucius and Ben Hogan. In: A. Wible (Ed.), *God and Philosophy: Lessons from the Links* (pp. 33–48). Lexington, KY: University Press of Kentucky.

Lever, J. (1983). *Soccer Madness: Brazil's Passion for the World's Most Popular Sport.* Long Grove, IL: Waveland Press.

Levinas, E. (1989). *Difficult Freedom: Essays on Judaism* (S. Hand (Ed.)). Baltimore, MD: The Johns Hopkins University Press.

Lewis, S. M. (1999). Cycling in the Zone. *Journal of Sport Psychology, 1*:3, 1–5.

Lifton, R. J. (1976). *The Life of the Self: Toward a New Psychology.* New York: Basic Books.

Lunsford, R. (2010). Golf and the Meaning of Life. In: A. Wible (Ed.), *God and Philosophy: Lessons from the Links* (pp. 223–237). Lexington, KY: University Press of Kentucky.

Mahler, J. (2013). Is the Game Over? The *New York Times* Sunday Review, http://www.nytimes.com/2013/09/29/opinion/snday/is-the--gam..., Retrieved 10/1/13.

Mahler, M., Pine, F. and Bergman, A. (1975). *The Psychological Birth of the Human Infant: Symbiosis and Individuation.* London: Hutchinson & Co.

Mapes, J. (2009). *Pedaling Revolution: How Cyclists are Changing American Cities.* Corvallis, OR: Oregon State University Press.

Marcel, G. (2005). *Music and Philosophy.* (S. Maddux & R. R. Wood (Trans.)). Milwaukee: WI: Marquette University Press.

Marcus, P. (1988). *Autonomy in the Extreme Situation: Bruno Bettelheim, the Nazi Concentration Camps and the Mass Society.* Westport, CT: Praeger.

Marcus, P. (2008). *Being for the Other: Emmanuel Levinas, Ethical Living and Psychoanalysis.* Milwaukee, WI: Marquette University Press.

Marcus, P. (2014). *They Shall Beat Their Swords Into Plowshares: Military Strategy, Psychoanalysis and The Art of Living.* Milwaukee, WI: Marquette University Press.

Marcus, P. (2015). *Creating Heaven on Earth: The Psychological Experience of Immortality in Everyday Life.* London: Karnac.

Marcus, P. & Marcus, G. (2011). *Theater as Life: Practical Wisdom Drawn From Great Acting Teachers, Actors and Actresses*. Milwaukee, WI: Marquette University Press.

Martin, B. (2008). The Difficult Ways of God and Caissa: Chess, Theodicy, and Determinism in Gadamer. In: B. Hale (Ed.), *Philosophy Looks at Chess* (pp. 89–118). Peru, IL: Open Court.

Martin, J. S. (1968). *The Curious History of the Golf Ball: Mankind's Most Fascinating Sphere*. New York: Horizon Press.

Mason, T. (1995). *Passion of the People: Football in South America*. London: Verso.

McCary, R. (2010). *The Challenge of Modernity: Nietzsche's Freedom: Self-Overcoming*. www.challenge of modernity.blohspot.com/2010/01/nietzsches-f..., pp. 1–22.

McNaron, D. L. (2010). Quiet...Please! In: A. Wible (Ed.), *God and Philosophy: Lessons from the Links* (pp. 49–63). Lexington, KY: University Press of Kentucky.

McNaron, D. L. (2014, July 21). Personal Communication.

Menninger, K. (1942). Recreation and Morale: A Subjective Symposium. *Bulletin of the Menninger Clinic*, 6:3, 65–102.

Miller, L. (2013, July 17). Pitching God. *New York*, p. 22.

Miller, S. & Hill, P. M. (1999). *Sport Psychology for Cyclists*. Boulder, CO: Velo Press.

Moore, B. E. & Fine, B. D. (Eds.) (1990). *Psychoanalytic Terms and Concepts*. New Haven: The American Psychoanalytic Association and Yale University.

Moore, P. (2000). Soccer and the Politics of Culture in Western Australia. In: N. Dyck (Ed.), *Games, Sports and Cultures* (pp. 117–134). Oxford, UK: Berg.

Morgan, W. J. (2004). Baseball and the Search for an American Moral Identity. In: E. Bronson (Ed.), *Baseball and Philosophy* (pp. 157–168). Chicago: Open Court.

Murray, H. J. R. (2012). *A History of Chess*. New York: Skyhorse Publishing.

Nabokov, V. (1993). Speak, Memory. In: B. Hochberg (Ed.), *The 64-Square Looking Glass: The Great Game of Chess in World Literature* (pp. 25–29). New York: Times Books.

Nachmanovitch, S. (1990). *Free Play: Improvisation in Life and Art*. New York: Penguin Putnam.

Nguyen, A. M. (2010). Barc's Treble or: How I Learned to Stop Worrying and Love the Heat. In: T. Richards (Ed.), *Soccer and Philosophy: Beautiful Thoughts on the Beautiful Game* (pp. 265–277). Chicago: Open Court.

NPR. (n.d.). *Arts & Life: Books: Author Interviews*. www.npr.org, retrieved 1/28/14.

Nuttall, M. (2008). Arsarnerit: Inuit and the Heavenly Game of Football. In: J. Turnbull, T. Saterlee & A. Raab (Eds.), *The Global Game: Writers on Soccer* (pp. 274–282). Lincoln, NE: University of Nebraska Press.

O'Donohue, J. (1998). *Eternal Echoes: Exploring Our Hunger to Belong.* London: Bantam.

O'Donohue, J. (2004a). *Anam Cara: A Book of Celtic Wisdom*. New York: Harper Perennial.

O'Donohue, J. (2004b). *The Invisible Embrace: Beauty. Rediscovering the True Sources of Compassion, Serenity, and Hope.* New York: Perennial.

O'Neil, B. with Wulf, S. & Conrads, D. (1996). *I was Right On Time*. New York: Simon and Schuster.

Oberndorf, C. P. (1951). Psychopathology of Work. *Bulletin of the Menninger Clinic, 15*:3, 77–84.

Olaya, C., Lammoglia, N. & Zarama, R. (2010). A "Messi" Way of Life. In: T. Richards (Ed.), *Soccer and Philosophy: Beautiful Thoughts on the Beautiful Game* (pp. 278–289). Chicago: Open Court.

Palmer, P., Gillette, G. & Shea, S. (2006). *The 2006 ESPN Baseball Encyclopedia* (1st ed.). New York: Sterling.

Paret, P. (1986). Clausewitz. In *Makers of Modern Strategy: From Machiavelli to the Nuclear Age*. Princeton, NH: Princeton University Press.

Parke, S. (2012). www.thirdwaymagazine.co.uk/editions/julaug-2012/featur..., retrieved 6/19/14.

Pelé with Fish, R. L. (1977). *My Life and the Beautiful Game*. New York: Double Day.

Penn, R. (2010). *The Pursuit of Happiness on Two Wheels*. New York: Bloomsbury.

Pepple, J. (2010). *Soccer, the Left, & the Farce of Multiculturalism*. Bloomington, IN: AuthorHouse.

Perry, C. (2005). Concentration: Focus Under Pressure. In: S. Murphy (Ed.), *The Sport Psych Handbook: A Complete Guide to Today's Best Mental Training Techniques* (pp. 113–125). Champaign, IL: Human Kinetics Publishers.

Person, E. S., Cooper, A. M. & Gabbard, G. O. (2005). *Textbook of Psychoanalysis*. Washington, DC: American Psychiatric Association.

Petrucelli, J. (2010). "Serve, Smash, and Self-States": Tennis on the Couch and Courting Steve Mitchell. *Contemporary Psychoanalysis, 46*, 578–588.

Price, J. L. (2006). *Rounding the Bases: Baseball and Religion in America.* Macon, GA: Mercer University.

Rachels, S. (2008). The Reviled Art. In: B. Hale (Ed.), *Philosophy Looks at Chess* (pp. 209–226). Peru, IL: Open Court.

Rachels, S. (2014, July 20). Personal Communication.

Reider, N. (1960). Chess, Oedipus, and the Mater Dolorosa. *International Journal of Psychoanalysis, 40,* 320–333.

Robson, K. (1998). Introduction. In K. S. Robson (Ed.), *A Great and Glorious Game: Baseball Writings of A. Bartlett Giamatti* (pp. 1–6). Chapel Hill, NC: Algonquin Books of Chapel Hill.

Rosen, M., with Bruton, J. (2012). *Best Seat in the House.* Minneapolis: MVP Books.

Rotella, B. (1995). *Golf is Not a Game of Perfect.* New York: Simon and Schuster.

Ruiz, J. A. V. (2010). *God is Round.* Editorial Planeta Mexicana Sa De cv.

Rycroft, C. (1995). *A Critical Dictionary of Psychoanalysis.* London: Penguin.

Saidy, A. (1994). *The March of Chess Ideas: How The Century's Greatest Players Have Waged War Over Chess Strategy.* New York: David McKay Company.

Seidel, M. (1991). *Ted Williams: A Baseball Life.* Lincoln: University of Nebraska Press.

Selinger, E. (2008). Chess-Playing Computers and Embodied Grandmasters: In What Ways Does the Difference Matter? In: B. Hale (Ed.), *Philosophy Looks at Chess* (pp. 65–88). Peru, IL: Open Court.

Senor, T. D. (2004). Should Cubs Fans Be Committed? What Bleacher Bums Have to Teach Us about the Nature of Faith. In: E. Bronson (Ed.), *Baseball and Philosophy* (pp. 37–55). Chicago: Open Court.

Sexton, J. with Oliphant, T. & Schwartz, P. J. (2013). *Baseball as a Road to God: Seeing Beyond the Game.* New York: Penguin.

Shahade, J. (2005). *Chess Bitch: Women in the Ultimate Intellectual Sport.* Los Angles: Siles Press.

Shakespeare, W. *Henry,* Act 1, Scene 2.

Sheehan, G. A. (2013). *Running and Being: The Total Experience.* New York: Rodale.

Shenk, D. (2006). *The Immortal Game: A History of Chess.* New York: Doubleday.

Smith, R. (1951, October 4). Miracle of Coogen's Bluff. *New York Herald Tribune.*

Stanislavski, C. (1989d). *Stanislavski's Legacy.* (E. R. Hapgood (Ed. & Trans.)). New York: Theatre Arts Books.

Stanislavski, C. (1998a). *An Actor Prepares.* New York: Routledge.

Stanislavski, C. (1998b). *Building a Character.* New York: Routledge.

Stanislavski, C. (1998c). *Creating a Role.* New York: Routledge.

Stewart, M. (2012). *Team Spirit: The Houston Astros.* Chicago: Norwood House Press.

Strickland, B. (2001). *The Quotable Cyclist: Great Moments of Cycling Wisdom, Inspiration and Humor.* Halcottsville, NY: Breakaway Books.

TCM.com. (n.d.). They Were Expendable (1945). www.tcm.com/tcmdb/title/2070/They-Were-Expendable, Retrieved 9/30/13.

The Week. (2013, July 19). 13(626).

Tinley, S. (2010). LeMond, Armstrong, and the Never-Ending Wheel of Fortune. In: J. Ilundáin-Agurruza & M. W. Austin (Eds.), *Cycling: Philosophy for Everyone: A Philosophical Tour De Force* (pp. 68–80). Malden, MA: Wiley-Blackwell.

Treanor, B. (n.d.). Gabriel Marcel. *Stanford Encyclopedia of Philosophy*, http://plato.stanford.edu/entries/marcel/#13, Retrieved 10/29/13.

Tsouras, P. G. (Ed.) (2005). *The Book of Military Quotations*. St. Paul, MN: Zenith Press.

Turnbull, J., Satterlee, T. & Raab, A. (Eds.) (2008). *The Global Game: Writers on Soccer*. Lincoln, NE: University of Nebraska Press.

Valentini, T. (2010). Love-Love: A Fresh Start at Finding Value and Virtue in Tennis. In: D. Baggett (Ed.), *Tennis and Philosophy: What the Racket Is All About* (pp. 125–141). Lexington, KY: The University Press of Kentucky.

van Creveld, M. (1991). *The Transformation of War*. New York: The Free Press.

Vargiu, L. (2010). Kant at the Maracana. In: T. Richards (Ed.), *Soccer and Philosophy: Beautiful Thoughts on the Beautiful Game* (pp. 172–184). Chicago: Open Court.

Vecsey, G. (1995). Foreword. In: J. Jennings (Ed.), *Tennis and the Meaning of Life: A Literary Anthology of the Game*. New York: Breakaway Books.

Wallace, D. F. (1997). Tennis Player Michael Joyce's Professional Artistry as a Paradigm of Certain Stuff about Choice, Freedom, Limitation, Joy, Grotesquerie, and Human Completeness. In: D. F. Wallace, *A Supposedly Fun Thing I'll Never Do Again* (pp. 213–255). New York: Back Bay Books.

Wallace, D. F. (2010). Federer as Religious Experience. In: D. Baggett (Ed.), *Tennis and Philosophy: What The Racket Is All About* (pp. 6–25). Lexington, KY: The University Press of Kentucky.

Wallack, R. M. & Katovsky, B. (2005). *Bike for Life: How to Ride to 100*. Cambridge, MA: De Capo Press.

Wardle, I. (1992). Introduction. In: K. Johnstone (Ed.), *Impro: Improvisation and the Theatre* (pp. 9–12). New York: Routledge/Theatre Art Boos.

Warner, C. T. (2001). *Bonds That Make Us Free: Healing Our Relationships, Coming to Ourselves*. Salt Lake City, UT: Shadow Mountain.

Waterman, A. (1993). The Poetry of Chess. In: B. Hochberg (Ed.), *The 64-Square Looking Glass: The Great Game of Chess in World Literature* (pp. 13–24). New York: Times Books.

Weinstein, F. (1990). *History and Theory after the Fall*. Chicago: University of Chicago Press.

Wells, H.G. (1901). *Certain Personal Matters*. London: T. Fisher Unwin.

Welsh, A. (1999). *The Soccer Goalkeeping Handbook*. New York: McGraw-Hill.

Whitman, M. D. (2004). *Tennis: Origins and Mysteries*. Mineola: Dover Publications.

Whitman, R. W. (1969). Psychoanalytic Speculations about Play: Tennis—The Duel. *Psychoanalytic Review*, 56:2, 197–214.

Wible, A. (2010). More Than a Playing Partner. In: A. Wible (Ed.), *God and Philosophy: Lessons from the Links* (pp. 239–251). Lexington, KY: University Press of Kentucky.

Wilkinson, D. J. (2006). *The Ambiguity Advantage: What Great Leaders Are Great At*. New York: Palgrave.

Will, G. F. (1990). *Men at Work: The Craft of Baseball*. New York: Macmillan Publishers.

Will, G. F. (1998). *Bunts: Curt Flood, Camden Yards, Peter Rose and Other Reflections on Baseball*. New York: Scribner.

Winters, E. (2010). How to Appreciate the Fingertip Save. In: T. Richards (Ed.), *Soccer and Philosophy: Beautiful Thoughts on the Beautiful Game* (pp. 149–160). Chicago: Open Court.

Winters, E. (2014, May 6). Personal Communication.

Womack, C. A. & Suyemoto, P. (2010). Riding Like A Girl. In: J. Ilundáin-Agurruza & M. W. Austin (Eds.), *Cycling: Philosophy for Everyone: A Philosophical Tour De Force* (pp. 81–93). Malden, MA: Wiley-Blackwell.

www.360soccer.com/pele/peleplay.html, retrieved 1/28/14.

www.4dfoot.com/2012/02/05/the-greatest-football-quotations/, retrieved 4/1/14.

www.allgreatquotes.com/cycling_quotes.shtml, retrieved 7/5/14.

www.allgreatquotes.com/tennis_quotes2.shtml, retrieved 5/20/14.

www.archive.org/stream/.../tenthousandmile01baggoog_djvu.t..., retrieved 7/1/14.

www.backpagefootball.com/clean-sheet-grand-final-countdown/56929/, retrieved 1/30/14.

www.barnet123.wix.com/the-goalkeeper#!__page-1, retrieved 4/3/14.

www.bicyclekingdom.com/bikes/quotes/cycling_1.htm, retrieved 7/3/14.

www.bikefortcollins.org/enjoyable-riding, retrieved 6/30/14.

www.bikehub.co.uk/news/.../cycle-tracks-will-abound-in-utopia/, retrieved 7/13/14.

www.biography.com/.../billie-jean-king-936487... retrieved 5/12/14.

www.biographyonline.net/sport/tennis/billie-jean-king.html, retrieved 5/12/14.

www.bleacherreport.com/.../1642636-5-traits-every-great-golf..., retrieved 6/17/14.

www.born-today.com/Today/09-02.htm, retrieved 5/21/14.

www.brandongaille.com/36-famous-golf-quotes-and-funny-golf-sayi..., retrieved 6/16/14.

www.breakingnews.ie/.../safin-davis-cup-win-better-than-se, retrieved 5/22/14.

www.camus-society.com/camus-football.html, retrieved 4/5/14.

www.chess.com : Forums : General Chess Discussion, retrieved 5/5/14.

www.chess.com/article/view/the-five-schools-of-chess, retrieved 4/29/14.

www.chesscorner.com/quotes/chess_quotes.htm, retrieved 4/18/14.

www.chessgames.com/perl/chesscollection?cid=1001992, retrieved 4/8/14.

www.chessgames.com/player/alexey_suetin.html, retrieved 4/10/14.

www.chessgames.com/player/lev_alburt.html?kpage=14, retrieved 4/29/14.

www.chesslessons4beginners.com/additional.../lesson_7_middlegame.htm, retrieved 5/2/14.

www.chessmaniac.com/index.php/2012/.../how-many-chess-players/, retrieved 4/29/14.

www.chessquotes.com/player-alekhine, retrieved 4/25/14.

www.chessquotes.com/player-capablanca/, retrieved 5/3/14.

www.chessquotes.com/player-fischer, retrieved 4/18/14.

www.chessquotes.com/player-kasparov, retrieved 5/2/14.

www.chessquotes.com/player-lasker, retrieved 5/4/14.

www.chessquotes.com/topic-humour, retrieved 4/10/14.

www.chessquotes.com/topic-kings, retrieved 5/3/14.

www.chessquotes.com/topic-middlegames, retrieved 5/2/14.

www.chessquotes.com/topic-pawns, retrieved, 5/4/14.

www.chessquotes.com/topic-psychology, retrieved 5/2/14.

www.chessquotes.com/topic-sacrifices, retrieved 4/30/14.

www.chessquotes.com/topic-studies, retrieved 4/30/14.

www.cmgww.com/sports/ashe/about/quotes1.htm, retrieved 6/1/14.

www.cockermouthtennis.org/quotes.html, retrieved 5/23/14.

www.coloradoavidgolfer.com/50-best-golf-quotes-of-all-time, retrieved 6/13/14.

www.compleatgolfer.co.za › From The Magazine › Legends of Golf, retrieved 6/11/14.

www.correspondencechess.com/knudsen/quote.htm, retrieved 4/29/14.

www.cyclingnews.com/.../froome-believes-team-sky-was-too-cautious-at..., retrieved 7/13/14.

www.cycling-passion.com/2012/09/10/best-cycling-quotes/, retrieved 7/1/14.

www.cyclingtips.com.au/2011/04/paris-roubaix-l'enfer-du-nord/, retrieved 7/4/14.

www.dailymail.co.uk/.../Andy-Murray-interview-Martin-Sam..., retrieved 6/4/14.

www.dailymail.co.uk/.../Andy-Roddick-retires-A-Rods-greates..., retrieved 5/22/14.

www.dailymail.co.uk/sport/article.../The-game-glory-Jose.ht..., retrieved 2/10/14.

www.digitalcommons.mcmaster.ca/.../viewcontent.cgi?, retrieved 3/19/14.

www.dreamhawk.com/dream-dictionary/bicycle/, retrieved 7/16/14.

www.edition.cnn.com/TRANSCRIPTS/1107/03/pmt.01.html, retrieved 6/16/14.

www.en.chessbase.com/post/vladimir-kramnik-che-is-so-deep-i...feel...-/2, retrieved 4/19/14.

www.endlessbacon.com/quotes/342710, retrieved 6/9/14.

www.endlessquote.com/category/bjorn-borg/page/2/, retrieved 5/12/14.

www.espn.go.com/espnw/athletes-life/article/.../always-learn-masters, retrieved 6/13/14.

www.espn.go.com/espnw/quote/6391571/264/let-racket-do-talking, retrieved 5/23/14.

www.exeterchessclub.org.uk/content/chess-tactics-quotes, retrieved 4/30/14.

www.expertfootball.com/wp/soccer-playing-styles/, retrieved 4/22/14.

www.facebook.com/GolfballsDotCom/posts/10151222153028710, retrieved 6/13/14.

www.fansided.com/.../nelson-mandela-sports-power-change-world/, retrieved 3/26/14.

www.fifa.com/.../players/player=63869/, retrieved 1/28/14.

www.fifa.com/world-match-centre/.../7/, retrieved 1/27/14.

www.footballtoptens.wordpress.com/2010/09/.../top-ten-footballers-nick-names..., retrieved 3/23/14.

www.forbes.com/sites/brentbeshore/2012/.../golf-the-game-of-life, retrieved 6/12/14.

www.free-project.eu/.../the-last-man-standing-a-tribute-to-the-goalkeeper..., retrieved 4/1/14.

www.geniusrevive.com/en/geniuses.html?pid=142&sid...Football, retrieved 1/28/14.

www.goalkeepersaredifferent.com/keeper/wordframe.htm, retrieved 4/3/14.

www.goalkeepersaredifferent.com/keeper/words.htm, retrieved 4/4/14.

www.goalkeepersarediffferent.com/keeper/words.htm, retrieved 4/2/14.

www.golf.about.com/cs/golfterms/g/bldef_handicap.htm, retrieved 6/16/14.

www.golf.about.com/od/golfersmen/a/hogan_quotes.htm, retrieved 6/11/14.

www.golfdigest.com/.../impact-the-place-where-sam-sne.html, retrieved 6/14/14.

www.golfdigest.com/.../impact-tom-watson-rocks-the-tu.html, retrieved 6/11/14.

www.golfdigest.com/golf...07/greenberginterview, retrieved 6/10/14.

www.golfdigest.com/golf-tours.../jack-nicklaus-on-design, retrieved 6/13/14.

www.golfdigest.com/golf-tours-news/.../jack-nicklaus-quotes, retrieved 6/9/14.

www.golfdigest.com/golf-tours-news/.../jack-nicklaus-quotes, retrieved 6/12/14.

www.golflifelessons.com, retrieved 6/6/14.

www.golflifelessons.com/famous_golf_quotes.html, retrieved 6/13/14.

www.golflifelessons.com/famous_golf_quotes.html, retrieved 6/15/14.

www.golfmagic.com/features/ten-of-the-best-golf-quotes/16705.html, retrieved 6/17/14.

www.golf-mavin.com/.../ChiChi-Rodriguez_Good-Shot_Golf-Tips.html, retrieved 6/12/14.

www.golftoday.co.uk/noticeboard/quotes/trouble.html, retrieved 6/16/14.

www.golftoday.co.uk/noticeboard/quotes/wodehouse.html, retrieved 6/13/14.

www.hachettebookgroup.com/.../978140131..., retrieved 5/12/14.

www.hansleitert.com/en/quotes.php, retrieved 4/4/14.

www.hdfootballwallpaper.com/quotes.php, retrieved 1/28/14.

www.heraldtribune.com/article/.../703080381, retrieved 6/13/14.

www.how2playsoccer.com/goalkeeping-quotes/, retrieved 4/3/14.

www.huffingtonpost.com/.../lucas-black-interview-golf-tiger-woods-seve..., retrieved 6/13/14.

www.ifhof.com/hof/banks.asp, retrieved 2/1/14.

www.independent.co.uk/.../football-the-philosophers-co., retrieved 4/1/14.

www.indoorcyclingassociation.com/.../on-suffering-and-pain-two-great-..., retrieved 7/15/14.

www.isleofholland.com/read/sports/14-classic-johan-cruyff-quotes-explained, retrieved 1/29/14.

www.izquotes.com/quote/127048, retrieved 7/13/14.

www.izquotes.com/quote/194617, retrieved 6/12/14.

www.izquotes.com/quote/291919, retrieved 9/15/13.

www.izquotes.com/quote/44218, retrieved 6/10/14.

www.izquotes.com/quote/52360, retrieved 1/30/14.

www.izquotes.com/quote/79780, retrieved 6/13/14.

www.just-one-liners.com/sports/golf-activities/100395, retrieved 6/12/14.

www.justquotes.com/quotes/martina_hingis/74586, retrieved 6/1/14.

www.kba.tripod.com/quotes.htm, retrieved 7/11/14.

www.kramnik.com/interviews/75, retrieved 4/29/14.

www.library.arlingtonva.us › Articles › Collection Arlington County, retrieved 7/4/14.

www.lushquotes.com/author/lionel-messi/, retrieved 1/28/14.

www.m.bikeradar.com/gear/article/best-bike-quotes-34881, retrieved 7/5/14.

www.manchester.com:Sport:United, retrieved 1/27/14.

www.news.bbc.co.uk/sport2/hi/funny_old_game/quotes_of.../3617400.stm, retrieved 3/18/14.

www.newsmax.com/RonaldKessler/.../2011/.../398929, retrieved 4/29/14.

www.newyorker.com/reporting/2010/07, retrieved 5/4/14.

www.newyorknatives.com/vintage-gossip-tennis-the-love-game-that-dre..., retrieved 5/22/14.

www.notespublication.com/2012/08/16/173/, retrieved 3/12/14.

www.observer.theguardian.com/osm/story/0,,1053339,00.html, retrieved 4/1/14.

www.online-literature.com › HG Wells › The Wheels of Chance, retrieved 7/1/14.

www.open.salon.com/.../review_of_rafa_my_story_an_autobiography_of_raf..., retrieved 5/12/14.

www.ottawagolf.com/files/lineoftheday.txt, retrieved 6/11/14.

www.ottawagolf.com/files/lineoftheday.txt, retrieved 6/12/14.

www.oxnardtenniscenter.com/Fun/TennisQuotes.htm, retrieved 5/28/14.

www.pedalqueens.com/links.html, retrieved 7/18/14.

www.philosiblog.com/.../after-the-game-the-king-and-the-pawn-go-in..., retrieved 5/4/14.

www.philosophyfootball.com/quotations.php, retrieved 3/21/14.

www.pilgrimsrestgolfclub.co.za/gallery.html, retrieved 6/11/14.

www.pinterest.com/pin/259308891017930436/, retrieved 3/30/14.

www.pinterest.com/pin/508273507916040657/, retrieved 1/30/14.

www.pitchero.com/.../buckinghamunitedfootballclub/.../football-quotes, retrieved 4/22/14.

www.planetworldcup.com/LEGENDS/banks.html, retrieved 4/1/14.

www.project4cycling.com/.../david-millar-john-malkovich-of-cycling.ht..., retrieved 7/14/14.

www.psychologytoday.com/.../how-do-we-make-the-..., retrieved 4/30/14.

www.quoteinvestigator.com/2010/07/14/luck/, retrieved 6/3/14.

www.quotery.com/billie-jean-king/, retrieved 5/24/14.

www.quotes.lifehack.org/quote/mike.../i-dont-try-to-intimidate-anybody-befor..., retrieved 5/2/14.

www.quotestorage.com/JackNicklaus252326, retrieved 6/11/14.

www.quotestorage.com/JohnElway52237, retrieved 6/14/14.

www.quotestorage.com/TigerWoods342813, retrieved 6/13/14.

www.quotestree.com/tag/sports, retrieved 6/1/14.

www.realclearsports.com/.../pure_joy_hitting_sweet_spot_76626.html, retrieved 6/13/14.

www.ronaldo7.net/extra/quotes/cristiano-ronaldo-quotes.html, retrieved 1/28/14.

www.saidwhat.co.uk/keywordquotes/chess, retrieved 4/18/14.

www.samuel-beckett.net/speople.html, retrieved 5/4/14.

www.searchquotes.com/search/Committed_To_Excellence/, retrieved 5/28/14.

www.shankly.com/article/2517, retrieved 2/1/14.

www.shmoop.com/literature-glossary/carnivalesque.html, retrieved 4/4/14.

www.shortlist.com/.../sport/50-greatest-sir-alex-ferguson-quotes, retrieved 3/29/14.

www.sirbikesalot.com/index.php?s=5348&np=9, retrieved 7/21/14.

www.socialenterprise.org.uk/.../how-will-you-..., retrieved 6/30/14.

www.sparknotes.com/drama/endgame/themes.html, retrieved 5/4/14.

www.sportplan.net/.../Keeping-Session-Dealing-with-Crosses-and-much-, retrieved 4/2/14.

www.sportscardforum.com/.../the-psychology-of-sports-memorabilia-wh..., retrieved 6/13/14.

www.sportsfeelgoodstories.com/sport-quotes/sports.../tennis-quotes/, retrieved 5/28/14.

www.sportsfeelgoodstories.com/sport-quotes/sports.../tennis-quotes/, retrieved 6/1/14.

www.sportsillustrated.cnn.com/.../siflashback_p..., retrieved 1/28/14.

www.stevensadowskijr.com/forget-your-opponents-always-play-against-par, retrieved 6/13/14.

www.strava.com/activities/30057735, retrieved 7/4/14.

www.tampabay.com/...nbc...johnny-miller/1158553, retrieved 6/13/14.

www.telegraph.co.uk, retrieved 4/4/14.

www.tennis.com/pro-game/2013/12/boris-bet/50020/, retrieved 5/21/14.

www.tennisnow.com/.../Roger-Federer-As-Philosophical-For, retrieved 5/12/14.

www.tennispanorama.com › Features, retrieved 6/1/14.

www.tennispsychology.com/motivational_tennis_quotes_greatest_champ..., retrieved 5/27/14.

www.tennisquote.com/page/6, retrieved 5/25/14.

www.tennisquote.com/post/.../sportsmanship-for-me-is-when-a-guy-walks-off-..., retrieved 5/28/14.

www.thebestyoumagazine.co/serena-williams-guidance-and-brilliance/, retrieved 5/21/14.

www.thebicycleworks.org/10-10ClimateChallenge.html, retrieved 7/12/14.

www.thebikebeat.com/quotes-about-bicycles/, retrieved 6/30/14.

www.thedivineponytail.com/.../roberto-baggio-and-the-moment-that-def..., retrieved 4/1/14.

www.theglobalgame.com/.../shostakovich-football-is-the-ballet-of-the-m..., retrieved 1/27/14.

www.thegoaldiggers.weebly.com/legends-of-the-game.html, retrieved 1/28/14.

www.theguardian.com : Sport : Football : Eric Cantona, retrieved 3/28/14.

www.theguardian.com/.../seven-deadly-sins-cantona-kung-..., retrieved 3/28/14.

www.theguardian.com:Sport:Football, retrieved 1/28/14.

www.thetennisspace.com/top-10-jimmy-connors-qu..., retrieved 5/22/14.

www.topendsports.com/sport/soccer/quotes.htm, retrieved 1/27/14.

www.topendsports.com/sport/tennis/quotes.htm, retrieved 5/25/14.

www.totalfootballforums.com : ... : Off The Pitch : The Pub, retrieved 4/2/14.

www.unm.edu/news/2012/oct/05soccer.html, retrieved 4/2/14.

www.usgolftv.com/great-golf-quotes, retrieved 6/14/14.

www.vanguardngr.com/2013/01/messi-ive-changed-so-much/, retrieved 1/28/14.

www.velonews.competitor.com/.../lee-rodgers-langkawi-diary-the-sacrifice_20..., retrieved 7/11/14.

www.vigyanprasar.gov.in/vipnet/mar2012/vipnet_mar2012.pdf, retrieved 4/30/14.

www.voices.yahoo.com/sports-dont-build-characterthey-reveal-john-w..., retrieved 6/19/14.

www.west-point.org/class/golf58/Golf%20Stuff%201/Quotes.htm, retrieved 6/10/14.

www.winwisdom.com › Author Index › L – Authors, retrieved 7/13/14.

www.worldgolfchampionships.com/accenture...play.../tour-insider.html, retrieved 6/12/14.

www.worldliteraturetoday.org/.../wheels-fire-writers-bicycles-a..., retrieved 6/30/14.

www.worldsoccer.about.com/od/Soccer.../The-Zidane-Headbutt.htm, retrieved 3/28/14.

www.worldwidebikeride.com/index.php?option=com...view=article..., retrieved 7/14/14.

www.yourgolftravel.com/19th.../arnold-palmer-quotes-from-the-king, retrieved 6/12/14.

Young, W. (2004). Taking One for the Team: Baseball and Sacrifice. In: E. Bronson (Ed.), *Baseball and Philosophy* (pp. 56–68). Chicago: Open Court.

Zupan, U. (2008). Beauty Is Nothing but the Beginning of a Terror We Can Hardly Bear. In: J. Turnbull, T. Saterlee & A. Raab (Eds.), *The Global Game: Writers on Soccer* (pp. 172–181). Lincoln, NE: University of Nebraska Press.

Zweig, S. (1976). *Chess Story*. New York: New York Review of Books.

INDEX

T

U

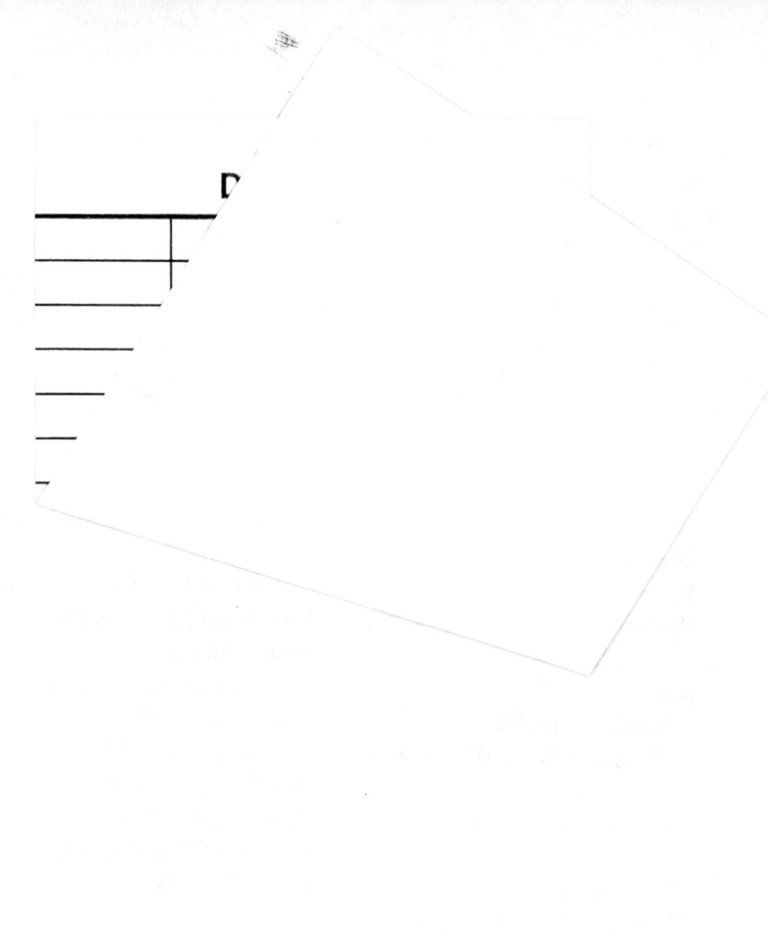